The
LONG
BOOM

A VISION FOR THE COMING
AGE OF PROSPERITY

PETER SCHWARTZ
PETER LEYDEN
JOEL HYATT

PERSEUS PUBLISHING
Cambridge, Massachusetts

To Ben, Emma, Zachary, and Jared,
Our Long Boom Generation who will inherit
the world we create today, and who can
expect to see both the beginning and
the end of the twenty-first century.

Catalog Card Number is available from the Library of Congress
ISBN: 0-7382-0364-5
Copyright © 1999, 2000 by Peter Schwartz, Peter Leyden, and Joel Hyatt

Perseus Publishing is a member of the Perseus Books Group

Text design by Heather Hutchison
Set in 10-point Stone Serif

1 2 3 4 5 6 7 8 9 10—03 02 01 00 99
First paperback printing, August 2000

Perseus Publishing books are available at special discounts for bulk purchases in the U.S. by corporations, institutions, and other organizations. For more information, please contact the Special Markets Department at HarperCollins Publishers, 10 East 53rd Street, New York, NY 10022, or call 1–212–207–7528.

Find Perseus Publishing on the World Wide Web at http://www.perseuspublishing.com

Find more on the Long Boom at http://www.longboom.net

CONTENTS

Preface

A Shared Political Vision

Since the publication of the hardcover edition of this book a year ago, each week seems to bring another positive story: The American economy continues its longest expansion ever. Unemployment is down, wages are up, and inflation is nowhere to be seen. Federal surpluses are projected to top $3 trillion over the next decade. Crime rates are plummeting in the inner cities. The expected Y2K computer meltdown never happens. The crashed Asian economies are bouncing back. Europe is booming and its chronic unemployment rates are finally coming down. China moved much closer toward acceptance into the World Trade Organization. Terrorist North Korea comes in from the cold. Russia succeeds in democratically electing a capable leader. Mexico breaks the lock of one-party rule. Scientists complete mapping the human genome. The Microsoft monopoly is broken. The list goes on and on.

These remarkable events happening all around the world make more sense when understood as part of a larger story that has been playing out for the past twenty years—that of a technological revolution that has helped create a new kind of economy, a more high-tech, high-growth economy. That New Economy is now creating the conditions for a Long Boom, a vast economic expansion that could go for decades, spreading prosperity around the world and lifting billions into middle class lifestyles. These same forces that have transformed the economy—technological change, rapid innovation, and global integration—are now moving beyond the economy and beginning to change our society, our politics, our culture, and ultimately, over the course of the coming century, even our civilization.

The Long Boom tells this larger story of how the world steadily has been getting better as we move away from the Cold War and other divisions of the twentieth century, toward the more interconnected and open world of the twenty-first century. But it doesn't stop there. *The Long Boom* puts today's stories—like the breakup of Microsoft and the rise of open source software—in historical perspective by telling the story of our entire Long Boom era from 1980 right through to 2020. The book lays out what happens in the next twenty years if positive developments consistently win out over negative ones. It explains how all regions of the world make the transition onto the new digital infrastructure and become part of the globalizing New Economy. It shows how three new waves of cleaner technologies—biotechnology, hydrogen energy technology, and nanotechnology—will sustain the boom while greatly reducing damage to the environment. *The Long Boom* is the positive story of the future history of the world.

But this book is more than just a story—it's a political vision. In the wake of the Cold War, no global vision has emerged that gives people hope about how we can collectively improve the world. We spent much of the twentieth century in great intellectual battles and real wars over which systems—capitalism or socialism, communism or democracy, totalitarianism or anarchy—would be better for all people. Ten years have passed since the fall of the Berlin Wall and still we define current thinking in terms of what it is not: "Post-Cold War." We still don't have any agreed-upon term to call the current era, yet our era is not derivative of any other. We need a new vision to fit these very different times. This year at the World Economic Forum in Davos—a gathering of many of the world's most powerful business and political leaders—President Bill Clinton was asked after his keynote address what he thought was the most important thing the world needs today. Without hesitation, he replied: "A shared vision."

The Long Boom provides a starting point for that shared vision. This is a global vision that transcends the politics of any one party or country. It's built on values that can be held in common by different cultures and within different civilizations. This is important because one of the most crucial developments happening in the world today is that everything is going global. Although it's happening initially on the technological and economic plane, it's increasingly affecting other spheres of human endeavor as well. We're now constructing a highly integrated global system that will define how the world is organized in the twenty-first century. This globalization phenomenon will mark an historical watershed that will be well understood by people looking back on our times from 50, 100, or even 1,000 years in the future. They'll say that before the year 2000, humans organized themselves within nations or even smaller localities. After the year 2000, humans increasingly organized on the global level.

What is this twenty-first century global vision? The Long Boom vision shows how we can harness the new technologies and the New Economy to greatly spread prosperity, dramatically lower the damage to our environment, and lessen the chances of large-scale violence and war. These are three major goals that the West and the East, the ideological right and left, and all religions could value and embrace. *The Long Boom* articulates a big, bold, ambitious vision that is not constrained by the preconceptions of our twentieth-century thinking. The vision fits the new realities of an emerging Politics of Prosperity, which will be based on the immense wealth being created in this global boom. We can afford to start thinking more expansively, more generously, and more long-term. The vision also places the value of openness at its core. In our highly interdependent global future, the open options will tend to be the best ones: open trade, open borders, open alliances, open access, open code, open minds. This book lays out the open philosophy that should inform many important decisions that lie ahead. *The Long Boom* shows the open way to go.

When the book first came out in hardcover in the fall of 1999, some skeptical reviewers accused us of being overly optimistic. Our view of the future is indeed positive—but no more so than the times warrant. We live in extraordinary times. The opportunities that are opening up in the next twenty years are enormous. The potentials of the technologies we're developing and the human resources we're amassing are nothing short of astounding. If anything, in the last year the Long Boom vision has only been strengthened by positive developments all over the world that bolster the book's arguments. Nothing of consequence has arisen that undermines our premises.

Take economics. There may have been a legitimate debate in the late 1990s about whether the new computer technologies were increasing productivity and whether what was going on in the economy was new. That debate seems largely over now in light of the amazing economic boom in the United States, which was the first country to thoroughly adopt the new technologies and restructure its economy around them. The United States is still surging in the longest economic expansion the country has ever experienced—and it shows no inherent signs of slowing down. After more than nine years of uninterrupted growth, with the last four years of stellar 4 percent growth rates, the $9 trillion American economy exploded in the fourth quarter of 1999 at more than an 8 percent rate, and in the first half of 2000 accelerated to a 5 percent growth rate.

This high growth is partly built on high productivity boosts that are finally registering in the government statistics. In fact, in the last year the government has continued to upwardly revise productivity rates for the second half of the 1990s based on new information that it is only now collecting. Since the mid–1970s, average annual productivity increases had hovered at a measly 1 percent. However, the new numbers show that after 1995, average productivity often has increased by between 3 to 5 percent per quarter, with the numbers steadily increasing from year to year. And those official numbers are probably still underestimating the true productive impact of computer technologies because the effect on the service economy and knowledge work is so difficult to measure accurately.

The economies of other regions of the world that recently stalled if not collapsed have also started growing rapidly in the last year. When we were writing the book, much of Asia was flattened by the financial crash of 1997 and many of its economies were contracting; today almost all of them have bounced back to high growth rates. Thailand, Malaysia and Hong Kong are expected to grow more than 5 percent in 2000. South Korea, which needed a $57 billion bailout by the International Monetary Fund in December 1997, grew more than 10 percent in 1999 and is expected to grow almost 8 percent in 2000. Even Indonesia is expected to grow more than 4 percent in 2000 after going through the transformation to democracy. China, which did not crash, continued to grow at consistent 7 percent rates and is poised for even higher growth with its likely acceptance into the World Trade Organization. Europe also is back in a boom as it follows the path to the New Economy blazed by the United States. The eleven-nation Euro bloc is expected to collectively grow at more than a 3.5 percent pace in 2000. Even the chronic unemployment that has bedeviled Europeans has been steadily coming down. France has cut its unemployment rate from almost 13 percent three years ago to about 9 percent today. Germany also is now about 9 percent. Smaller countries like the Netherlands have an unemployment rate of 2 percent, and Ireland, once a land exporting emigrants, is now importing immigrant workers.

The technological developments in the last year were even more encouraging. As expected, biotechnology, the next big technological wave to power the Long Boom, stole the headlines. The Human Genome Project—the cracking of the human genetic code—was completed a full five years ahead of its original schedule. The first practical genetic therapy was successfully completed on several hemophilia patients and appears to have effected a cure. This development could pave the way for many other genetic therapies. Advanced Cell Technology made a possible breakthrough in life extension by creating clones from the cells of an adult cow. These cows have cells that do not seem to deteriorate, and so they have a high likelihood of living much longer than normal. Meanwhile, more than 500 new biotech therapies have moved into the late stages of testing and are poised to enter the market in the next five years. In addition, the year saw a resurgence in investment in biotech companies as capital migrated to take advantage of a wide range of scientific advances.

Fuel cells, the clean energy technology that could well supersede the internal combustion engine, went from a controversial technology to a mainstream one in the last year. Today virtually every major auto and energy company has a serious investment in bringing fuel cells and the accompanying infrastructure to the market. Governments and universities are hosting conferences about how to prepare for the coming hydrogen economy. And in the last year, micro fuel cells, which can sustain power to laptops and the like for far longer than batteries, have been demonstrated for the first time.

No technology has accelerated faster in the last year than nanotechnology, which is the whole new field of molecular engineering, or making devices at the atomic level. Developments in just the last year have astounded even longtime proponents and cutting edge researchers. In physics labs across the country and the world, electronic devices and workable machines are actually being built atom by atom. Even insiders thought the ability to do this would be five years, ten years, or perhaps decades in the future. Instead, companies are now being formed in this nascent new industry and we're being told to expect the earliest nanotech products within the next two to three years. In January 2000, President Clinton announced the National Nanotechnology Initiative, which will invest about $500 million in research money in this promising new field.

In the last year, the world has easily survived many so-called crises that were touted as impending disasters. The Y2K computer meltdown and global recession never materialized. In fact, the date passed almost without incident—proving that our technological infrastructure is much more robust than many people thought. It turns out that our networked computer systems are not fragile and our ability to manage looming problems is quite good. In August of 1998, Russia defaulted on its foreign loans—many thought the entire global financial system might collapse. It didn't. And in the last year Russia has carried out its second democratic election that peacefully passed power to President Vladimir Putin, a strong leader who has presented a progressive economic plan that is very reassuring to the West. Even the rogue state of North Korea—high on everyone's list of actors who could start a war or drop a terrorist bomb—has come in from the cold in the last year. North and South Korea seem started on the journey towards reunification of that troubled peninsula.

We survived the correction of the stock indexes, particularly the technology-heavy NASDAQ, in the spring of 2000. At the time, analysts were quick to say that maybe the boom wasn't going to be so long after all. But there is a clear distinction that must be made between the stock market boom and the more fundamental economic boom that underlies it. The Long Boom that we write about refers to the more fundamental economic boom in the bedrock economy. Our Long Boom vision is not about the stock market. However, people who just skimmed the book or read the book's title often misunderstood that we had written about the long stock market boom, which we had not. The stock market is generally related to the core economy but only within limits. As that core economy grows, the companies within that economy will grow in value. A growing economy is usually reflected in a growing stock market over time. And a stalled or shrinking economy will undermine the stock markets. But the correlation is not exact, and the timing is seldom perfect. The stock market and the stock of any particular company can rise and fall for many reasons unrelated to the health of the core economy. For example, the hyper-accelerated growth and dramatic fall of some Internet stocks in the last year is very typical of the creation of new industries, where many innovative new businesses are formed only to eventually consolidate with others or die. We've seen it before in other new industries, like the auto industry in the first half of the twentieth century, when hundreds of new auto companies evolved to less than a half dozen companies, which then entered a period of huge increases in shareholder value. In fact, the spring shakeout of some Internet companies and the correction in the valuations of others is actually good for the Long Boom. This forces people to analyze their investments more on the solid fundamentals and gets investors thinking more long-term. For the economy as a whole, not to mention for the society as a whole, it's better when investors realize steady profits over five years rather than spectacular profits in five weeks.

Of course, not everything that happened in the last year has been positive or supportive of the Long Boom. There is growing resentment of American power and hegemony by former allies—not to mention enemies. If Americans do not tune into this, a serious backlash could result. Globalization has run into considerable resistance from a coalition of labor, environmental, and human rights groups who mounted large protests not only at the World Trade Organization meeting in Seattle in December 1999, but also at a gathering of the World Bank and International Monetary Fund in Washington in April 2000. These groups represent constituencies who truly fear the effects of increased global integration and who could do much to undermine it. Their concerns are understandable and must be dealt with—without undermining the clear benefits that come from globalization. Also, the tragedy in Africa is getting worse with jaw-dropping numbers of AIDS cases being projected. Reports around the time of the 13th International AIDS conference in South Africa in the summer of 2000 projected that one-third of all 15-year-olds in the eight hardest hit African nations can expect to die from the disease. Even in many of the most developed African nations, large numbers of the well-educated adults—teachers, business people, and government officials—also have the HIV virus. Something dramatic must be done by the entire global community. A political response is imperative.

Ultimately, *The Long Boom* is a book about politics, not just business or economics or technology. This is a book about how people can come together, how the *world* can come together, and deliberately try to achieve the Long Boom vision of a prosperous, peaceful, global future. Technology and economics are not the problems right now. As we laid out above, developments in those fields are right on track. The problems are arising in the sphere of politics. There comes a time in every historical transformation of this scale when all sectors of society need to understand the forces swirling around them. New institutions need to be devised to deal with new realities, like a global economy beyond the borders of nation states. We're in that sort of historical transformation right now. We need to be demonstrating that kind of political leadership.

We offer this paperback edition in September 2000, in the midst of the Presidential race in the United States. If ever there was a watershed election, this is it. This election will mark the beginning of what will be a new four-year, if not eight-year, administration. It will mark a new beginning for American politics, the beginning of a new decade, of a new century, of a new millennium. But this is not just the confluence of cute symbolic dates. Americans are moving from a politics of scarcity to a politics of prosperity and this shift changes everything. It changes a people's sense of limits, of benchmarks, and of attainable goals and lofty aspirations. Not just the United States but the entire world could be on the cusp of something truly different, truly remarkable. Never have all countries been integrated into the same economy with the capacity for such huge wealth creation for such a sustained period of time. And now the people who have experienced first a foreshadowing of the coming prosperity, the ones who will have great influence on the prospects for the rest of world, are getting ready to elect their political leaders. This election is a big deal.

The Long Boom was originally written to be neutral about partisan politics in all countries, including the United States. We worked hard to think through a politics that would transcend the twentieth century's ideological division between left and right, between conservative and liberal, between Democrat and Republican. We put together an agenda that people coming out of all factions could conceivably find attractive. It was a new political agenda that we thought reflected the emerging new ideology of people rooted in the New Economy—an ideology that had yet to find a political home. This new mindset had many distinctive characteristics: thinking globally, thinking inclusively, thinking long-term, thinking more positively and ambitiously about the future. Theoretically, candidates from either the Republican or Democratic parties could speak to it. However, as the Presidential campaign has developed through the primaries and now into the general election, the theoretical outcomes have materialized into actual ones. We have two candidates for President, and one is clearly better able to realize the Long Boom vision. The stakes are too high not to take sides.

The two presidential candidates have very different views on the roles of government, with Al Gore understanding its importance far better than George W. Bush. Achieving the Long Boom vision will require a positive role for government, wise government policies, and strategic public investments. The high rates of economic growth of the Long Boom have created huge government surpluses that can be leveraged in powerful ways. At last count, the federal government expected to have more than $3 trillion—yes, *trillion*—in surpluses over the course of the next ten years. That's based on estimates that do not factor in the higher growth rates we think will become prevalent soon. The next President will determine the most productive investments for this extraordinary national wealth.

This election highlights the difference between looking forward to the future or looking backward to the past. Bush tends to look toward the past, primarily by resurrecting the formula Ronald Reagan rode to power twenty years ago. Cutting taxes may have been appropriate back then to stimulate an economy in recession, but cutting taxes significantly in our high growth economy of today is unwise. The Federal Reserve Bank is seeking to do the opposite—tightening credit to slow growth and ward off inflation. And most of the new government spending that Bush proposes is to beef up the military, again something that was more compelling in Reagan's time when we had an "evil empire" to battle. These are not Long Boom policies.

Al Gore looks more to the future. He understands the digital technologies at the base of this Long Boom. As early as the 1970s, he worked as a Congressman to shift what was known as ARPANET from elite military applications to what became the Internet. As a key member of the Clinton Administration through the 1990s, he helped nurture the New Economy, understanding that higher growth rates can be sustained with lower unemployment, and lower inflation, through the productivity gains of technology. That explosion of innovation and growth happened on his watch—partly due to the right government policies. The economy of today doesn't need redirection or a jolt. It needs continuity and prudent government investment in education and scientific research.

Gore's politics are the more inclusive ones, which are the right ones at this stage of the boom. If ever there was a time to extend opportunities to everyone and build a healthier society, this is it. Gore has continued Clinton's legacy of judiciously rebalancing the market orientation of traditional Republicans with the social orientation of traditional Democrats. He has stood up to the anti-globalization constituencies of his party on such issues as opening more trade with China, but also proposes more initiatives to help those groups make the transition to the global economy. Most importantly, Gore is much better prepared for the challenges of the next decade. We're heading towards a more global future and Gore's foreign policy experience is far more extensive than Bush's. And Gore is much more knowledgeable about global warming and environmental issues, which we think will emerge as a *bona fide* crisis in the next decade and pose one of the greatest challenges ever faced by the global community. Al Gore could rise to that challenge.

Whatever the outcome of this election, though, the Long Boom could carry on. The Long Boom is bigger than any one person, or one party, or one country. The Long Boom can and will absorb setbacks—electoral disasters, regional economic downturns, stock market bubbles and crashes. The Long Boom will not be ended easily. There have been too many positive developments in the last twenty years that are providing momentum that will help carry us through the next twenty. There are too many positive trends in motion today and too many people already out there creating a more positive future. The Long Boom vision is not about dramatically changing course, but about continuing on our current trajectory. It's about making the world as good as it truly can be.

We're in the middle of a magnificent story about a world that could be leaving behind the wars and divisions of the past and moving toward a more connected and harmonious future. We're in a transition from a past that was marked by deprivation and scarcity to a future characterized by prosperity and plenty. It's hard to live in a transitional era trapped between these very different twentieth- and twenty-first-century worlds. It's difficult to shift our world views and mindsets so abruptly. That's why we've written this book—to help everyone envision the times of peace, social progress, and prosperity that lie ahead, and show a way that we all can get there.

Peter Schwartz, Peter Leyden, Joel Hyatt

August 2000

The San Francisco Bay area

Introduction

The Historic Moment

THE LONG BOOM IS A POSITIVE meme about a better future. A meme is a contagious idea that can quickly spread around the world and influence what people think and do. A concept that borrows heavily from biology, a meme skips from host to host and quickly works its way through a population in ever-widening circles until it affects the vast majority, seemingly overnight. A meme takes that biological concept into the realm of ideas—and gives it a positive spin.

The Internet has evolved to the point where it now acts like a giant circulatory system for ideas. Someone can introduce a new idea to his or her circle of friends or colleagues, who in turn spread the idea through their own networks. The idea soon takes on a life of its own, out of anybody's control, flitting from computer host to computer host in an exponential expansion that spreads around the world. It may not retain any identity with the originator, and it may mutate into a different form. This is one of the most powerful yet underappreciated aspects of the Internet. It provides the infrastructure that allows an idea to be introduced, tested, improved, refined, and distributed far faster than in any other era. It speeds up a process that previously took years or even decades.

The Internet is now closely monitored by the global media of television and print, which often latch onto the latest ideas and move them into their even more accessible venues. So in a very short time, a meme can leap from the realm of the 200 million or so Internet users into the consciousness of the hundreds of millions of people reading their local newspaper or watching television or listening to the radio. A meme has the potential to reach the brains of billions. The power of memes comes not simply from their speed but from their potential impact. It takes a long time to build a new technological infrastructure and an even longer time to restructure an economy and grow to new levels of prosperity. But in a relatively short time, a meme can change people's perceptions from negative to positive, from anxious to hopeful. It can help people understand their situation differently and reconsider the possibilities of their era. It can help them reframe how they think about the future. That's what we hope to do with *The Long Boom*.

The Long Boom starts with the recognition that the world is faced with a historic opportunity. What we call the Long Boom—the years from 1980 to 2020—is a period of remarkable global transformation. No other age ever possessed the tools or the knowledge to do what we can do today. Since the 1980s, a new computer and telecommunications infrastructure has been built that significantly increases the productive capacity of our economy and promises to deliver much more. Through the 1990s, Americans restructured their economy to take advantage of those technologies and to sustain high levels of economic growth. Corporations are reorganizing, essentially shifting from centralized hierarchies to flexible networks. And a veritable revolution has transformed the world of finance, bringing a hyperefficient use of capital. In addition, the thawing of the Cold War spurred increasing integration of what is becoming a truly global economy, as well as the emergence of many new democracies. These megatrends—technological change, economic innovation, global integration, and spreading democratization—have picked up momentum since the early 1980s, particularly in the developed countries best positioned to take advantage of them.

We've now seen how this new kind of economy can work on a large scale through the experience of the United States, and more recently in parts of Europe, two regions that have been booming. With the right choices and actions, this economic boom can take off on a global level, and we could be entering another couple of decades of vast economic expansion—a boom to rival all past booms. It could easily outdo the last great global economic expansion, which came in the wake of World War II and which mostly benefited about 500 million people in the United States, Europe, and Japan. This new boom has the potential to pull the whole world into it, allowing literally billions of people to move into middle-class lifestyles. And that spreading prosperity will help bring about beneficial changes far beyond the economy, changes that could truly make this a better world. This is no ordinary opportunity. This is not just a once-in-a-generation opportunity. Only occasionally in the great sweep of history is there an opportunity like the one before us now.

The Long Boom assumes that major technological developments are coming in the next couple of decades. There are at least three major waves of new technologies that are going to roll into our lives. All the focus today is on computer and telecommunications technologies, which, indeed, are revolutionary. In many ways networked computers are the great enablers of the other technologies that are to come. But developments in biotechnology—that is, manipulation at the genetic and molecular level—are going to create a revolution similar to the digital revolution we're in now. Biotechnology will transform medicine and health care, leading to many wonders, including life extension to more than 120 years. The fuel cell and other new energy technologies are already proving that the world can lessen its dependence on oil as the primary energy source and can rely instead on the much more environmentally benign hydrogen. The fuel cell will soon replace the internal combustion engine—transforming the global auto and oil industries, which are already starting to prepare for the transition. Nanotechnology—that is, manufacturing one atom at a time—will take another decade or so to develop but will have equally profound consequences. This process promises to take pressure off our natural resources and ultimately eliminate pollution over the course of the twenty-first century.

When you build things from the atom up, the way nature does, there is no waste. None.

The potential lies not just in technology but in human resources, where other inexorable developments are largely underestimated. The scientific and engineering community now numbers in the tens of millions, and our universities are producing more people with advanced degrees than ever before. These people are simultaneously pushing the boundaries of knowledge in every field and preparing to solve many of the challenges that lie ahead. A new Global Middle Class has been burgeoning with numbers now approaching 1 billion. These people share many values that transcend national borders and increasingly act as a positive force reducing world population growth, building pressure for democracy and less extreme politics, and directing great attention to education. The rise of women has kept up a steady trajectory in the developed world. This promises ultimately to bring half the planet's population into the global economy, and to tap the talents of people largely ignored in many societies. And we can count on a massive generational transition that will bring to power people who implicitly understand the new technologies and the New Economy.

The View from 2050

The best way to reframe the present is to try to think about how people in the future will look back on it. Taking that historical perspective should bring a certain clarity to the confusing events of our time. That's because the rhythms of history are slow, deep, and calm. When you look back on history, you're not disoriented by the cacophony of the contemporary media. You're not influenced by the mercurial moods of the public reacting to what they knew and—more often—didn't fully appreciate. When looking back on history, you can see a clear story line that emerges out of the snippets of stories that tried to make sense of their times. You can see the relationship of seemingly disparate events taking place over years and decades. And from that historical vantage point, you can see positive developments just as clearly as negative ones. There's nothing like the perspective of history to clear away the clutter and draw out what's ultimately true. That's why it's so important that we adopt this historical perspective in trying to figure out what's going on in our world today.

People living in the middle of the next century—say, the year 2050—will look back on our times and understand that a monumental transformation took place. They will see developments in the decades around the turn of our century as nothing short of a sea change in the nature of capitalism. We will have gone from an economy driven by the production of tangible things to one driven by intangible ideas. They will see the forty-year period from 1980 to 2020 as encompassing a critical shift from an Industrial Age economy to an Information Age economy, or a Knowledge Economy, or what we simply call the New Economy.

Those people in 2050 will also see the world in a tense transition right around the turn of the century, just as the twentieth century rolled over into the twenty-first. They'll understand this millennial anxiety as more than just a reaction to the collapse of the economies of Asia and other developing regions. They'll see the turmoil as a struggle of the world trying to go global by taking those new technologies, taking the redesigned New Economy that had been seen most clearly in prototype in the United States, and trying to expand it to the world at large. They'll see the larger story as the attempt to create a truly global economy that for the first time in history integrated every region of the world, almost every single country, into one highly interconnected economic unit. But they'll see the transition as even more fundamental than that. The economic integration will have been the first stage of a more complex social and political integration over the course of the new century.

The Long Boom, from our perspective today, is half in the past and half in the future. We refer to the Long Boom in both senses throughout the book. We describe historical developments of the last two decades as laying the groundwork for the incredible opportunity we face today. Those are based on facts and analysis. But the Long Boom going forward is a vision of a better world. It is an unapologetic attempt to lay out the realizable goal of a better, more prosperous and peaceful world. We can consistently grow the new global economy at unprecedented high rates that will greatly expand prosperity, in the process drawing in people previously marginalized in both the devel-

oped and the developing countries. We can establish much more inclusive policies because there is now a strong practical incentive to
integrate everyone into this global economy. Just as important, we
can grow this economy without damaging the environment. We can
migrate to readily available technologies and energy sources that will
supersede the old polluting industrial technologies. We can set the
world on a trajectory that will, over the course of the twenty-first century, get the economy completely in balance with nature. We can do
this not simply for ecological reasons but because it makes good business sense. And we can create the conditions necessary for long-last-
ing geopolitical stability and decreasing levels of violence. The more
technologically interconnected and more economically interdependent we make the world, the lower are the chances for large-scale war.
The Long Boom vision engages seemingly intractable problems like
global warming, Third World poverty, and the persistence of war and
shows how they can be solved over time. These problems need to be
confronted because the only way to sustain a healthy global economy in the long run is to include everyone, to make this economy
environmentally sound, and to avoid the destruction of war.

The Politics of the Long Boom

The Long Boom is more than a pure vision. It acts as a first-draft plan.
It gives shape to a new agenda through what we call the "Politics of
the Long Boom." Technology is not the problem. That's proceeding
quite nicely. The economy is not the problem either. We may need to
fine-tune this New Economy, but the basic developments are sound.
No, the problem is with politics, defined in the broadest sense as the
realm where people come together to pool resources and collectively
solve problems. We're not just talking about electoral politics; we're
talking about all the activities of people who are trying consciously
and deliberately to change their world for the better. Politics can either make or break this Long Boom. We can do the right things and
sustain it, or we can do the wrong things—or do nothing—and cause
it to peter out.

The Politics of the Long Boom deals with each major region of the
world and highlights the assets that can be leveraged to make the

transition to the new global economy work. The cultures rooted in Western civilization, the Europeans and the Americans, invented modern capitalism and have been innovating new forms of it for the last several hundred years. So in the move to this global capitalism, it makes sense for the Americans and the Europeans to be the first to figure out the new methods and master them. And because their economies are the most developed and the most intact going into this transition, they can be the economic bastion that brings stability to the world economy as we move through this difficult period. They have the resources to be more selfless and generous in providing leadership to the world at large.

The cultures rooted in what could be broadly categorized as Asian civilization can also do their part to pull the world into the Long Boom. The many peoples within Asian civilization obviously mastered the rules of the old economy, the Industrial Age's manufacturing economy, during the 1980s and 1990s. Now they can master the rules of this emerging New Economy. The Japanese could shift first because of their high level of development and immense resources; the Chinese next, because of their key cultural assets like reverence for learning; and then the entrepreneurial Indians could soon follow. These societies will bring their considerable talents to the table and with time will also innovate in this new twenty-first-century capitalism.

Other regions and countries, now considered problem areas or potential spoilers, could join this Long Boom by 2020. The Russians, currently backsliding from the market economy, could be drawn back into the global arena with their huge natural resources and highly educated human capital—if the Europeans and Americans make vitally important decisions to help them through this critical juncture. The Arabs, long locked in traditional cultures and resistant to modernization, could move beyond the oil economy and unleash the pent-up yearnings of their still small middle classes and their young people. And Africans, long on the fringes of the economic mainstream, have the opportunity to begin the long march of development by taking over the entry-level industries like textiles. We can see how the world could methodically move through the anxiety of this current millennial transition and reconnect with the trends that emerged in the

1980s and 1990s and that have been waiting to break out and take off again.

The actual politics that can help bring about this global transformation starts with a new kind of ideology that goes beyond the traditional ideologies of the right and the left. This ideology is characterized by people who think globally and long-term, and who are open-minded. The politics seizes on the logic of the New Economy and pushes it toward its ultimate conclusion, which has benefits far outside commerce. The business world understands the rationale of "expanding the network," with each additional member bringing added value to everyone. The new politics seeks to assure everyone access to information technologies and opportunities in the New Economy. Business is now coming to understand that in the new knowledge economy, "production is learning." The new politics initiates an overhaul of education and the creation of a new learning society. Business understands the merits of competition. The new politics extends that understanding to what we call the "rule of twos," the necessity of competition, the internal logic of self-correcting systems that lies behind the historical success of democracies and market economies. Applying the rule more broadly and rigorously in politics and economics would energize many countries that are now languishing and would accelerate the Long Boom.

The book outlines ten guiding principles that inform the new politics and that anyone, in any capacity, can use to thrive in this new era. They are simple but powerful principles that apply to nations, to large and small businesses, to schools, to communities, and even to families and individuals. They are core values that should be embraced, attitudes to be adopted. They can be honed down to their essence—each of them just two words. We'll elaborate on them at the end of the book but frequently refer to the general concepts. For now, here are the basics: Go Global in all things. Open Up in every capacity. Let Go of all tendencies to control. Grow More both in economic and personal terms. Always Adapt to all the changes swirling around. Keep Learning in order to thrive. Value Innovation at every juncture. Get Connected to all kinds of networks. Be Inclusive because it will benefit everyone, including you. And Stay Confident because we are fully capable of solving all the challenges ahead. Keep these guiding principles in mind as you read on.

The Long Boom is not a prediction. This can't be emphasized enough. It is a first-draft idea—with the emphasis on the "first-draft"—that is intended to show people a positive future that is desirable and attainable. It is meant to inspire people with a vision of what's possible and to outline some of the critical choices we all must make to enable the realization of that vision. But this is a vision proposed with the explicit understanding that it is incomplete. It is meant simply to provide an initial framework that others can improve. We want to get you thinking about the present in a new light, from this Long Boom perspective that sees great opportunities all around us. We want to lead your mind down a path toward a better world. But remember, this is a malleable meme. Take it and run.

We're sitting smack in the middle of this Long Boom, partly paralyzed by the anxiety surrounding the millennial transition. In many countries, people are feeling stymied by the magnitude of the changes coursing through the global economy. Once-booming Asia is still desperately trying to recover from its 1997 collapse, and other developing regions are even more overwhelmed. People in the developed countries are nervously preparing for the possible computer meltdown in the year 2000. And if all that weren't enough, the world is beginning to come to terms with an even more daunting problem: severe environmental damage, particularly global warming, which seems to be getting worse. We want this book to be many things, but in the end, we want it to get people to act. We want it to convey a feeling of gravity and deep responsibility toward both today's communities and the generations that will follow. We have a historic opportunity that, if seized, can bring unprecedented benefits, but we must rise to the occasion and act. We must choose to create a better future. It won't come without us.

The Logic of the Long Boom

The Long Boom is an argument based on scenario thinking. Any thoughtful scenario must be based on several key elements, all of which we rigorously followed in making this book. We started by posing a crucial question: What is a positive yet plausible scenario for the world in the next two decades? What is the scenario that can bring us to a world where prosperity has significantly increased and spread widely, based on an economy that is ecologically sustainable, in an atmosphere of less violence? Because prosperity is an indispensible part of the equation, the central question is: How fast can the world grow on an economically and ecologically sustainable basis?

The Long Boom is based on the idea that the growth potential of the world is increasing rapidly because of several major drivers of change, most notably globalization and technological innovation. The key uncertainties that could undermine the scenario have to do with whatever limits that growth potential. Historically, the biggest constraints on growth have come mainly from three sources: political conflict rooted in a clash of interests or ideologies; social stress arising from economic disparities that produce misery amid wealth; and, finally, and increasingly in the future, ecological constraints on growth. So the challenges to sustaining today's burgeoning prosperity lie mainly in these three arenas. What are the politics that sustain growth? How do we ensure that the benefits of that growth will be widely shared? How do we deal with the environmental consequences of growth? A central message of *The Long Boom* is that increasingly sustainable prosperity for most people in the world is possible—but not inevitable. We have to make a choice to go for growth.

This book is organized in four sections. The first section, "Track the Inevitable," looks at several trends that have come together in the last two decades to create the foundation for thinking much more ambitiously about our future. Section II, "The Politics of the Long Boom," builds off that foundation and explores the new political realities needed to sustain the Long Boom over the next couple of decades. The third section, "The Engines of the Twenty-first Century," looks at the coming waves of exciting new technologies that will continue to drive economic growth and also lower damage to the environment. The final section, "Birth of a Global Civilization," looks at some of the far-reaching consequences on people everywhere that flow from the high growth of the Long Boom.

This book is a story. It weaves together three distinct strands that continue across all the sections. The main strand, written in the contemporary voice of the authors, is an integrated narrative that follows developments in disparate fields all over the world. It makes the overarching argument and speculates on developments in the future.

At certain junctures, we shift to the second strand of the book, which tells the story of our future in the form of a documentary from the year 2050. "Twenty-first Century Choices: The Making of a Long Boom" is a journalistic look back on the first two decades of the twenty-first century. It provides the long view on key historical events that the audience in 2050 will look back on with the same perspective that we look back on the 1950s and 1960s. Think of a future version of today's television documentaries that look back on grainy black-and-white film footage of Martin Luther King and the civil rights movement while the soothing voice of Peter Jennings describes the historical significance of that twentieth-century struggle. "Twenty-first Century Choices" talks about our era in that way.

The third strand of the book is a series of letters written by a fictional character in ten-year intervals starting in 1980 and continuing through 2020—including one final one in 2050. These letters are written to a close circle of friends as the character struggles to make sense of the confusing world around him and deal with the anxiety created by uncertainty. He remains trapped in time and unable to see the larger, more positive forces at work. He's a reminder to us all that we frequently are trapped in time and lose perspective on the big picture. Looking back ten, twenty, or thirty years, we can laugh at some of our unfounded fears—as does he.

The Really Long Boom

In the long view of history, the story of the Long Boom will be seen as part of a much larger story that starts at least as far back as the nineteenth century. It will be seen as reestablishing the trajectory of progress that started way back then. The industrial revolution of the late nineteenth century cranked up the notion of "progress," the idea that the world was getting better and would continue to do so far into the future. Those were giddy times. Almost every year, fundamental scientific breakthroughs and widespread technological innovation astonished people with some amazing new technology: electricity, the radio, the telephone, the internal combustion engine, the airplane. Can you imagine how people felt when they learned for the first time that humans can fly? That they can communicate across hundreds of miles through thin air? That cities chronically engulfed in darkness could be lit up by electric lights? That new medicines could cure diseases, extend life, and reduce suffering? The modern mind-set became rooted in the notion of progress. Who could argue? Everything seemed to be getting so much better.

Then came World War I. That conflict shattered the sense of optimism and progress. The great countries of the world took those new technologies and used them to wage total war. The carnage and destruction were unprecedented. The world mourned. A sense of tragedy came to balance the sense of progress. World War I could have been one brief detour from the path of progress. Instead, it was the first in an agonizing series of detours. The vindictive resolution of the war set the world on a path of increasing nationalism, which manifested itself in insular economic policies and isolationist politics. After a burst of growth in the 1920s, the world economy collapsed into the Great Depression of the 1930s. That created such severe deprivation that nationalism in some places turned into fascism, which forced the world into yet another total war. World War II was far more savage and comprehensive than World War I: An estimated 45 million people died, including 20 million in Russia and 6 million Jews. No region of the world was unaffected, and Europe and Japan were left decimated. That trajectory of "progress" that had begun in the nineteenth century took a nosedive through the first half of the twentieth. By 1945, many thought progress had ground to a halt.

The post–World War II era began to restore the sense of optimism and progress. In the wake of the war, the world economy picked up, particularly in the Free World. The United States, whose soil had been virtually untouched by the destruction, made the transition from a war economy to a booming mass consumer one. The countries of Europe and Japan, with the visionary help of the Americans, went into a frenzy of rebuilding that stoked their economies. This boom continued through the 1950s and 1960s, drawing large numbers into the middle class and raising wages for almost all workers. Many of the technologies that had been invented in the 1930s and during the war in the 1940s moved into the mainstream, including television, atomic energy, and mainframe computers. The boom also saw the emergence of a generation—the Baby Boom generation—that reaped all the benefits of this prosperity. But just about the time that the first Baby Boomers finished their formal education and began to enter the economy, the boom began to falter. The oil price shock of 1973 started the stumble, pushing the economy into stagnation coupled with inflation, so-called stagflation. The second major oil shock, in 1979, which brought another quadrupling of prices, dashed any hope that the boom could pick up again.

For the rest of the twentieth century, the post–World War II boom was the standard that we always wanted to attain. If only we could achieve the level of growth enjoyed in that era. If only prosperity could spread as quickly. If only all workers could enjoy such improvement in their prospects and standards of living. The common understanding during the last decades of the twentieth century has been that the postwar boom was an anomaly, never to be achieved again. At best, we could muddle along and flat-line the arrow of progress out from the 1970s. But many people adopted an even more pessimistic view: The future was going to bring more poverty, wider gaps between the haves and have-nots, more conflict rooted in scarcity. The conflicts between nations and cultures were going to be more intense and intractable. And, of course, we were going to keep trashing the environment.

It All Began in 1980

The real story of the twentieth century is that the post–World War II boom simply brought the world back to the threshold we could have been at decades before. That boom mostly filled in the crater created

by successive wars and wrongheaded economics, and by the end of
that boom, the world had reached a plateau from which to really
grow. The 1980s, then, were not the beginning of a slide into obliv-
ion, but the start of something much more positive: the very long
journey of the Long Boom. We authors think that increasing numbers of people will pick up on this meme and start to see our times
this way. They will finally see that their generation is not just trying
to re-create some past glory or perpetuate an earlier generation's accomplishments. They will understand that they are inventing yet another wave of technologies that are even more astounding than the
ones they have inherited. They are building a new and better world.

But that attitude is a far cry from the prevailing attitude in 1980,
when this whole Long Boom story starts. The world in 1980 was filled
with much agony and soul-searching. In America, the economy was
in shambles. The inflation rate was 14 percent, and the unemployment rate was 10 percent; combined, they created what Americans
called the *misery index*. On top of that, interest rates were 21 percent.
Europe was in worse shape, with the added problem of militant labor
wreaking more havoc. The communist USSR, too, had an anemic
economy, but we didn't find out until later because they put out
phony statistics. What we could see was that they had invaded
Afghanistan the year before and seemed bent on expanding their empire. Meanwhile, the United States couldn't get Iranian revolutionar-
ies to release American hostages held for more than a year. Jimmy
Carter was the president in 1980, running against Ronald Reagan,
whose campaign slogan was "Are you better off today than you were
four years ago?" The resounding answer was no, and Reagan won in a
Republican landslide. Four years later, he changed the slogan of his
reelection campaign to "It's morning again in America." Reagan was
onto something with that slogan, apart from showing the power of
confidence and optimism. After all the darkness of the 1970s, some
rays of hope started to break out in the 1980s. The first had to do
with technology.

The story of the future of the world begins with technology. Go
back to the starting point way back in 1980. This was a time before
music CDs, compact discs, were introduced. The CD came along in
1981—and now they make up everyone's music collection. This was a

time before the FAX machine. There were no faxes until 1985. By 1987, they were nearly ubiquitous in business. This was a time before VCRs and video stores got off the ground. The VCR was still in an experimental phase and in a standards battle between VHS and Betamax. This was before cable television really got started. The very earliest stations like HBO were playing to small audiences, but there was no CNN or MTV. Mobile phones did not exist—businesses had to use radios with dispatchers. For that matter, the world of telephones in the United States was still controlled by a monopoly, Ma Bell, and state companies in other countries. The Walkman was not even around. Mobile music was in the same place as mobile telephony. And most important of all, the world lacked the personal computer. This was the machine that would start to really transform the world. That's where we start this story.

PART ONE

TRACK THE INEVITABLE

A REMARKABLE ALIGNMENT of events with profound historical consequences happened around 1980. They took place in the fields of technology, economics, and politics and on the surface appear unrelated. Together, though, they warrant our thinking of 1980 as the beginning of the Long Boom. The world had been moving in the direction of greater and greater centralization throughout the twentieth century, and that process only accelerated after World War II, driven in part by increasingly centralized technologies that had been developed to achieve greater economies of scale. But by 1980, the crowning achievements of that inexorable process had all begun to flounder. This simultaneously happened to giant corporations, the gargantuan welfare states, and the even more colossal systems of communism. The stage was now set for the epochal changes to come in the following two decades.

This section of the book, "Track the Inevitable," follows the major developments in technology, economics, and politics that have brought us to our present situation and appear ready to propel us forward. We look at the fundamental advances in computers and telecommunications that have laid the groundwork for much that is to come. We make the case for the New Economy, showing how the reorganization of work around these new technologies is bringing productivity gains and the potential to sustain high growth over the long term. And we explain the nature of the current millennial transition in capitalism as the expected difficulties in creating a truly global economy. In short, this section tells the story of how we moved through the first half of the Long Boom to arrive at the historic opportunity we face today, and how we have laid the foundation for the more complete global transformation to come in the next two decades.

1

The Great Enabler

Computer and telecommunication technologies are creating a fundamentally new infrastructure upon which our twenty-first-century world will be based. This technological base makes possible a much more efficient and productive knowledge economy and leads to rapid advances in other technologies and fields.

THE SINGLE MOST IMPORTANT EVENT to fall on the 1980 dateline was the introduction of the personal computer. Apple Computer had technically introduced its first personal computer in 1977, and the first IBM PC came out in 1981. At the time, the personal computer didn't seem like all that big a deal—despite the revolutionary rhetoric of its proponents. Apple's cofounder, Steve Jobs, had said the personal computer would change the world, and frankly, he was right. The introduction of the personal computer will probably go down in history with other key dates like the introduction of the printing press in the 1450s. The personal computer, like the printing press, had the potential to change almost everything. The personal computer was the key tool that allowed the "centralisms" of bureaucratic corporations and welfare states and communism to be undermined. We had had computers long before—ever since World War II—but they had been huge mainframe computers that centralized all tasks and were run by elite engineers and technicians. The significance of the personal computer was that it decentralized computer-processing power—and thus facilitated the decentralization of decisionmaking and raw power itself, which had previously tended to move toward the center. The personal computer was the key tool that began to reverse that trend and to allow the spread of power to the periphery. It would become The Great Enabler in more ways than one.

To be sure, those first personal computers were no match for the mainframes in their processing power. But personal computers were riding an amazing developmental dynamic unheard of in other industries. This dynamic was known in the computer industry as *Moore's law*, after Gordon Moore, one of the founders of Intel, the maker of microprocessors, which are the brains of personal computers. Moore was the first to recognize that every eighteen months, on average, engineers were able to double the number of circuits and components that fit within the same computer chip, essentially doubling the speed, or power, of that chip. The effect of Moore's law was that every eighteen months, a new computer chip came out that essentially doubled in power for the same price. This dynamic has been playing out ever since the very first microprocessors were invented in the 1970s. The results are truly astounding: Microprocessors for today's $250 video games are as powerful as mainframe computers that cost $14 million in about 1985.

Right before the advent of the personal computer, the movie *Star Wars* came out and created a modern mythology set in a distant time of interstellar space travel. The film has classic archetypal characters and deals with transcendent themes like the never-ending struggle between good and evil. The evil is personified in Darth Vader, a huge, hooded villain dressed in sweeping black robes. The good is personified in Luke Skywalker, a young, smart, struggling hero who pulls together a scrappy band of rebels with good hearts. In a strange way, that movie mirrored the drama that would play out in the technological world, a drama that, squeezed down to its essence, was the battle over technological openness. The bad guys were into control and proprietary standards. The good guys fought to open up technology for everyone. They fought for open standards, compatible technology, interoperable computer languages, and, ultimately, open source code. So far, the good guys have won each round, though we're at another crucial juncture right now. We argue that openness *always* wins in the end. The most open strategy in technology as well as in other areas like economics is always the one to bet on—especially in the long run. But the forces for evil, those trying to hang onto control, often seem invincible—until they fall.

Act I: IBM, Bad; Microsoft, Good

The technology drama has had several main acts, and as in all good drama, the good guys have sometimes turned into bad guys. But in the end, we could have a happy ending. In the first act, the curtain rises on 1980, with IBM as the bad guys. They controlled the computer world and came dangerously close to being deemed a monopoly. Because they were so big and powerful, many thought that the only countervailing force of sufficient power was the U.S. government. In fact, like two sumo wrestlers in an endless match, the government and IBM had been locked in an ongoing anti-trust lawsuit through the late 1970s. The real protagonist, though, turned out to be a character right out of *Star Wars*. In 1975, Bill Gates, with his college buddy Paul Allen, had founded a software company called Microsoft, selling an operating system for personal computers. These two approached IBM offering to provide their operating system for the personal computer that IBM was reluctantly going to manufacture using Intel's chips. IBM had little more than disdain for these personal computers, which seemed so pathetic compared to the powerful mainframes, but realized that the PC might provide yet another market to move into. So IBM enlisted Microsoft and Intel to help put together the IBM PC.

Darth Vader had opened himself up to a mortal saber thrust. The personal computer exploded in popularity through the 1980s as businesses bought the increasingly powerful machines. Both Microsoft and Intel were perfectly positioned to ride that boom. They became known as Wintel because every personal computer sold with an Intel chip also came with Microsoft's evolved operating system, called Windows. And by the 1990s, more than 90 percent of all personal computers were Wintel. What happened to Apple Computer? It was supposed to be the revolutionary, and it was for much of the 1980s. But Apple and Microsoft played out a little minidrama through that decade around the same theme of technological openness. Those two companies had the two most prominent operating systems, and Apple's was technologically better, but this time, Apple stayed on the dark side of control and would put its software only on its own hardware: If you wanted the Apple software, you had to buy the Apple machine. Microsoft stayed out of the hardware business altogether and designed its software applications to fit any computers—including those of Apple. So Apple took the closed strategy and Microsoft took the open one. Apple ended up almost bankrupt and became a niche player. By the end of the 1990s, Microsoft had become the most valuable company in the United States, and Gates the richest man in the world. Open clearly won that time.

Another key development took place around 1980 in another technology field: telecommunications. In 1982, the U.S. government, while grappling with IBM, entered into a consent decree that broke up the monolithic AT&T, the "centralism" that had dominated telecommunications for decades. That breakup of the Bell phone system, which formally happened in 1984, was the watershed event that unleashed a great wave of innovation in this crucial field. In the wake of that breakup, we saw the rise of competing long-distance phone firms like MCI and Sprint, which scrambled to build their own networks of high-capacity fiber-optic cables around the country. We saw the building of vast wireless phone networks that led to the mobile phone craze. We watched the construction of a parallel cable television network in every city in the country. In short, the 1980s produced an explosion of entrepreneurial zeal that had been long lost in telecommunications. And the best was yet to come as the telecommunications world began to align with the world of computers.

Throughout the 1980s, the increasingly powerful personal computers had spread throughout the business world. Businesses, which were able to afford the relatively expensive new tools and could capitalize on the investment, became the early adopters of this new technology. By the early 1990s, though, a key development had taken place. The isolated personal computers began to be tied together in networks. At first, they were in small networks within offices, but soon they were networked between offices and within larger organizations. Ultimately they began getting tied together in even larger public networks. Until then, the personal computer had essentially been a glorified typewriter or a number cruncher. Through networking, the personal computer became a communicator, and that shift from calculator to communicator made all the difference in the world. Calculators are useful, but limited. Most people don't really want to sit around and crunch numbers. They want to communicate, and communication is at the heart of everything we humans do. So with a change in the way we communicate comes a change in the way we do almost everything else.

The advent of the Internet, the networking together of all computers and the merging of the computer and the telecommunications worlds, led to an explosion of growth in both fields throughout the 1990s. Almost anything that had to do with digital technologies and telecommunications showed the same unmistakable growth through the 1990s. You can track the number of microprocessors sold, the feet of fiber-optic cable laid, the rise in cell phone subscriptions, the explosion in Web sites—anything to do with these fields has taken off since 1990. The number of Internet hosts, or servers, alone has been doubling almost every year since the introduction of the Mosaic Web browser in 1993. By 1998 that number had passed 30 million and was continuing to climb. The number of Internet users that year topped 160 million. Personal computers have saturated the business world, have moved from business into the home, and have begun spreading from the developed to the developing world.

Impressive as the growth has been so far, the really big expansion is yet to come. The personal computer still appears in only about half of all American homes. Compared to the adoption of other key technologies like television, personal computers are only halfway up the adoption curve. And the adoption percentages for households are much less in almost all other developed countries—let alone the developing countries, which are only now adopting personal computers for their businesses. From a global perspective, the bulk of the growth in personal computers is clearly ahead. Also, microprocessors are increasingly being embedded in all the tools and appliances that we use in our lives. With time, the personal computer per se will fade in its significance, and these computerized tools will take over the functions of the old personal computer. But that shifting is just beginning, and the growth in the use of these embedded chips lies almost all ahead of us. Ultimately, in the first two decades of the twenty-first century, we will create what is called *ubiquitous computing,* an environment where we are surrounded by these cheap, powerful chips and almost effortlessly interact with them—taking them completely for granted.

The forty-year period between the introduction of personal computers and the full arrival of ubiquitous computing is not arbitrary. Previous technology adoption patterns such as with television and radio had similar four-decade spans. Businesspeople in Silicon Valley frequently use a graphic called the *technology adoption curve* to show the slow ramping up of any new product's penetration in a market from zero to 100 percent. It starts out slowly with early adopters, then rapidly expands when the majority catch on, and then tapers off as even laggards finally buy the product. Historically, we've seen this pattern happen again and again. It takes roughly forty years for a fundamentally new technology to be fully adopted by a society. One of the primary reasons has less to do with technology and more to do with people. Over the course of forty years, societies see a complete changeover between generations. The generation that enters the era as young people in their twenties and thirties just out of formal training end the era moving into their sixties and seventies and letting go of their positions of power and entering retirement. Meanwhile, their children, who were born in the first couple of decades of the era, emerge at the end as young adults ready to make their full impact on the world. The new generation spends their entire young lives surrounded by the era's new technologies and steeped in the new ways of doing business and running the world. They implicitly understand the new system by the time they reach their twenties and thirties and begin to make meaningful contributions to the economy and society. When they take over, the whole system really works. In fact, one of the key reasons we define the Long Boom as a forty-year era is that a complete generational changeover will occur in that time span. That generational transfer will come on top of a full adoption of this revolutionary computer infrastructure.

The growth in telecommunications is mostly ahead as well. We still haven't wired up even half the personal computers. Only about a third of adults in the United States use the Internet now. And we are still struggling to beef up the bandwidth, or capacity of the wires, to handle even adequate levels of digital traffic for basic graphics. We are at the beginning of a huge effort to greatly expand that capacity so that within the coming decade we will be able to move the huge computer files that carry video images and full-length movies over our landlines and into our homes. We're just now embarking on efforts to establish satellite networks that will allow phone and Internet access from every square foot of the planet. The Iridium global phone was the first of this generation to become operational in the fall of 1998. Despite the problems with Iridium, there are still several other projects in motion to provide a global phone or to expand the capacity from phones to full, high-bandwidth Internet access. The most promising of these is the Teledesic project, due for completion in 2004 and partly bankrolled by none other than Bill Gates.

Meanwhile, the telecommunications infrastructure is moving toward a common open standard, if you will. Until now, the main traffic on the global telecommunications grid has been the human voice, and telephone traffic has far overshadowed computer data. But that balance has started shifting during the 1990s—prompting a huge technological debate. Voice has always been transmitted via fixed circuits in the world of telephony. That means that a person placing a phone call to someone across the country first establishes an open connection that reserves a circuit of the telecommunications grid that literally spans that distance. Computer data, on the other hand, are transmitted via packets over the Internet and other protocols. All computer messages or transmitted data on the Net are broken into smaller bits, called *packets,* that then individually make their way across various routes in the telecommunications grid, to be reassembled at the final destination. These are fundamentally different approaches to using the telecommunications infrastructure, yet they are not equally useful. For one thing, telephony can be transmitted via packets and, many argue, much more efficiently. For another, all other media are going digital. Music is already digital on compact disks. Digital television is being developed in parallel to old analogue TV. Mobile phones are shifting to digital options. The common language is the bits and bytes of computer code. So we're starting to see some of the key players in the world of telephony positioning themselves for the leap. The world is now heading toward a future in which one common telecommunications infrastructure of a network of networks will be able to handle all communication. This development, too, will stimulate growth.

Bill Gates understands better than most that we're on the front end of growth in digital technologies—not the back end. In a conversation in 1998, he remarked that everyone seems fixated on the growth Microsoft had enjoyed in the previous twenty-five years. True, by 1998 Microsoft was the world's most valuable company based on its astronomical stock prices, but Gates said the real growth all lay ahead. He compared the computer industry in the late 1990s to the auto industry in the late 1920s. The auto industry had enjoyed substantial growth in the previous twenty-five years, but nothing like the growth of the next twenty-five and beyond. The same holds true for the computer industry today. The real growth is ahead, not behind. What's more, that growth is inevitable. *Inevitable.* Gates attributed the success of his company to that insight. He said Microsoft simply "tracks the inevitable." It looks where the technology is obviously heading, then positions its business plan to correspond to that technological trajectory. Once the breakthrough was made, it was inevitable that computer power was going to decentralize into personal computers. Microsoft saw that decentralization early and capitalized on it. Once the power of networked computers was demonstrated, it was inevitable that all computers would be wired up through the Internet. When Microsoft recognized that, it rapidly repositioned its business strategy. Looking forward, it's inevitable that computer chips will spread throughout the business world, into our homes, and across the planet. They aren't going to stop spreading. We aren't going to quit computerizing. You can count on it. It's inevitable.

Act II: Microsoft, Bad; Silicon Valley, Good

As in any good story, though, Act II, in the 1990s, brought a surprising role reversal—in this case involving Gates and his company. Microsoft had grown into an upgraded version of IBM: the control freak, the bad guy. Microsoft sat on top of a virtual cash machine because the costs of replicating software were minimal, yet Microsoft could charge a premium for its software, which every machine needed. So it regularly would rack up after-tax profits of between 30–40 percent of revenues, and it had cash reserves of billions of dollars to hire any top programmer, or buy any promising company, or move into any new market. Gates had long ago moved his company to his hometown of

Seattle, which became a burgeoning base for the Microsoft crowd. The perceived good guys at this time were the network of smaller companies rooted in California's Silicon Valley, though they included some companies technically outside the area. In effect, this camp was the anybody-but-Microsoft crew, and in an odd twist of fate, a wised-up IBM threw its still substantial weight behind these innovators. What unified this coalition, beyond fear and hatred of Microsoft, was the belief that the Internet had shifted the paradigm of computing. They believed the Net, or the network, would undermine the importance of Microsoft's operating system by moving beyond the world of isolated personal computers. When every computer was an island, Microsoft ruled the land. But once all computers became connected, many other possibilities open up.

The first major shot fired in this battle came from Netscape, a company that produced the first user-friendly interface with the World Wide Web. The Web allowed a graphic dimension to the Internet, which until then had been all text. Once the Internet became visual and easy to navigate, its popularity took off. Netscape rode that initial takeoff and became a very valuable company almost overnight. But Gates shifted strategy quickly, coming up with a competing Web browser, and the huge base of Windows users started migrating to it. Netscape's fortunes soon began to fade. The next major shot from the Silicon Valley coalition came from Sun Microsystems, which came up with a computer language called Java that was specially suited to the Internet and that could work on any machine. Sun preached that "the Network *is* the Computer," meaning that personal computers would increasingly do less work on their own and would connect with larger computers, called *servers,* that would do the bulk of the work. As a result, the operating system and the applications on the personal computer would diminish in importance, as would Microsoft, and applications that worked over the Internet would increase in importance, as would the servers, which Sun happened to make. Alas, Microsoft made server software, too, and Microsoft's marketing muscle brought it an expanding piece of that pie. And then Microsoft adopted the Java language but developed a modified version that worked best with the rest of the Microsoft applications suite.

There were other major thrusts and parries throughout the 1990s. No matter what the Silicon Valley coalition did, Microsoft somehow countered. So the Silicon Valley crew eventually turned to its last weapon. This group, which had often prided itself on its libertarian impulses and its disregard for government, looked to Uncle Sam for help at the end of the 1990s. As in the battle with IBM twenty years before, the U.S. government seemed to be the only player big enough to take on Microsoft. But as in that other saga, the government may not provide the real answer. In the end, a new cast of characters probably will.

ACT III: OPEN SOURCE, Good

Act III in the battle over technological openness is taking place right now and is starring some new actors. The good guys are a ragtag band of programmers, hackers, and idealistic computer nerds spread all over the world. Some of them work in big companies, some in smaller firms, and many of them on their own. The label *ragtag* is no reflection on their skills. They are as smart as anybody when it comes to understanding computers—as smart as the best that Microsoft or Silicon Valley has. It's just that these people are completely into the technology, not just making money from their skills. They just love the challenge of creating great code, sharing their discoveries with a community of peers, and getting the feedback that will improve their innovations. They pay their bills with what could be called day jobs, but their real passion is the code, the code. The software innovations that they design in the day to solve their particular problems, they then pass on to the community over the Net at night. Much of their spare time is spent working on collective software projects. The Net has become the means of unifying this network of techies. It is the tool through which these people self-organize.

There has long been a code of honor on the Internet to share ideas for the greater good. When the Internet was little more than an academic medium, this code of honor simply continued the tradition of the scientific method. In science, those who make a discovery are obligated to share the results and to explain clearly how they arrived at their conclusions, so that the entire scientific community can subject the discovery to rigorous analysis. If the discovery passes that scrutiny, it becomes common intellectual property, and everyone gets to reap the benefits. This mentality is not due to some socialistic impulse but is the best way that science can move forward. If the results of one person's discovery are quickly distributed, then no time is wasted in rediscovering that piece of knowledge. It can just be used, refined, built on, or taken in another direction that pushes the boundaries of collective knowledge further still. Many computer programmers work the same way. When they write a great piece of code that solves a common problem, they want to share that knowledge, partly for the kudos but mostly because they want to help everyone out. If they figure out a software patch that fixes a bug in an existing program, why hide the results? The benefit of having the exclusive solution is minimal in the long run. Besides, if everyone hides results, everyone fails to benefit from the thousands of great ideas being discovered all the time. If we all share our code and our ongoing innovations, we all get to benefit from the great collective mind, and together we'll be solving thousands of problems simultaneously.

This open, collective approach is very powerful. As the Net has spread and the number of contributing programmers has expanded, the brainpower of this group has begun to rival that in the biggest corporations, including the top firms in Silicon Valley and even mighty Microsoft. The quality of this group's software has begun reaching the level of that put out by highly organized corporations. The corporate software goes through rigorous quality control. The collective software, though, attains a similar rigor through the experiences of many thousands of independent eyeballs poring over it. And you certainly can't beat the price. The collective software is absolutely free. Nobody owns it, or, rather, everybody does. In fact, at first this kind of software was called *free software,* and the people who created it called themselves the *free software movement.* But the average layperson's notion of anything "free" is that it is less valuable, somehow inferior, and this software isn't. So over time the names have evolved into *open source software* and the *open source movement.* The terms refer to opening up to everyone the source code that is the basis of any software program. Once you can see the source code, which explains exactly how a software program works, you can understand why the program performs as it does—and how to modify or improve it. You can't see the source code of software designed by corporations like Microsoft. Their code is completely proprietary, so you always have to go to them and pay them for modifications or for solutions to your problems. To growing numbers of techies, this way of operating is unacceptable.

An open source operating system called Linux emerged in the late 1990s to compete with Microsoft's Windows. The core of the program was designed in the early 1990s by a Finnish graduate student, Linus Torvalds, to operate on all personal computers. The system has now grown to include hundreds of other open source packages that have improved and expanded the system's capabilities. By 1998, Linux was claiming more than 7 million users and was the world's fastest-growing operating system. Meanwhile, an open source Web server called Apache was running on more than 50 percent of the Web servers exposed to the Internet. This software had been developed by and was being maintained by a core group of about a dozen Web site administrators and an active group of contributing users. For a while, the corporate world ignored these and a growing number of other open source options. But with the continued success of the open source movement and its increased exposure in the mainstream media, that corporate resistance has begun to shift. The drama has begun to unfold.

Twenty-First Century Choices: The Making of a Long Boom

Part One: "Openness Wins"

Welcome to our documentary series "Twenty-first Century Choices: The Making of a Long Boom." I'm your host, Salma Aboulahoud, and like many of you viewers today in 2050, I lived through the turbulent two decades after the turn of the century, the 2000s and 2010s. I was a girl coming of age in Egypt just as the new millennium dawned. I remember well the anxiety of those times.

Those first years of the new millennium were ones of explosive growth and rapid innovation. They were filled with widespread changes that rolled through almost every field. And they brought their share of trauma, including moments of great peril when it wasn't clear the global community would rise to the challenges.

Our eight-part series will look back at the major stories that defined those times and led to the creation of ours. We will look at some of the critical choices that helped produce a half century of peace and prosperity.

We'll look at how the people in the first part of this century made many far-sighted choices that proved to be the right ones. Far more often than not, they chose the more open and inclusive alternatives that led to greater integration and higher growth. We'll look at how they struggled to restructure what was a new global economy, and to build a bold new politics, and to create the flexible learning society.

However, we'll also look at how they might have gotten it wrong. At several key junctures, they could have chosen more closed or hostile alternatives that might have produced decades of horror like the first half of the twentieth century.

We'll tell the stories of how they solved the Caspian Sea Crisis and fixed global warming in the wake of the Shanghai Winter of 2012. We'll remember their efforts to launch the new Space Age with the first mission to Mars. And we'll revisit their attempts to redress the gross inequities between the world's affluent and poor, a division that is much less severe today.

But we'll start our series with a look back on the construction of the technological infrastructure that now lies at the foundation of our twenty-first Century society. It was quite a feat to computerize and connect the entire world in such a short time span—just a couple of decades. But it was all the more important because it enabled many of the unexpected developments that were to come. We owe them much.

The Chips Spread

It's funny, but today we don't even think about computer technology. Back then, in the late twentieth century, people were obsessed with it. There were hundreds of magazines about all the latest gadgetry and whole television programs about "the computer and you."

It was like the early twentieth-century obsession with electric motors. By the end of the century, no one even thought about the electricity coursing through all walls or about the tiny electric motors silently powering a home's fifty or so appliances—from food blenders to dishwashers to every clock on the wall. We feel the same way now about computers: They are just tiny chips embedded in everything and connected together wirelessly. We don't notice them or even think about them.

At the end of the twentieth century, the ultimate goal of the technology world was to spread computers and computer chips around the entire globe and to connect them all together. This was the dream of technologists and an increasing number of businesspeople, but it was by no means a done deal. Some crucial choices had to be made. That megaproject can be understood as three major stories: in computer hardware, telecommunications, and software. The overall project was largely completed by 2015, though some of the final solutions were unpredictable until the very end.

First comes the hardware story, which concerns the basic machines. Just after the turn of the century, basic personal computers approached the cost of a good television set. The razor-thin profit margins put computer manufacturers under extreme competitive pressure but allowed businesses and families in developing countries to buy computers—which boosted the number of global sales and kept revenues flowing.

Meanwhile, the first half of the first decade saw advances in chip technology that increased the downward pressure on prices and kept boosting power. By 2006 virtually every new top-of-the-line personal computer was driven by a chip 100 times more powerful than the chips of the 1990s. The chips also kept shrinking in size, and by 2002 all a computer's functions could be housed on a chip the size of the head of a screw. This shrinking helped propel a proliferation of small computerized devices that unbundled the functions that had previously been the sole province of the PC.

The net effect was incredible mobility. Essentially by 2005 computers had become extremely small, extremely powerful, and extremely cheap. Combined with a vast expansion of wireless telecommunications, all computer users became free to roam.

The exploding power also allowed computers to become much easier to use. The most stunning break came with reliable voice recognition in the early part of the decade. The keyboard had long kept the growth of computing in check. Many highly literate people had never learned to type; illiterate or barely literate people had no way to interact. And, of course, most keyboards were designed for European languages, especially English.

By 2005, the majority of new computerized devices were voice-enabled and could recognize a limited vocabulary. By the end of the decade, powerful dictation systems caught nearly every word, even in languages not well suited to keyboards. This advance was a special boon to the Chinese, whose language is based on characters representing words rather than on letters. The 4,000 character keyboard was a thing of the past.

The final hardware threshold was crossed with the development of high-resolution flat screens, which approached the crispness of paper. Experimental flat screens had been developed in the 1990s, but their price didn't drop to reasonable levels until 2003.

Flat screens of all kinds soon appeared everywhere: in displays at work, in walls at home, in automobiles. Some were flexible like electronic paper; some were large and rigid—the size of entire walls of buildings. These became the many windows into the myriad corners of the world that came with the astounding developments in telecommunications.

Free Communications

The telecommunications story in the late twentieth century was all about bandwidth—as it was called in those days. Computer data at that time traveled in a relative trickle to many small businesses and almost all homes. This bandwidth bottleneck caused much consternation at the time because so much of the promise of networking depended on moving large files.

Many competing projects were initiated in parallel to deal with this problem. This proliferation of ideas became both a problem and, in the end, a boon. It was a problem for regulators because the different systems needed to be standardized and interoperable. It was a problem for individual companies because the fierce competition caused many to lose money. But it was a boon to everyone else because bandwidth, indeed, became plentiful—and then some.

By the middle of the decade in North America and Europe, half the population, depending on the density of the area, had high-speed access, some via telephone lines, some via cable modem, some by wireless connections, some by satellite connections.

The trends toward increasing mobility and increasing bandwidth came together in the arrival of overlapping satellite systems just after 2005. By that time, there were eight different competing systems providing major conduits for both voice and video data traffic. When the projects had been initiated in the 1990s, they were all highly proprietary and cutthroat—expecting to corner a piece of the market.

This competition spurred the early arrival of the means to cheaply connect to the new digital infrastructure from anyplace in the world. But the individual companies found their markets all merging, which led to a temporary glut of capacity, a big shakeout, and eventual consolidation. So around 2009, there was no meaningful distinction among any of them. They all had become just one more strand in the Net.

This building out the capacity of the digital pipes, if you will, would have been welcome enough. But at the same time, many firms were competing to compress digital files to stream through the bottlenecks. These two developments combined to bring an unexpected big bang in telecommunications in 2007.

Telecommunications in general and bandwidth in particular became so cheap that no one thought about the cost. There was so much capacity that virtually anything could be sent over the Net. Demand soared in what became known as the Telecom Takeoff.

Anybody with any idea about how to take advantage of the bandwidth had the opportunity to do so. The most visible development was the proliferation of full-motion video connections between millions of nodes in the Net.

This essentially opened up huge video windows between ordinary people on distant parts of the planet. With screens the size of walls, people in the frigid Arctic Circle could look out the equivalent of their back doors and experience a beach bar in the balmy Bahamas.

Open versus Closed Software

The final piece in the equation of creating a global network of computers had to do with software. The hardware was spreading as fast as possible. The capacity of the infrastructure was also expanding exponentially. But software was what tied everything together—or did not.

At the turn of the century, the big software battle was between free and proprietary software. If the open source movement, as it was called, could consistently produce high-quality software for free, then why would anybody pay good money to the proprietary crowd? Microsoft had the most to lose by moving in the direction of free software. The Silicon Valley group, though, potentially had the most to gain. If it moved early to give away software and expose its source code, it might be able to dramatically shift the status quo and unseat Microsoft. But that move would mean coming up with new strategies for making money around freely distributing the basic software.

At the time, there were several models for creating value through services and ongoing relationships, but they were largely untested and quite risky. The breakthrough came not long after the turn of the century, after the spread of the open source software had taken off. The Anybody-But-Microsoft crowd took a deep breath and adopted the new model.

The timing could not have been more fortuitous. The entire developing world was ready to take a leap into the digital age, yet the costs had been prohibitive.

How was some poor person in Bangladesh going to come up with $100 to pay Bill Gates for the use of his operating system—or $200 more for every application? Suddenly people found out that software was now free. At first, they couldn't believe it. Why would anyone do that? Then, when the suspicion dissipated, they became quite voracious in their use of it.

In addition, a de facto amnesty for software piracy was declared. Piracy had become a huge problem for software companies in the last part of the twentieth century, and they had spent enormous amounts of money trying to stop it. With the advent of open source software, the crackdown didn't make sense. In fact, use of a company's software was an asset: A business wanted people to spread its code—and its name—around. The wide acceptability of a company's software enabled the introduction of new products and services that were the real source of economic gain.

So by 2006, a common base of open, interoperable computer code spread across the planet to run virtually all digital machines. This had been the goal from the very beginning. The entire world was computerized, and all the machines could talk to each other and interact. With the shift to open source software and the accompanying explosion of growth, the goal was attained.

What had happened to Bill Gates? By the turn of the century, he had moved into the league of the great barons of the earlier Industrial Age, the Rockefellers and Carnegies, and he started becoming a serious philanthropist, donating billions to eradicating childhood diseases in developing countries. Gates wanted to be perceived as a good guy who had helped bring the world into the computer age. That's what he had wanted from the beginning. He hadn't gotten into software simply to make money; he had been like all those early young dreamers wanting to bring about a computer revolution. Yet Gates could not shake his sinister image.

There was one daring way forward: Gates could let go of his control and embrace the open route, the open source software model. He could let go of his ambitions for more proprietary control of the basic software running on desktops, and on the Internet, and on handheld gadgets. He could even release the source code for Windows and therefore his so-called monopoly of the personal computer world.

This option could actually help solve some nagging problems. Computer code was becoming so complex that the best way to solve the problems arising from complexity was to open the code up to all across the Net. Also customers were demanding interoperability and the ability to tailor code to their needs. By

PUTTING ITS CODE ON THE INTERNET, Microsoft would fully MOVE INTO THE INTERNET ERA AND leave behind THE PC ERA THAT IT Had dominated. THE COMPANY would THEN COMPETE ON THE QUALITY AND PRICE OF ITS APPLICATIONS THAT RAN ON THE COMMON BASE CODE. IT would RISE AND fall ON ITS SERVICE AND THE GENUINE VALUE IT brought TO THE MARKETPLACE. IT would RELY ON ITS Ability TO CONSTANTLY INNOVATE AND reinvent itself. Microsoft WAS A TRUE COMPANY OF THE New Economy. IT Had MORE brainpower AND RESOURCES THAN virtually ANY OTHER ORGANIZATION OUT THERE. If IT couldn't move confidently INTO AN UNCERTAIN future, who could?

The bulk of Microsoft EMPLOYEES WANTED TO MOVE IN THAT MORE risky direction. MANY Of THEM WERE TOP PROGRAMMERS who Had GROWN UP IN THE OPEN tradition Of THE software world. They WANTED TO work ON THE CUTTING EdGE OF THE COMPUTER REVOLUTION, NOT TO BE THE CARETAKERS OF THE Old CODE. THE PROblEM for Microsoft WAS ITS shareholders. THE COMPANY'S ASTRONOMICAL STOCK VALUES WERE based PARTLY ON THE STRATEGIC ADVANTAGES OF ITS Windows software, AND ANY MOVE TO GIVE IT AWAY would PROMPT A shareholder mutiny AND OUTRIGHT lawsuits.

Luckily for GATES AND COMPANY, THE U.S. GOVERNMENT STEPPED IN. THE JUSTICE DEPARTMENT'S ANTITRUST SUIT, BEGUN IN THE LATE 1990S, ENDED WITH A DEAL THAT broke Microsoft UP INTO TWO COMPANIES AND forced IT TO OPEN ITS OPERATING SYSTEMS SOURCE CODES. ONE WAS A COMPANY THAT kept improving THE OPERATING SYSTEMS for PERSONAL COMPUTERS AND OTHER COMPUTERIZED devices. THE OTHER COMPANY WAS THE ONE THAT would COMPETE IN APPLICATIONS, SERVICES, AND OTHER NEW MARKETS IN THE New Economy.

Though THEY complained bitterly AT THE TIME, THE Microsoft shareholders ACTUALLY profited Handsomely IN THE LONG RUN. BOTH SUCCESSOR COMPANIES WENT ON TO THRIVE—PARTICULARLY THE New Economy ONE. THE RESULT WAS VERY REMINISCENT Of WHAT Had Happened TO THE shareholders OF THE Old AT&T WITH THE breakup OF MA Bell AT THE BEGINNING OF THE ECONOMIC boom IN THE 1980S. THEY RECEIVED STOCK IN THE REGIONAL Baby Bells, which TOOK Off IN GROWTH. AND THE REMAINING PARENT long-distance TELEPHONE COMPANY Also woke from ITS slumber AND kicked INTO GROWTH, EVENTUALLY splitting INTO ANOTHER THREE COMPANIES THAT furTHER ENriched THE shareholders.

Wise public policy worked BOTH TIMES. Everyone, INSIDE AND OUTSIDE THE COMPANIES, benefited. NONE OF THEM benefited AS MUCH AS A REHABILITATED GATES. His shift IN STRATEGY brought A dramatic improvement IN His REPUTATION. He could TAKE His RIGHTful place IN Helping THE world MAKE ITS difficult TRANSITION. He WAS THE MAN IN black NO MORE.

2

The Millennial Transition

A new high-speed, highly innovative economy is transforming how business is done and redefining the rules of capitalism. Change of this magnitude is always accompanied by great turbulence and anxiety. As this New Economy tries to make the transition to a truly global one, we need to fully understand the dynamics and make the transition work.

December 1980
London, England

My Dear Friends,

I'm writing this year's end-of-the-year letter not on a typewriter, but on a brand new personal computer. You may have heard about them. Before I left the States, I went out and bought what's called an Apple II computer and lugged it all the way over here. I remember banging out college term papers on those god-awful typewriters late into the night, starting over with a new page or grabbing the bottle of white-out every time I made a mistake. We thought the great innovation was the arrival of erasable paper. But the real innovation is this personal computer, which really speeds up the process of typing and correcting mistakes. I'll never go back.

I finally made it to London, the place I've been reading about since I was a kid. I'm sitting right now in a bona fide garret that was probably built in the eighteenth century sometime. It's just one room tucked under a steep roof, and it's absolutely freezing all the time. I often sit here under a blanket, blowing cigarette smoke up to the ceiling, thinking about how much I miss you guys, my circle of best friends. The reason it's so cold is that it drizzles almost constantly. The city is shrouded in heavy clouds that make noon seem like dusk. It's an eerie feeling, like living inside a Dickens novel. I always had the image of London as this place of industrial gloom and crammed tenements, with smokestacks belching smoke, grim workers staggering to their jobs, and haughty rich people sneering at everyone. I always felt a heaviness when I thought about England—a heaviness that I feel now.

I spend a lot of time in the pub down the street. There's not much to say about British food, but the beer is great, and the characters you meet in the pubs are fantastic. The British women are pretty cool, too. Anyway, I sit in my corner of this working-class hangout, sipping my pint and watching the faces all around me. These people look so worn out, so beaten down. They do joke around and tell some pretty good stories, but their eyes are worried, and worried for good reason. England is getting to be a pretty miserable place. You step outside the pub and there's garbage piled in the streets. The garbage collectors have been out on strike the last couple of weeks. The air just reeks with the stench everywhere you go. Not that you can get anywhere. The transport workers seem to be on strike half the time as well. The tube sometimes works, the trains less often. I have no idea what's going on with the buses. You have to wake up and turn on the radio to see what's down for today. Not that I blame these people for going on strike. I'm one of those supporting them. I stood outside with everybody else at a rally for the coal miners the other day. Those poor guys are getting screwed. They're just decent people trying to make a living. Can you imagine how hard it must be to go down in tunnels to dig coal? Yet instead of thanks, they're getting tossed out of their jobs. I'd be angry, too.

It's all Margaret Thatcher's fault. I can't stand this woman, even the sight of her. She looks like a macho version of the queen. She's cracking down on all the people we identify with: the students, the regular workers, the poor. She's busting up the unions and laying people off. She's attacking the welfare system and cutting benefits all around. I understand that the welfare state was running into problems, but there must be ways to fix it. At least with a

Labour government in power, the right people were leading the country in the right direction with the right basic ideas. But Thatcher is just scrapping the whole approach. She's selling off publicly owned companies to rich people at bargain prices. She's deregulating big business and letting it run rampant. How can you trust those guys? They're going to completely exploit the situation, grind the workers into the ground, squeeze every last penny out of the consumer, and then leave us living in a cesspool of pollution. It's going to be an utter disaster. And the disaster is not just looming here in England. You guys must be seeing the same thing happening back in the states. For god's sake, Ronald Reagan was elected president of the United States a month ago. What are Americans thinking by electing a bad movie actor as leader of the Free World? He's going to out-Thatcher Thatcher, plus get the world into a war. He's promising to build up the military and take on the Soviets. Give me a break—the Soviet Union has 40,000 nuclear bombs.

What kind of a world are we living in? I spent my life raised in middle-class middle America—in a strict Catholic household no less. All my life my family told me what a wonderful world I lived in. God is great, America is great, my life is great. What did I know? I just believed everyone. Then I finally grew up, left home, started college with you guys, and began thinking on my own. The world I started encountering didn't map onto what I had been taught. And then I went to study abroad for this year and my mind really got blown away. I realize now that almost everything I was taught about the world simply isn't true. The world just doesn't work the way they told me—and I'm angry about it. The United States turns out not to be this land of equality and justice. Sure, I did pretty well growing up in my middle-class home, but how about all the poor people, or blacks in the inner city, or Latino immigrants? They can barely survive in the so-called land of opportunity. And what about women? They are permanently locked into a second-class status. And the United States was supposed to make the world safe for freedom and democracy. So why did we support dictators and go across the world to napalm the Vietnamese? This is insane, yet this is my country. Soon God disappeared for me, too. The religion that I had faithfully followed no longer made sense.

I feel duped. I feel like a foolish kid who spent his youth studying about how the world worked—only to emerge from isolation and find what I studied completely obsolete. The old systems of religion and politics and economics don't seem to work anymore. Capitalism sure isn't all it's cracked up to be. It's barely working for the people making money, let alone the bulk of us, who are struggling to survive. On the other hand, what could realistically replace it? Communism? No one really wants to live as a proletarian in the Soviet Union. I mean, the goals are noble, but life is grim over there, too. There doesn't seem to be much difference between the futures of Ronald Reagan capitalism and Soviet Politburo communism. They both seem bleak. I suppose there's the ideal form of socialism that's been talked about for decades. But in Europe that's just turned into a lame form of capitalism. And in the Third World, it's just turned into never-ending warfare. Who really wants to be a Marxist? Marxism seems so rigid and harsh and rather bleak, too.

I don't have the answers. In fact, I realize now I don't know much of anything about the world. I've been traveling a bit around Europe and have encountered all these different people speaking different languages. Half the time I have no clue what is going on. I was recently in Paris and watched a bunch of riot police storm some protesting students and beat them with clubs. The police started coming after me, and I didn't even know what we were fighting about. At least the Europeans speak languages that have some identifiable words and a culture that I generally recognize. Every once in a while I come across Asians or other foreigners speaking languages that are absolutely impenetrable, from cultures that seem exotic. In London there are all these people from India and Bangladesh and Pakistan. In France, there're all these Africans and Arabs. I have no idea what is going on in those distant parts of the world. I've got to get a better handle on what's happening on this planet because right now nothing makes much sense. At this point, I just need to find a way to somehow survive. I just need a few simple things. I want to find a way to make a living and find a partner to share my life. And I really want to stay connected to you guys.

Here I am twenty years old in the year 1980, and I'm just finishing up my formal education, confused as hell. Right now I'm supposed to be launching into my life, moving confidently into the world. Yet I feel depressed if not terrified. I feel that the world is a mess and that the future will only get worse. I missed all the really great moments in history. I wasn't around for World War II, the good fight against fascism, and the rebuilding of the Free World. That struggle gave the lives of my father and mother's generation so much meaning that our generation doesn't have. Plus they were able to enjoy a postwar economic boom that's over. They had rising prospects and great hope. We Baby Boomers are entering a very different world. Our world is one of decreasing expectations and seems to have no such higher calling or deeper meaning. Our future is going to be stark. I can't think of a worse time to start my adult life.

The New Economy Rumbles

Just as the year 1980 marked a watershed in technology, it also marked a watershed in the political economy. That was the year Ronald Reagan was elected president of the United States. And just the year before, Margaret Thatcher had been elected prime minister of Great Britain. These two conservative politicians began a historic assault on the welfare state that had become predominant in the West after World War II. They began to dismantle the old bureaucratic industrial economy and to lay the groundwork for the more entrepreneurial New Economy of today.

At the time, their approach was extremely controversial. After all, they were fighting decades of economic orthodoxy about how to run the economy from the commanding heights of big government. And their methods were often raw—if not brutal. They both took on the labor unions—Thatcher's most memorable battle being with the coal miners, and Reagan's with the air traffic controllers. They privatized portions of the government that many members of the public had come to consider their own. They deregulated businesses that many still deeply distrusted. And they jacked up the unemployment rates by tightening monetary policy in an attempt to rein in inflation. In short, they threw their countries into a traumatic transition that many people did not fully understand at the time. However, looking back on their efforts of the early 1980s, they clearly helped initiate a critical shift in the direction of the economy that had to be made one way or the other. Not all that Reagan and Thatcher did worked, nor was all wise and equitable. Indeed, President Bill Clinton and Prime Minister Tony Blair, the leaders of the opposition parties who eventually came to power, had to clean up many of the mistakes—such as high government deficits—and deal with the collateral damage by helping those most affected by the changes.

But Reagan and Thatcher did create the political and economic context for the beginnings of the transformation of capitalism. Although they would not explain themselves in this way, they acted as mid-wives in the birthing of the New Economy, the knowledge economy, out of the old industrial economy. The old economy was relatively static—change came more slowly. The New Economy became increasingly entrepreneurial and innovative. Those who succeeded were those who moved quickly. Pre-1980s, we lived and worked in an industrial and service economy, where we mostly made stuff, tangible things, and provided services with them. Post-1980s, we are moving increasingly to a knowledge economy, where the new value added comes in the realm of ideas, which are intangibles. We still make physical things—food, cars, houses—but the growth and dynamism of the economy increasingly comes from the information sectors, the emerging knowledge sectors.

REVOLUTION I: REORGANIZING WORK

Computers played a big part in this transformation. Personal computers allowed, or facilitated, two major reinventions in capitalism: in corporate organization and in the world of finance.

The first reinvention had to do with how we organize work in our economy, and in the individual companies that compete in that economy. The central way this reorganization manifested itself was in a shift from hierarchical, bureaucratic organizations, where information moved up an elaborate chain of command and decisions came back down the chain, to networked ones, where information and the concomitant decisionmaking moved horizontally, within more flattened organizations. This kind of reorganization could not have happened without the new information technologies. But such fundamental corporate reorganization caused a lot of traumatic repercussions. For example, many middle managers in that earlier chain of command, along with many secretaries and clerks, were no longer needed to move information around the organization: The technology did it faster and cheaper.

So throughout the 1980s, and particularly in the recession of the early 1990s in the United States, corporations went through a downsizing—a new managerial term that fit the new reality. There were other new terms and concepts that people did not fully understand at the time. We began "outsourcing" work to smaller businesses, working with contract workers and temporary workers who could fill constantly shifting needs. We began creating "virtual" corporations, with people telecommuting out of their homes. The language and the experiences were strange, but with hindsight, we can see that corporations were reinventing themselves to become leaner, more focused, more efficient economic units that were heading into a new kind of economy, the networked economy. Many people were hurt by these transitions, and Reagan and Thatcher were insensitive to their plight. These changes could have been accomplished with greater concern for those who fell through the cracks. Going forward, they should be.

What happened in corporate America during this period can be understood better through a football analogy. American businessmen are obsessed with football, partly because the game is not just a sport but a metaphor. Essentially, the game has many similarities to the competitive business world. Each team is like a corporation. The head coach is like the chief executive officer, or CEO, whose coaching staff is like top management. The players—much like a good firm's employees—are carefully selected to bring together a diverse skill set. The key to winning in both the game and the market depends on several factors. First, you need the right mix of talent. Then, all personnel have to work together and operate as a highly coordinated team. And finally, you need the right strategy.

One football strategy that emerged in the early 1980s quickly became an unprecedented winner. Its inventor was Bill Walsh, whose first head coaching job was at Stanford University in the heart of Silicon Valley. After success at the college level, he became head coach of the professional San Francisco 49ers. Out of his base in the Bay area, Walsh created what became known as the *West Coast offense,* which was based in great part on speed. Other teams might grind up the field by running for short gains up the middle, or protect the quarterback while he threw long passes that were occasionally caught. The 49ers darted up the field with quick short passes to the sidelines that were very difficult to defend against and that brought consistent midrange gains. The West Coast offense was also about smarts. The key player was the quarterback, who had to act independently and make split-second decisions in reaction to the defense. Other players also had to play with their heads and exploit unforeseen opportunities. The West Coast offense was also about constant innovation. Every week the team came up with different plays and strange combinations of players that the other teams, with more static strategies, did not know how to cope with. And finally, the offense was dynamic. It changed approaches not just week to week but during the game. Walsh would purposely run a preordained set of twenty-five plays at the start of the game so that he could immediately adapt to the reactions of the defense.

Using that strategy, the 49ers became phenomenally successful, winning their first Super Bowl championship in 1981, and eventually adding another four. But the success of the West Coast offense was not limited to that one team. Soon the disciples on Walsh's coaching staff moved on to become head coaches of other teams and, by replicating the offense, made those teams powerhouses as well. By the 1990s, virtually all the best teams in pro football were running the West Coast offense and racking up Super Bowl championships. The strategy had spread through the heartland of America to Denver, Green Bay, and Minnesota, among other teams. The West Coast offense was now just the winning one.

The parallels to the world of business are so striking that they're almost eerie. At almost the same time that Walsh was creating his new offense in Silicon Valley, the business community there was creating a new business model, too. This model shared many of the same attributes: The Silicon Valley business model was about speed in everything from the initial design phase to manufacturing to getting products to market. It was also about smarts. For one thing, new business ideas in the Valley often spun off from research at Stanford University and other academic institutions in the Bay Area. In addition, the firms were not nearly as hierarchical as traditional corporations. Control devolved from the center, with everybody in a company trusted to come up with ideas and to contribute. And the new economic model was about constant innovation: If it ain't broke, then *still* try to improve it. These companies were extremely dynamic—quickly responding to minute changes in their industries.

Other hallmarks of the new economic model did not have direct parallels to football. For example, unlike sports teams, the companies in Silicon Valley tended to form cooperative networks that shared ideas and worked together on projects—while still competing intensely in other areas. The workers and top talent frequently changed jobs, bringing about further cross-fertilization. In essence, the business model for what became the underpinning of the New Economy was developed in Silicon Valley throughout the 1980s. As the model proved its success, it started migrating out of the Valley—first, via disciples who had experienced its magic. Bill Gates replicated the formula in one company up in Seattle. Microsoft combined the same speed, smarts, and constant innovation in one corporation. Instead of a valley of independent small companies, Microsoft had a campus of decentralized divisions that operated with much autonomy amid sharing. Over time, Microsoft spawned and attracted other companies that formed a Valley-like network in the state of Washington. By the early 1990s, you could definitely distinguish a West Coast offense in the business world. Other high-tech hubs like Boston and Austin and Minneapolis were early adopters, and the firms there began to thrive. Soon the West Coast model became just the winning one.

Revolution II: Revamping Finance

The other aspect of capitalism that went through a major reinvention was in the world of finance. Here, too, computers played a central role. Starting in the 1980s, finance began a giddy fifteen-year run of innovation using the new information technologies. The computers themselves, the number crunchers, were used in new ways to assess risk and to create increasingly sophisticated financial packages. So we saw the appearance of new financial products like junk bonds and derivatives, as well as the proliferation of increasingly specialized mutual funds. More powerful computers allowed experimentation in computer models of the market that led to computers trading by themselves, with little direct human control. Then the telecommunications side of the networked computer revolution opened up whole new possibilities. The information used to make financial judgments became much better, much more extensive, and amazingly more timely. The financial world benefited immensely from a wave of increasingly better ways to get information—from the rise of cable television's twenty-four-hour news cycles, to innovative news agencies like Bloomberg Financial Services, to today's up-to-the-second information on the Internet. The global information infrastructure itself not only allowed better information to arrive but also allowed the financial operators to react instantaneously to opportunities that were emerging anywhere in the world. So on a daily basis, literally trillions of dollars in investments could move around the world in response to the most promising opportunities. All these innovations made for an incredible increase in the efficiency, or productivity, of that capital. We started to get a lot more bang for each buck.

The Productivity Paradox

Taken together, these two major innovations in the nature of global capitalism—in finance and organization—began to boost the productivity of the economy at large. But this did not happen right away, nor was it obvious. In fact, there's still quite a bit of controversy surrounding what is called the *productivity paradox*. Basically, the investment in new technologies typically translates into higher productivity for the workers who use them. That's why businesses invest in them in the first place. However, by the late 1990s, although businesses had invested an estimated $4 trillion in information technologies, the standard government productivity measurements showed only a slight rise, and that had come only since about 1996. Critics of the New Economy charge that these networked computers are not all that productive—and they point to the government statistics. But New Economy advocates, like us, say the computers are highly productive and are getting more so as we figure out the best ways to work with them. The problem lies in the government measurements, which are rooted in old ways of counting the number of widgets—tangible things—coming off the assembly line, rather than the intangible products of the New Economy, like software and financial packages. On the one hand, we're waiting for new methods to be devised to properly measure productivity in an information economy. On the other, as with any fundamentally new technology, it takes decades for a workforce to reorganize its work to get the most productivity out of new tools. We're now increasingly seeing those kinds of work-flow breakthroughs.

The real proof of the productivity of the new computer technologies—and by extension, the New Economy—is in the overall performance of the economy that houses them. In that respect, the economy of the United States in the late 1990s made the case. The U.S. economy has now sustained the longest peacetime expansion without a recession in the nation's history. In fact, technically, the economic expansion has been uninterrupted since 1983 because the so-called recession of the early 1990s did not meet the formal criteria of three consecutive quarters of negative growth—it just flattened growth for about a two-year spell. From 1996 to 1999, this mature $8-trillion economy sustained gangbuster growth of about 4 percent. Growth rates even hit more than 5.5 percent in some quarters. Meanwhile, a quarter million new jobs were consistently created in every quarter. Unemployment rates bottomed out at around 4 percent—levels not seen for nearly thirty years. After stagnating for nearly two decades, wages for the average worker began increasing in the mid-1990s. Yet, despite all that, inflation remained very low. According to basic economics, that kind of growth and tightened labor conditions almost certainly leads to rising inflation unless the productivity of workers keeps growing at an even faster pace. We say that productivity clearly is kicking in. Economists may not be able to measure it accurately, but the effects of that productivity are obvious for all to see.

Many people have equated the boom with the stock market, which has burgeoned past all records. The Dow Jones industrial average had pushed past the 10,000 mark by the spring of 1999, having doubled in less than four years, and having increased almost tenfold since the beginning of the Long Boom. But the boom has affected everyone, not just the rich and the well-off with investments. The higher employment levels and rising wages have boosted consumer confidence, and people are spending on a vast array of retail goods. The spending has swept through the housing market, and new construction can hardly keep up with demand. Poor people have moved into decent job opportunities, and the welfare rolls are at their lowest levels since the late 1960s. There are opportunities all over the place, in both high-end and low-end jobs. Smart people all over the world have seen the openings and have been moving toward the action. People from

Latin America have migrated northward to the United States to start better lives by taking the ample domestic work and other low-end jobs. Those who know about technology have been coming to the United States, to be welcomed with open arms. This New Economy clearly has been working in the United States, but the looming question is whether it will work for the world.

Globalization Begins

The changes in technology and the political economy of the West paralleled the third set of events that fell along that 1980 axis—*globalization*. Technically, these events also fell in the realm of politics and economics, but with more global implications than what Reagan and Thatcher represented. In 1980, Mikhail Gorbachev became a Politburo member and began the process that led to the Soviet Union's move toward democracy and capitalism. And in 1978, Deng Xiaoping wrestled control of political power in the People's Republic of China and began moving the Chinese toward the market economy. It's hard to exaggerate the significance of these two events. They created the starting point for our truly globalized world.

The world had made other attempts to integrate on a more global scale. There was the creation of colonial empires in the late nineteenth century, but they integrated only slices of the overall global economy of that time. Half the world, the so-called Free World, was integrated into one interdependent international economy during the Cold War, but the incorporation of the other half of the world, the Communist World, into the global market economy took globalization to an even higher level. For the first time in history, every region of the world—and almost every single nation—is tied into the same economy. This integration is historically unprecedented—with unprecedented consequences to come.

This globalization, this global economic integration, combined with the new networked computer technologies, is powering the Long Boom. They are equally important forces in our economy and our lives, and they are interdependent: The information technologies spread the media and data that allow the globalization to work. To understand the power of these twin forces, we can compare the Long

Boom era to the last time the world experienced such a great global economic expansion: the forty-year era after World War II. Some remarkable parallels warrant a closer look. In the years after World War II, two metatrends emerged that transformed the decades that followed. In the first, an array of new technologies that had been developed during the war, or that had been developed before but had been bottled up by the war, suddenly moved from the hands of the military into the private sector. We've already mentioned mainframe computers, atomic energy, and television, but there were many others, like radar, commercial aviation, and plastics. The second, equally important development was that we integrated the economies of the Free World to a level not seen before. We interconnected our currencies through the Breton Woods accord, and we devised international institutions that had no precursors: the International Monetary Fund, the World Bank, the European Economic Community, and, for that matter, the United Nations itself. The net effect was to more closely calibrate the interactions of these national economies.

Those twin developments of the second half of the 1940s were the main causes of the economic boom in the United States in the 1950s. Why the United States? It was the first country to adopt the new technologies aggressively, and it had the most open borders, so it could take advantage of the enhanced trade environment. And so the U.S. economy just took off on a tear. To this day, Americans look back on the 1950s as the economic Golden Age. But that economic boom didn't stop in the United States, and it didn't stop in the 1950s. That same boom spread throughout the Free World in the 1960s. Europe got back on its feet after the war, and Japan also rebuilt. All these economies were booming throughout the 1960s—causing huge repercussions in their social and political arenas as well. This high growth continued until the oil shocks of 1973, when the quadrupling in price of oil, the lifeblood of the Industrial Age economy, helped choke off the growth and push the economies of the developed world into the stagflation of the 1970s. Still, the economic expansion had had a good twenty-five-year run.

Those same two megatrends are driving through our Long Boom era today. In the wake of the Cold War, that quasi-war of military preparedness, another array of new technologies is flooding into the private sector—not the least of which is the Internet. The Internet was developed by the military to link university researchers around the country who were doing defense work. Now it stitches together most U.S. businesses. The early research on the microprocessor was funded in the 1960s by DARPA, the Defense Advanced Research Projects Agency, to help direct guided missiles. But those aren't the only new technologies moving into the public sphere. The military sank hundreds of billions of dollars into satellite technology—from spy imaging, to global positioning systems, to Star Wars laser defense. We don't even know the exact amounts because they are still classified. But now all that technology is being turned over to enterprising businesses, which are innovating like mad to bring them to you. Global economic integration as well as the technology bonanza are the two major forces behind that U.S. boom of the 1990s. But again, we don't expect that boom will end in the 1990s or with the United States. We think this Long Boom model will reach beyond the United States and go global. However, that development lies in the future, and taking that step, it turns out, is easier said than done.

Which brings us to the global crisis. All that innovation in the New Economy, that reinvention of the corporation and of finance, happened in the West's developed countries. All the heavy adoption of computer technologies that undergirded the New Economy was a Western phenomenon. In fact, most of it happened first in the United States, only later spreading to Europe in the late 1990s. The Asian economies clearly had benefited from globalization, which spurred their economies, albeit industrial ones. But they had not adopted the new computer technologies or begun the process of reorganizing work around them. And their financial systems remained trapped in a time warp—not keeping pace with those in the developed West. These financial systems lacked transparency and accountability, which are essential to the efficient use of capital. Those countries also needed better regulatory and legal systems for oversight and conflict resolution. In essence, they had not shifted quickly enough to the institutions of civil government necessary to operate in the more open networked economy, which began to emerge as the future system for the world. They had not gone far in their transition to the economy of the Knowledge Age. And when the herd mentality in global finance recognized this, everyone began to pull out their funds.

Starting in Thailand in July 1997, Western international investors began to withdraw money from the developing Asian nations, collapsing their currencies. After Thailand, came Indonesia, and Korea, and Hong Kong, and Malaysia. The cause was not the bad judgment of one nation, but a structural problem that spanned almost the whole of Asia. And the Asians weren't alone. The Russians floundered soon afterward. There was a continual scare that Brazil would also go under, thereby hanging Latin America in the balance. By the late 1990s, almost the entire developing world was reeling. To most people in the world, the new global networked economy seemed like a wild animal out of control. No one had ever dealt with the movement of such great sums of capital at such speeds, and the international community had no good mechanisms for dealing with the phenomenon. The individual developing countries had no idea what to do. And the whole thing really put the world in a deep funk.

The Millennial Anxiety

The millennial anxiety is just that: It is as much about anxiety as it is about actual problems. Certainly, the global economy has run into some serious difficulties, but they are clearly manageable, definitely solvable. What has pushed these solvable problems into the category of a crisis is the anxiety that has mushroomed around them, causing people to overreact and misunderstand what is really going on. What started with a growing anxiety among currency traders and global financiers in the summer of 1997 developed into a near panic as the world edged closer and closer to the turn of the century—and to an apparent nervous breakdown. The worst prognosis of some analysts was that we were heading into a global depression.

There's good reason why the term *depression* is used to describe an economic situation in which the economy contracts into negative growth with no end in sight. The term comes from the world of psychology and refers to a mental state where the patient is hopeless because he has an inability to see a positive way out of his situation. That lack of a vision leads to his debilitating condition. All he wants to do is curl up in a ball and sleep. The global community could be seen as edging toward a state of depression, largely because of the lack of a positive vision of how to move ahead into a better world.

Ever since the collapse of the Cold War, the world has not had a clear, coherent vision of how it could turn out better than it is now. We can say now that the dreams of communism and socialism were utopian, but at their beginnings, they gave their adherents a better world to strive for. And without communism to contrast with, the capitalist liberal democracies have not advanced their vision beyond more of the same—what we have now, writ larger.

The lack of vision is compounded by a lack of leadership—particularly political leadership. It's one thing to crystallize a new vision of how the world should evolve in the coming decades, and it's another thing to communicate that vision to a wide mass of people and convince them that the vision can come true. The world has run into some particularly bad luck in the last few years when it comes to leadership. At exactly the time when the world needed powerful leaders to see through the confusion of the global crisis and articulate clear directions as to how we could move ahead, we instead had a paralysis in the corridors of power. President Bill Clinton, who has come as close as any current leader to understanding the nature of the economic transition the world is moving through, was forced to spend much of 1998 and 1999 preoccupied with defending himself from impeachment. At the same time, the Republican leadership in the U.S. Congress thought of little else besides the President's impeachment. And the leadership vacuum was found not just in the United States: While Japan kept rotating through the same batch of tired old politicians, Europe stayed preoccupied with its own regional integration challenge.

If we pull back from the specifics of the global crisis and from all the anxiety churning in the air, like our hypothetical person in 2050, we can better see the essence of the problem. Let's go slow here. We're watching a transformation in the nature of global capitalism. There are two basic legs of capitalism: capital and labor. On the capital side, we've seen radical innovation since 1980. The world of finance has undergone tremendous change. And huge amounts of capital have been invested in new technologies, which have undergone even more extreme changes. Certainly the world of capital—particularly finance—needs to be refined and perfected. For example, developing countries need to establish regulatory institutions for their financial systems. But the real thrust of the work ahead lies on the other side of the equation, the labor side. Ordinary human beings, working hard and living their lives, also need to understand the magnitude of the changes taking place in the economy and through the new technologies. People have to understand how the way we work is being transformed, where this New Economy is heading, and how it will change our lives and the lives of our families. This is where the politics of the Long Boom comes in. A clear vision needs to be articulated by strong leaders to everyone, humanity at large, not just an elite of financial traders or knowledge workers. Everybody has to have a general understanding of the direction we're heading. That's the way through the anxiety and back onto the Long Boom.

As if the anxiety over the turndown in the global economy weren't enough, there's the mounting anxiety over the state of our technology. As the new century approaches, the year 2000, or Y2K, problem looms large. Talk about a lack of historical perspective! Here's a problem generated by the mass of computer programmers who collectively could not foresee that the computer code they were creating might need to survive more than the decade or two until the turn of the century. Their mistake affects programs with millions of lines of code that need to be tweaked. And many of the programs are housed in embedded chips that can't easily be reprogrammed—they are inside an electrical power grid, or a navigation system in a plane, or within the pipes pumping oil across Alaska. The failure of multiple computer systems, or even the expectation of such failures, could prompt a broad public backlash—or it may not.

There's a very good chance that the Y2K problem will act like the 1973 oil crisis, which cut the supplies of oil, quadrupled the prices almost overnight, and forced almost every person in the world to recognize that the global economy's dependence on oil affected everyone. That shock was a thunderous wakeup call that focused the world community on developing and deploying more efficient technologies. The same will be true of the Y2K problem. Most people do not understand how hooked we already are on computers, but if widespread failures affect services of every kind, and if the global economy goes into a real wobble, they'll get the message. Even if the actual failures are relatively contained, the increasingly hysterical discussions leading up to the big day ("You mean my electricity, my food supply, the phones, hospitals, airplanes, everything could go down?") will drive the point home almost as well. The Y2K crisis will also accelerate the shift from the problematic computer systems that are a legacy of the past to the newest generation of networked computer systems, which are a solid foundation going forward into the new century. These will be the new baseline for the twenty-first century computer age—and for the centuries that come next.

The nature of crises in general is that they accelerate change. That's the silver living in entering what by most accounts is a situation that nobody wants to go through. Crises tend to clear the decks of old leaders and old ideas. These people and ideas are often rightfully blamed for helping create the crisis in the first place. Crises tend to force inevitable changes that societies will not voluntarily make in noncritical times. That's what's happening in Asia right now. For example, because the Japanese could not summon the political will to go through a painful and expensive, but inevitable, restructuring of their financial systems, their economy increasingly stagnated in the 1990s. It may take a full-blown crisis to finally force that restructuring.

Out of crisis comes opportunity. Instead of dwelling on the potential disaster, think about how to leverage the situation to bring about needed change. That's the Long Boom attitude: When faced with a crisis in global capitalism, move full speed ahead—forward through the transition, not backward. The Russians don't want to go back to communism. No one has to tell them that it didn't work—they lived under it for seventy-five years. As long as they can find a reasonable transition to a decent form of capitalism, as opposed to the wild form of gangster capitalism that they have experienced, they'll move forward. The peoples of Southeast Asia don't want to go back to crony capitalism—certainly not if it will get them back into the same kind of trouble they experienced in the late 1990s. They want to do whatever it takes to get back to a high-growth economy, back into a boom—only this time a sustainable one built on solid financial foundations.

The Imperative of Growth

The millennial transition in global capitalism presents a choice to the world community: Do we proceed to a high-growth economic strategy; or do we maintain the status quo, a less dynamic economy of slow growth; or, as some radical environmentalists advocate, do we opt for no growth? The developed Western countries could cut and run right now. They could say that they got theirs. They have a broad middle class, and almost everyone is out of dire poverty—at least according to a global standard. They rode the economic booms of this century and inexorably raised their standards of living. They can drop that high-growth strategy now. But people in these countries contemplated a future of a perpetually stagnant economy and a two-tier society during the 1970s and 1980s, when it looked as though a high-growth economy was a thing of the past. None of us want to live in a two-tier society: people don't want to be rich in that kind of society—and they certainly don't want to be poor. The rich must live holed up within walled houses and armored cars, with security forces hovering over them and their kids. That's no way to live. And that's the rich. Think about how the poor live in that kind of world.

The bulk of the world today is destitute. The majority of people in the world are barely staying alive. For them, a high-growth global economy is the only possible way of attaining a decent standard of living, or perhaps even a middle-class lifestyle—and if not for them, then for their kids. Walk through the streets of Bombay and watch the thousands, hundreds of thousands—no, millions—of people with outstretched hands begging for anything that will just help them stay alive. And if not in Bombay, then Jakarta or Cairo or São Paulo or any of the other dozen megacities that you want to pick. Those cities are all packed with 15 million people or more—half of them barely hanging on—and there are millions more in the countryside who are in even worse shape. What can be done with the 2 billion or so poor people in the world? They're alive, and they're having children. Are they to be told that the global economy is going to stop growing? That their dreams of someday attaining a semblance of a middle-class lifestyle are now absurd? Are they to be left to die?

The Long Boom strategy is unabashedly progrowth. There's almost no other choice. We need to grow the global economy at high rates for a sustained period to get many more people up to a decent standard of living. We need to set in motion a dynamic where all people in the world have a reasonable expectation of making some incremental improvement in their, or their children's, standard of living. All people can expect to find opportunities to move up at least a notch over their lifetime. All—from the rich to the poor—can see progress possible in their own lives. At the very least, the global economy needs to sustain annual growth rates of 4 percent or more for the long haul. After revving up through the 1990s, the global economy did grow at about 4 percent by the peak years of 1996 and 1997, before Asia and the developing world crashed. Getting back to that baseline is certainly manageable and sustainable. The post–World War II boom consistently hit that 4 percent level. But global growth rates of as much as 5 or 6 percent are conceivable. China sustained average growth rates of 9 percent for twenty years. The world as a whole could do as much as 6 percent. That torrid pace would be based on a global economy creating whole new industries producing output, and many developing countries' growing rapidly. Growth at that 6 percent rate would double the base of the global economy every twelve years. We'd double it twice in twenty-five years. That kind of wealth creation changes everything, rapidly spreading prosperity and great hope.

The Long Boom strategy is also a high-tech one. It's high-tech partly because the networked computer technologies, among other new technologies, are going to be needed to improve efficiency and boost productivity in order to sustain that kind of growth. But it's also high-tech because new technologies are needed to mitigate the damage to the environment. A global economy growing at those high rates using old Industrial Age technologies would irreparably damage the environment and put our fragile ecology under unacceptable strain. We simply can't do that because another looming anxiety out there that's gathering force is the fear of global climate change. This fear is not as immediate as the anxiety over the global economy or Y2K, but long after these other anxieties dissipate, it will probably prolong the sense of urgency in the first decade of the twenty-first century and perhaps longer still. The environmental concerns are one more reason to go high tech. New technology will help lower the damage to the environment to acceptable and ever-improving levels at the same time that it helps drive the growth in the economy itself. It's a win/win situation. A hallmark of the Long Boom.

Going into the turn of the century, the world finds itself in a strange situation: The Americans have figured out an economic model that works marvelously and seems able to work in a global context, and the conduits of global media and technology are ready to spread the ideas. However, much of the world still struggles with the concept of globalization and sometimes equates it with Americanization. The new computer technology seems very American, the global media seem very American, and now the economic model is perceived as being American. Many nations fear that the United States is out to take over the world. The strange part of this perception is that Americans themselves seem to have no interest in anything outside their own borders. So the world is ambivalent about following the U.S. lead, and the American people are ambivalent about the necessity of leading.

We think the stalemate needs to be broken. The United States needs to provide real visionary global leadership, and the world needs to open up just enough to see that taking some new ideas and developing them further is in its best interests. In other words, everyone needs to let go of his or her fears and preconceptions and move on. If we break the stalemate soon, every region of the world will be able to make significant contributions to the global community. Over time, the increasingly globalized world will lose its American flavor and become something different, a hybrid. The transformation of the second phase of the Long Boom can proceed.

The Twenty-first Century Choices: The Making of a Long Boom

Part Two: "Going Global"

Welcome again to "Twenty-first Century Choices: The Making of a Long Boom." I'm Salma Aboulahoud, your host for the eight-part series that pauses at the midpoint of this remarkable century and looks back at the critical first two decades that laid the groundwork for much of what we enjoy today. Some of you in 2050 may already be looking ahead to the twenty-second century. Instead, we'd like to take you back fifty years and talk about economics.

Around the turn of the century, a clear consensus began to emerge that the global economy should be considered almost one body. Individual nations and regional blocs of nations should be regarded as body parts dependent on the whole. And individual cities, or clusters of cities, could be regarded almost as cells.

The new technology was seen as the nervous system of the newly integrated twenty-first century world, and what was called the New Economy was seen as the circulatory system that provided the sustenance for continued growth. The New Economy developed many different conduits for rapidly moving around the world everything from capital to products to parts and people.

This new conception of how to organize economically prompted what was called the Great Global Restructuring in the first decade of the century. Take the basic economic activity of selling things. Electronic commerce, or e-commerce, emerged in the late 1990s and exploded in growth for the next decade. If a person wanted to buy something—an airplane ticket or an automobile or tax advice—it was up for bid on the open market, and sellers anywhere in the world could make their pitch. By 2003, electronic commerce was already over $3 trillion dollars worldwide, roughly 10% of global GDP. In 2007, e-commerce was simply called COMMERCE because essentially every business transaction was carried out electronically.

By 2009, shopping malls were mainly sources of entertainment, the theme parks of materialism, where people went to examine and play with products— but not often to buy them. A full 51 percent of retail sales were on-line, and most purchases were delivered to the home or business. Still, almost half of all products were bought locally.

The new commerce also affected less tangible products that involved intellectual property. A system of currency called MICROPAYMENTS developed on-line and allowed the creators of original content to be compensated through tiny transactions of as little as one penny per view. The viewers were not burdened by such slight payments, but the creators were able to earn a decent living because the global market allowed the aggregation of those micropayments into substantial sums.

An elaborate network of publishing began to develop in virtually every medium. Artists could make available their paintings, videos, music, essays, poems— whatever they wanted to publish in any form. People around the world could then download the songs, articles, books, movies—all now in digital format.

The Revolution in Moving Bits and Things

In the new global environment, the production of things was transformed as well. Two major developments in information management and transport made for a revolution in logistics. The global information infrastructure led to a "glass pipeline," where the movement of all parts and products and people could be closely tracked through every stage of production.

Along with that fundamental change in communications, in moving information, came a big leap forward in moving things. A new generation of very fast freighters and large cargo planes beefed up the carrying capacity while keeping transport costs low. In 2003, a new class of superfreighter that could carry even bulk cargo, like wheat, went into service, cutting the time for transport from the East Coast of the United States to Europe from ten days to three.

Managers became much more efficient with just-in-time deliveries of everything from raw material to polished products, and avoiding high inventories which were all cost and little value. In addition, the entire world could be used to get the best prices on supplies; no business or consumer was trapped in a localized market.

In the early industrial economy, all major parts suppliers for a Detroit automaker had to be local. In the later industrial era, they all had to be within the same nation. The global logistics revolution allowed bids to come from Jakarta or São Paulo, and more and more products were assembled to order by the shipping companies themselves from components sourced all over the world. In distant locations these producers could specialize in some unique capability like plastic molding or auto electronics. This meant the world no longer needed as many steel mills, or car plants, or shipyards in each nation.

By 2010, a somewhat reluctant shift to specialization was well under way. Whatever people did best in the world, they tended to concentrate on. Competitive clusters, developed at the local level of cities or regions, became known in the global economy for their specialties. By 2020, most people saw the global economy as a network of thousands of these clusters rather than as a collection of hundreds of nations. For example, it was the hill region of northern Italy around Milan, not Italy itself, that was known for pottery. Now, in 2050, the clusters number hundreds of thousands, and nations' borders are much less relevant.

The Corporate Great Global Restructuring

The Great Global Restructuring was really obvious in the corporate world. The merger mania began in the late 1990s, starting with telecommunications, partly because that technology was the first to become global in every regard. The next industry up was financial services because capital was an early adopter of the possibilities provided by the new infrastructure.

The mergers then spread beyond the key industries of the New Economy and started affecting traditional industries like oil and cars. In late 1998, Exxon and Mobil announced a $60-billion merger—the biggest deal ever seen, though far bigger ones were to come. Ironically, these were two of the heirs of John D. Rockefeller's Standard Oil, which had been broken up in the trust-busting of the early twentieth century. Now, in the late twentieth, many people worried that they were merging to form a colossus again.

The auto mergers really began to push the alarms, starting with Daimler-Benz's merger with Chrysler. On the surface, this was just another transnational merger—only this one involved tanks. By the end of the twentieth century, before the merger, Chrysler was producing all the tanks for the U.S. military. After the merger, the company headquarters was in Germany, and most decisions were going to be made by foreign nationals. This situation really challenged the U.S. government to think in a different way about the realities of the new world: How was a national military to navigate this new global economy?

From our vantage point at mid-century, these mergers made perfect sense. In fact, they were just the most rudimentary responses to the new global opportunity. The new global companies needed the scale to operate at an optimal level in one global market. Consolidation was leading to much greater efficiencies and falling costs, and competition globally was actually increasing not decreasing.

A New Form of Global Governance

The global economy outran the political systems of oversight and the old institutions. Like everything, the systems of regulation had to evolve beyond the national arena.

The high-tech, high-growth economy of the Long Boom generated enormous flows of capital driven by a quest for investment opportunities. The Internet boom of the late 1990s was only the first of many that took place.

Soon huge pools of capital were sloshing around the world seeking the highest possible return—but overstressing the markets and regulatory systems.

The capital would collect around what came to be known as *white holes*. Certain companies or industries or entire countries would suddenly become attractive to the global investment herd, and huge amounts of capital would move their way—creating many instant millionaires. On the other hand, the capital also had a tendency to get sucked back just as quickly, collapsing the companies or industries and pulling down the economies of their countries with them.

The prevailing fear of that first decade of the twenty-first century was that the world was going to see a repeat of events that had taken place 100 years previously. Would this new frictionless form of capitalism lead to runaway booms and frequent busts? Would there be a rising challenge to the open global economy with calls for increasing constraints on capital and trade flows?

The twenty-first century could have been shaped by hypervolatility, with explosive transformations and unconstrained change. The challenge was to find a way to manage that change in a coherent way. It was to create the stable regulatory framework that enabled the free flow of capital to function without all the collateral damage. It was to build a framework of new institutions or new forms of governance.

How would the generation at that time respond to the new challenges of institution building? The obvious answer was to apply to the public sector the new form of networked organization that had already transformed corporate bureaucracies. These new ways of doing things were rapidly creating new forms of decentralized control and coordination.

The decade of the 2000s brought the emergence of the idea of global governance—not global government. Everyone realized that there was no likelihood of a global organization that controlled activity within nations. The need was for formal networks between the various governing bodies of those nations, networks based on two main things: using common standards of law and practices and voluntarily adopting mechanisms for conflict resolution when national practices diverged.

The new century brought a proliferation of networks that helped solve particular facets of emerging global problems. For example national environmental protection agencies and environmental groups formed a network to pursue constraints on pollution, which clearly spilled over borders.

THE VARIOUS bodies OVERSEEING SECURITIES, SUCH AS THE U.S. SECURITIES AND EX-CHANGE COMMISSION, FORMED THEIR OWN NETWORK OF EXPERTS IN FINANCE, WHO WORKED OUT SUCH THINGS AS COMMON STANDARDS FOR QUICKLY SETTLING STOCK AC-COUNTS SO THAT TRANSACTIONS WOULD MOVE FREELY IN THE NEW GLOBAL MARKET.

GLOBAL NETWORKS WERE ALSO FORMED BY QUASI-GOVERNMENT GROUPS, SUCH AS THE HEALTH PROFESSIONS, WHICH SET UP GLOBAL MEDICAL STANDARDS, AND THE LEGAL PROFES-SIONS, WHICH WORKED OUT EQUITABLE AND PEACEFUL MEANS FOR SETTLING DISPUTES.

THE OPEN NETWORKS OF GOVERNANCE MADE POSSIBLE THE BEGINNINGS OF EFFECTIVE DEMOCRACY ON A GLOBAL SCALE. IN THE TWENTIETH CENTURY, INTERNATIONAL AFFAIRS WERE HANDLED BY A SMALL GROUP OF ELITE DIPLOMATS. TODAY ALMOST EVERYONE IN THE WORLD CAN FIND WAYS TO PARTICIPATE IN THESE PROCESSES OF GOVERNANCE.

ALTHOUGH MOST MAJOR DECISIONS STILL NEED NATIONAL RATIFICATION, THE REAL POLITI-CAL CONVERSATION HAS FOLLOWED THE ECONOMIC ONE. TODAY EVERYTHING HAS GONE GLOBAL.

The Politics
of the
Long Boom

How are we ever going to pull off such a high-growth, high-tech strategy? How are we going to get the entire world through this Millennial Transition? Can we even do it? Yes. In fact, we're doing it right now. It's just difficult to see all the ways that people around the world are making it happen.

If Section I was about how we got to this point, then Section II is about how we go on from here. It lays out how every major region of the world can not only make the transition to the new global economy but eventually make major contributions to the global community as well. We take stock of the assets every civilization can leverage in the years ahead. We describe a realistic way forward, starting with some key acts of leadership by the more affluent countries that can help propel a chain reaction of bold moves by many others.

This section deals with the looming political problems that could make or break this Long Boom. We provide a basic plan for creating a more inclusive future, one that opens up opportunities for people from all sectors of society and from all regions of the world. And we end by taking on three major challenges facing the world in the short, medium, and long term: How do we decrease the chances of major war, change the conditions that breed terrorism, and finally confront the desperate poverty still trapping billions of people? This section begins to provide answers.

3

THE NEW
AMERICAN Ideology

The United States is playing a critical role in the global transformation as both a leader and an innovator. An emerging American political consensus is forming around a practical ideology that sustains high growth. A high-growth strategy for the New Economy needs to create a more inclusive politics, a new learning society, and opportunities available to all.

December, 1990
Tokyo, Japan
Dear friends,

I just got back to Tokyo from a trip through Asia with just enough time to get out my year-end letter. Molly finally left England to come live with me here, and we reconnected by spending several weeks on a remote beach in Thailand. Asia is a wild place to be right now. Every country is growing as fast as you can imagine. People are streaming in from the countryside to the big cities, which are bursting at the seams. You can't believe how chaotic Bangkok is. It takes half a day just to cross the city because of all the congestion from people driving new cars. But these people don't seem aggravated—they're extremely happy about their good fortune. They're radiating confidence and pride. By no means does this describe just Thailand. This same supercharged feeling pervades almost all these countries in Southeast Asia—let alone the original tigers that have been booming this way for a decade. And that's not to mention Japan, probably the richest, most together economy in the world.

Tokyo—what a mind-blowing city! Expensive as hell, much higher than even New York. You take a taxi and it's almost $100 to go across town—who in their right mind can do that? Most of the Westerners I know can't. Only the Japanese can. And the city is spotless. It's impossible to find litter. You go out on the street at 3 A.M. and there is a vending machine where you can get whatever you want, including beer. Some guy has been meticulously maintaining that beer machine. There's not a scratch on it. Everything works, and everything is on time. These people really have got their act together. It's so un-American. That said, life in the city is cramped. Asia is so crowded, it drives you crazy. Every street is totally packed, and every little house is packed, and every little square inch of every room has some kind of function. Wow, these people are squeezed. But, like everything, they've mastered it.

The future belongs to the Japanese. They have figured out how to build a society of amazing uniformity and work selflessly in teams. They have organized all their industries to be hyperefficient. They rip off many of the models and initial technology ideas from the States, but they perfect them and then just blow us out of the water. Their craftsmanship, quality control, design sensibility, and discipline give them a leg up every time. So now all the best cars, televisions, electronic goods are Japanese. Soon everything will be. We better start learning Japanese. They don't speak English even though they've learned it from second grade on. But they don't have to learn English anymore. It's over. It used to be that English was the primary language in Asia—with the British colonial influence. But no longer. At least the food will be a lot better than when Britannia ruled. If the future lies with the Japanese, at least we will be eating sushi, not smashed peas.

I hate to say it, you guys, but the United States looks in pretty bad shape from here. Man, these Asians dusted us. Basically the Asians are manufacturing everything. And what are we doing? We're in the classic decline of a great power. We've run up these huge government deficits and owe all this debt. The inner cities are rotting, and crack cocaine is spreading. The family unit is crumbling. The United States is decomposing. And then I see the Soviet Union collapsing—I have no idea what that's about. I guess the two old military superpowers are going down in flames. It probably makes sense: They've spent gazillions of dollars arming themselves to death, and now they're both gonna sink. And here's Asia with all its vitality, building things.

When Mol and I move back to the States in the summer, I'm totally screwed. I will be looking for jobs all over the country just when the economy's going into recession. They're laying people off all the time. Now they aren't laying off just the working-class people the way they did in the 1980s; they're laying off white-collar people and middle managers. Companies are shedding every single excess person. Soon they aren't going to employ anybody except this core group of the elite, and we're all going to be outside the fold and aren't going to have health care or insurance or any other benefits. It's going to be grim.

That's a bad enough environment, but employers will look at me and say, "You are well educated, well qualified, and really skillful, and we really like you, but we can't give you the job." All these companies are sticking to hiring quotas. They're trying to rectify the sins of the past. They're hiring minorities, blacks, Hispanics, Asians, and women. I know that's a good policy. They're doing it for the right reasons. But you know what? I'm dead meat because I'm a white male. I can't get a good job. I can't contribute. I totally missed the boat. All the older Baby Boomers filled all the job slots for white males, so the back-end Boomers like me are locked out. How am I going to support myself or Mol if she goes back to school? How am I going to be able to support a family? I can't even think of starting a family.

You guys are now almost my family. I severed many old connections back in the early 1980s when I was feeling really disillusioned and alone. You guys hung with me and helped me rebuild my value system and my life. You guys gave me emotional support when I needed it most, when my father died five years ago. And now our circle has expanded to a half dozen of us helping each other out. Max, who would have thought that a straight Christian kid from the heartland would have bonded so deeply with a gay Jewish kid from L.A.? Or Will, think of all we've been through. You started the decade in Nicaragua helping Third World peasants, and now you're trapped in the corporate law scene struggling to pay back your massive loans. Or Bud, you've been on an elusive quest to find an alternative career that can help bring environmental change and also earn you a decent living. Or Kate, way in Africa, trying to save the world. I hope you can win the good fight against apartheid, though I must say the odds seem stacked against you. Mol has been fighting the good fight for women here in Asia with similar results. She can't get a job in her field mostly because men won't take her seriously. Women around here simply serve as hostesses in the elevators or run around pouring tea.

I don't want to sound too bummed out about the world and my future, so I'll tell you one thing I am really happy about—my new laptop computer. You remember that portable Compaq computer I bought in 1985 that I hauled around like a suitcase? Now I have an extremely thin laptop made by—who else?—the Japanese. It's a Toshiba, but it is copied from the IBM PC and runs on this program by Microsoft called DOS. The best part about this computer is what they call a modem, which connects to the phone lines. So now I can use the international phone lines to actually connect to computers in the States. I'm doing some work for an American company over here, and I can call a local phone number and actually hook up to a satellite system and send messages through to New York within seconds. It's wild. But it's just for the elite corporations. I'm still sending this letter to you guys the regular way, through the postal system. You'll probably get this several weeks after New Year's. I hope it finds you well.

The First Among Equals

In a world stuck in the midst of a global transformation, a good first place to look for ways to get unstuck would have to be the United States. It would be hard to come up with a country better designed for the emerging twenty-first century than the United States. Its assets going forward are immense—some of them obvious, some not. In the wake of the Cold War, the United States emerged as the sole remaining superpower. Its sheer military superiority can't possibly be challenged until at least 2015. Its economy is the largest in the world—by far. Its gross domestic product is more than $8 trillion, compared with just over $2 trillion for Germany and under $400 billion for Russia. The United States has the world's largest market—which means that it disproportionately influences which products succeed or fail in the overall global market.

The list continues: The United States has the largest research establishment in the world, spanning everything from think tanks to corporate research to institutions of higher education. Its top tier of graduate-level research universities is unparalleled and educates the most brilliant students from all over the world. The United States spans a continent that is completely integrated economically across fifty decentralized states—all speaking the same language and sharing the same culture. In comparison, Europe is going through an excruciating process trying to get to that same threshold someday. The United States is both an Atlantic and Pacific power and a major trader in each region. The United States maintains high levels of immigration and has the relatively low population density that will allow it to keep that up indefinitely. As a result, it can welcome the best and brightest from all over the world and avoid the lopsided bulge of an aging population that threatens many European nations and Japan. And Americans tend to be early adopters of technology and consummate tinkerers. They are generally an innovative, entrepreneurial people. All these attributes clearly will be highly advantageous as the world goes into an age of high tech and the New Economy.

On top of all those strategic advantages, the U.S. economy has been on a tear throughout the 1990s, becoming unquestionably the healthiest national economy going into the transition. If ever there was a time when Americans could afford to be selfless, to be magnanimous, to exhibit true global leadership, to let go of narrow self-interest in their foreign policy, it is now. Now is the time to be visionary, to take a long-range view, to look out for the interests of the entire world—as befits the world's only superpower. In a global economy, such "selflessness" is just enlightened self-interest. The central challenge for Americans today is to recognize the historical opportunity thrust on them and to step into a global leadership role. Although U.S. politics has often tended to be parochial, the American people and American politics can think globally.

There was one other time when the United States emerged into the world scene with an awesome slate of strategic advantages. That came in the aftermath of World War II. The United States came out of the war as the only major industrial power whose soil had been untouched by the conflict and whose economic infrastructure had been left intact. Germany and Japan had been decimated. The Soviet Union, Great Britain, and France were not much better off. Any potential military or economic rival to the United States faced a long and arduous rebuilding process. The specter of the Great Depression haunted everyone with the fear that a slowdown of economic growth would come after the wartime boom driven by military spending. People feared a return of deflation, a free fall in international trade and financial transactions, and the layoffs and unemployment that had characterized the 1930s.

In the face of those fears, and in that geopolitical environment, Americans exhibited extraordinary global leadership. They had a long-term vision of how the world needed to evolve over the coming decades and understood that, by helping others, it would help itself in the long run. Because of this vision, the United States did several things similar to what is needed today. It committed itself nationally to a high-growth economic strategy to ward off deflation. It also rushed to rebuild its vanquished enemies, Germany and Japan, a move that was counterintuitive and unprecedented in the history of warfare. Certainly the intransigence of the Soviet Union and the acceleration of the Cold War played a part in this unprecedented strategy, but on a deeper level, U.S. leaders understood that they needed to get Germany and Japan back on their feet in order to stoke the engines of the global economy. They needed healthy, democratic countries out there buying U.S. products in order to sustain economic growth in the United States as well as the rest of the world.

That was the international dimension of the strategy. The domestic dimension was a similarly historic shift. The United States came around to the idea that the more inclusive the domestic economy, the better for everyone—rich and poor. So it established programs like the GI Bill, which provided higher education for veterans, and the Federal Housing Authority, which enabled them to buy homes. When the wealth is spread more generously throughout a society, workers become consumers who keep stoking the economic engines. That's obviously good for the workers but also for the owners and managers, as well as the investors. And so the mass consumer society took hold—and the economy took off.

Today the United States faces a similar situation and again needs to adopt a high-growth global strategy. The world economy is in a wobble, caught in slow growth and possibly tottering toward dangerous deflation. In the aftermath of the Cold War, the United States needs to support and invest in its former adversaries, Russia and China, so that they can make the full transition to the global market economy.

Russia is in particularly dire straits because of its near financial collapse, but in many ways, China, with its billion-plus people, has a more difficult task. Support is clearly in the long-term geopolitical interest of the United States and the rest of the world. Successfully helping these countries with potentially huge markets will generate more demand, which will get the global economy back on a trajectory of high growth. And the United States needs to make its own emerging New Economy more inclusive, but that won't happen this time through a crude redistribution of wealth. True to the times, there are new methods, rooted in a new mentality.

The Axis of Innovation

There's been a very interesting westward shift in the axis of Western civilization that has played out over the centuries. Three thousand years ago, the focal point was in ancient Greece. Then it jumped one peninsula west to Italy and ancient Rome. Then it migrated over to the rest of Europe. Then it left the continent and centered on England—later to move on to America. What was this "it," this center of the civilization? The center did not necessarily mean the population center—for the regions left in the wake of the migration usually had larger sheer numbers. The center has more to do with the center of innovation, of economic vitality. It was the center of power, but not necessarily formal power, rather power to influence the rest of the civilization in the long term. It was the place where the age's zeitgeist emerged, where the spirit of the times came out. It was the place where the future was being born.

By the late eighteenth century, the center of Western civilization hovered squarely over England. Here was the birth of the early industrial revolution. The new technology of that time, the new industrial tools, were being developed there. The new rules of that emerging capitalist economy were being roughed out by the economic actors there. And even the nascent forms of politics that would come to characterize the Industrial Age, what we came to know as liberal democracy, found its best expression there. Certainly innovation was happening in other places on the continent—and in the United States. But if you had to identify one place that best expressed the essence of the times, you'd have to go to England. That was ground zero for the early Industrial Age, say the critical forty-year period from 1780 to 1820 and even the decades after that. Over the course of the next 100 years, that center of the civilization shifted westward again, taking the very big leap across the Atlantic. For the later period of the industrial revolution, the one born in the late nineteenth and early twentieth centuries, the center hovered over the eastern seaboard of the United States, the New York and Boston corridor. This was the era of John D. Rockefeller, Andrew Carnegie, and J. P. Morgan—industrialists and financiers erecting a colossal new form of capitalism—and also of the innovators, such as Thomas Edison, Henry Ford, and the Wright brothers.

But then, in the second half of the twentieth century, the restless center shifted west once again, to the West Coast of the United States, where the digital revolution and the new knowledge age seem to have found their best expression. For the Long Boom period that we're describing, from 1980 to 2020, the West Coast corridor is ground zero. There's the megacity of Los Angeles, the home of Hollywood, the film and television capital of the world, certainly a place to watch at the beginning of an information age. There's Silicon Valley and the San Francisco Bay Area, home of the new digital tools and the emerging new media of the Internet. In fact, it's the entire coast from Seattle, home of Microsoft, to San Diego, home of key players in wireless telecommunications. Like England in the early Industrial Revolution or the East Coast in the later one, the West Coast is where the new tools of the new era are being hammered out, where the new rules of this New Economy are being worked out, and where the very earliest signs of a changing politics are emerging. Although there is plenty going on elsewhere in the world, the West Coast of the United States, and California in particular, is the first among equals, the new axis of world innovation. The future is being born right there, right now.

The future of the technology is becoming pretty clear to many people. The future of the New Economy is also coming to be relatively well understood by increasing numbers of people. But the future of the politics of the emerging era, the era of the Long Boom, is much less clear. A different political mentality seems to be emerging on the

West Coast, reaching its purest form, or most intense expression, in California. Although Americans might consider this a West Coast ideology, the rest of the world sees it as an American phenomenon, the New American Ideology.

California tends to be the place to study this ideology because the people who embrace it tend to congregate in large numbers there. These people are the technologists and programmers and engineers who are building the new technologies in Silicon Valley. They are creators of new and old media based in Los Angeles. They are the entrepreneurs and knowledge workers of this New Economy. They are the business elite and global finance class chasing after the massive opportunities. They are the young people creating this new digital, wired culture. California attracts a lot of them—from all over the world.

The draw of California has created the multicultural mix that has led to some of the key characteristics of the New American Ideology, such as its global mentality. California, more than any other state and all other countries, is home to immigrants from all over the world, so that thinking globally in California is a short hop from thinking locally. Along with diversity of cultures and backgrounds, the ideology is even more fervid in embracing the value of openness. Few cities in the world can claim to be more open than San Francisco.

California is not without its contradictions. For example, it supports both a thriving gay community and right-wing gun fanatics. Historically, the state has seemed to go from control by the Right to control by the Left. Conservative Ronald Reagan was elected governor for two terms, only to be followed by Jerry Brown, a very liberal Democrat. Outsiders can be forgiven for considering the state nearly schizophrenic. But this apparent shifting back and forth actually points to one of the ideology's central features.

The most distinctive thing about the New American Ideology is that it isn't an ideology—at least not in the way that term has been understood in the past. It's a political mindset that's not dogmatically ideological. An increasing number of Californians—and people across the United States—have disengaged from the old labels of Left and Right, liberal and conservative, and even, to a certain extent, Democrat and Republican, because these labels are not considered relevant to what these people believe and value. It's not that their beliefs are incoherent. There just are not yet any shorthand terms to describe this set of political ideas and values. And no current politicians artic- ulate all of them. So the people shift their votes to Democrats and Re- publicans, depending on who comes closest to their beliefs about particular issues at a particular time. Hence, we use the term *New American Ideology,* even though it's not a rigid ideology per se. This New American Ideology is the mind-set of the Long Boom.

The New American Ideology can best be stated this way: "It's not about left or right; it's about what works." The Long Boomers don't carry all the baggage from the political past about which side—the Left or the Right, the liberals or the conservatives—won what politi- cal battle and who needs to get back at whom. Get over it. Let it go. Give credit where credit is due. To the conservatives who helped fo- cus our energies on reforming our economy, thanks. To the liberals who helped foster an understanding of the strength of diversity, thanks to you, too. Both sides have had much to contribute. It's just that whatever only one side contributes simply isn't enough.

The New American Ideology draws from the traditional thinking of both the Right and the Left—particularly the libertarian tracks in both. Like those on the Right, the Long Boomers tend to be economi- cally libertarian: Whenever possible, pull government out of the economy and let the market, the millions of individual actors, per- form as best they can. But like those on the Left, the Long Boomers are socially libertarian: As much as possible, keep government out of a person's private life, and give everyone the maximum freedom to make his or her own choices of lifestyle. The consistent theme here is the value of freedom, being free from government or some other bu- reaucracy constantly organizing their lives, free to make their own decisions in their economic lives, their social lives, and their personal lives.

However, this libertarianism is *not* Libertarianism with a capital *L.* That formal Libertarianism has become associated in the United States with a party on the right-wing fringe that is fanatically antigovernment. Long Boomers are *not* antigovernment. They believe that good government can provide services that the market simply cannot provide. They understand that we need good government for security, for roads, for ensuring an education for all people and help for those in severe trouble. They understand that referees are needed in the marketplace and that occasionally conscious intervention is needed to steer markets for the public good. Long Boomers are even fine about paying taxes—they just want to be sure the money is going to be well spent. But when in doubt, when the choice is between two seemingly equal options of expanding government or letting people solve their own problems outside government—they'll always tilt in the more libertarian direction.

This libertarian strand of the Long Boom mind-set is more consistent than the right and left traditions it draws from. The Right—and more generally, the conservatives—believes religiously in economic libertarianism, and just as religiously believes that government should barge into people's private lives and dictate whether they can have an abortion, or with whom they can sleep. The Left and the liberals embrace social libertarianism but want to beef up government's role in telling businesses what practices are allowed. The Long Boom mind-set simply eliminates the inconsistencies and borrows what's best in both.

Another way to think about this Long Boom mind-set, this New American Ideology, is as a quest for balance. In many spheres, the entire twentieth century was marked with clashes of two antithetical sides: capitalism and communism, the liberals and the conservatives, the business class and the workers, the Right and the Left. Either one side or the other was in power. Either we followed one grand plan or scrapped that and proceeded with a completely different one. So the liberals had their heyday in the 1960s and 1970s, and the conservatives had their revenge in the 1980s and 1990s. But although a highly ideological agenda may start out as an effective counter to the excesses of the system that it replaces, over time that extreme agenda will run into its own excesses and become vulnerable again to a resurgence of the displaced group. The Long Boom mind-set says, "Enough. Stop lunging back and forth from right to left. Both have something to contribute, and the world has arrived at a point where we can take the best of both. We just need to get the balance right."

The world has arrived at this point of needing to draw from both right and left. Here's where the New American Ideology stops being

American and simply becomes the New Ideology. The only reason we call the ideology American is that the United States is where it coalesced first, among the people thriving in the New Economy. As the technological and economic developments spread to other parts of the world, the mind-set is becoming more consciously inclusive and more global.

TWENTY-FIRST CENTURY CHOICES:
THE MAKING OF A LONG BOOM

PART THREE: "Politics Adapts"

Hello, I'm Salma Aboulahoud welcoming you back to "TWENTY-FIRST CENTURY CHOICES, THE MAKING OF A LONG BOOM." FROM OUR VANTAGE POINT IN 2050, politics was the most critical element in the takeoff of the LONG BOOM in the early part of the twenty-first century. WE SEE NOW THAT THE TECHNOLOGICAL AND ECONOMIC developments WERE ALMOST INEVITABLE, BUT POLITICS WAS THE REALM WHERE PEOPLE EXERCISED CHOICE. And indeed, shortly after the turn of the century, the world made some big choices—the right choices in the end.

The people at that time could easily have stuck with the status quo and made the wrong choices. In fact, the tumultuous times favored the more fearful. But a new generation of leaders rose to power by promulgating a bold new vision that inspired confidence.

These new leaders knew that economic growth and social justice were not in conflict. Indeed, if social justice was to be achieved, economic growth had to be stimulated. These leaders knew that economic growth also was not in conflict with the environment and, that, in fact, new technology was required to turn over the old polluting industrial equipment and clean up the environment. The leaders offered a new sense of the potential of the twenty-first century—which has guided the world all the way to our times.

The clearest articulation of this new vision first surfaced in the year 2000 in the United States—specifically, in California. The closing years of the twentieth century had driven U.S. politics to new lows as conservative Republicans tenaciously attacked Democratic president Bill Clinton and even tried to oust him from office. The U.S. public came close to a complete repudiation of politics and deadlocked government.

In that poisoned atmosphere, a Silicon Valley software entrepreneur named David Brewster decided to run for Congress against the Republican incumbent. He chose to run as an independent because he felt both parties were too trapped in the past and beholden to entrenched interests to boldly lay out a political vision that met the challenges of the times. He understood the new technologies and the New Economy and fashioned a commonsense politics around them. His slogan, borrowed from popular Apple computer advertising of the time, was "Think Different."

His new Long Boom vision had three characteristics that set it apart. First, it was inclusive, aggressively reaching out to all segments of society and ensuring that everyone would be able to make a successful transition to the New Economy. His slogan: "Expand the Network."

Second, the vision was long-term, insisting that essential investments be made in education, technology, and scientific research even if they did not immediately bear fruit. His slogan: "Take the Long View."

Third, the vision was relentlessly global, thinking through the global implications of all national or local decisions and policies. His slogan: "Get Global."

And the vision celebrated the value of open trade, open borders, open debate, and open minds. His catchall slogan, which found its way on to popular bumper stickers, was "Open, good. Closed, bad."

The New Agenda for the World

Before we finish Brewster's story and its impact on U.S. politics, what specifically did those general themes mean? They clearly touched almost every nation in that first decade of the twenty-first century. What made them a break from the past?

In the United States, the Republicans had a good understanding of economics, except for their isolationist wing, but their party had become increasingly associated with intolerance and exclusion. The Democrats had a tradition of inclusion but still had large constituencies opposed to the increasing globalization of the economy.

The new vision was built on the realization that if the new global economy was to fulfill its potential, all people must have the opportunity to participate and benefit. So the new vision proposed a flexible social support network and a learning infrastructure that would help workers keep up with the churning New Economy.

IN EFFECT, A NEW kind of social bargain was proposed. People couldn't cling to old ways, old jobs, and old patterns of doing things, and society agreed to bear the burden of enabling people to continuously learn and adapt. With the spreading prosperity, generous support would go to those genuinely unable to do so.

THE long-term aspect of the Long Boom vision related to public investment strategies. In the late twentieth century, investments in basic research had dropped, partly because of large government deficits. With the huge fiscal surpluses of the first couple of decades of the twenty-first century, people began to think differently about investing.

THERE was a renewed commitment to investment in the future through scientific research and development—not through picking winners and losers in the marketplace, not through funding actual businesses, but through funding pure scientific research. After all, the two key innovations of the Long Boom era, both the microchip and the Internet, had come out of federally funded long-range R&D.

BY 2005, one of the key elements of the new politics in nearly every nation was a significant growth in R&D spending of all sorts as well as increased funding for the social sciences and the liberal arts. Universities and higher education were widely supported, and there was an intellectual renaissance fueled by economic necessity. Economic and human interests were now aligned.

THE global dimension of the vision infused everything. Foreign policy migrated from a narrow focus on a nation's self-interest to a broader focus on the entire global community. Geopolitics shifted from a clash of national agendas to a much more cooperative approach of aligning interests and increasing interconnections.

MANY developed nations began to take on responsibilities far outside their borders, not just because those actions directly benefited their citizens—which they did—but because other, less fortunate people needed help and the entire global community needed someone to act boldly.

ONE manifestation of this new resolve was the establishment in 2003 of the Global Corps, which was modeled on the old Peace Corps but included college graduates from many developed nations. These young people went abroad to help developing nations improve their technological and legal infrastructures and to adopt the new economic principles and practices. This program proved to be enormously successful, not just for the developing countries, but also for the participants, who returned home with a more global outlook.

The Race for the Long Boom

So what happened to Brewster back in Silicon Valley in the year 2000? How did American politics make such a rapid shift from near isolationism to global leadership?

Brewster won the Silicon Valley congressional seat and became a national celebrity in a country saturated with media but starving for new political ideas. His Long Boom vision quickly spread, to be debated far outside his district. His influence on ideas was magnitudes greater than the impact of his lone independent status in the U.S. House of Representatives.

The 1990s had seen the rise of independent populists, who appealed mostly to disgruntled working people fearful of globalization and rapid economic change. Ross Perot, a quirky tycoon from Texas, had made two runs for the U.S. presidency and attracted almost 20 percent of the electorate in 1992. A former professional wrestler, running as Perot's Reform Party candidate, had captured the governorship of one midwestern state in 1998.

It was not out of the question that a well-financed presidential candidate with an appealing new national agenda could give the traditional parties a run for their money. Brewster was such a potential candidate. He had his own fortune and the backing of Silicon Valley and Hollywood. He was a telegenic Baby Boomer. And most important, he had a compelling new vision.

By 2002, Brewster's Long Boom ideas were being adopted wholesale by candidates in states and cities around the country. His potential grassroots support was growing. A very active constituency was urging him to make a run for the presidency in 2004.

The professionals in the Democratic and Republican parties began to seriously worry—and to plot. One of the features of the two-party system in the United States had been the ability of parties to absorb ideas from the outside. Alternative parties had rarely succeeded in the United States because when their ideas became popular and threatening to the established parties, those ideas were adopted by those parties. Brewster knew this, and his goal was not to win personally, but to see his vision win.

The Long Boom ideas did not fit comfortably into the old ideological categories but could potentially have been adopted by both parties. Sizable factions in both parties were predisposed to adopt them anyway. By the 2004 election, both parties had candidates in the primaries championing versions of Brewster's Long Boom vision, so Brewster decided not to seek the presidency. The Democratic candidate, who had almost fully incorporated the Long Boom vision, won the election in the fall.

By 2008, the competition between the parties was over which was more Long Boomish. The redefinition of the political landscape was complete. American politics had shifted from being focused on division, partisan conflicts, and shrill moralizing. It now had a national consensus about how the United States should act in the world.

As the political drama unfolded in the United States, similar versions had played out in countries around the world. The U.S. economy had been the first to fully develop in the new direction, and so its national politics was the first to respond. However, when other countries began making similar economic transitions, they were quick to adopt similar political solutions.

The success of the American political ideology in the United States proved persuasive to change-oriented leaders in other countries. They adopted and modified many of the main tenets. By 2010, the ideology could no longer be called American. It was the New Global Ideology.

Expand the Network

There's a basic logic to networks that people in technology fields understand. The simplest way to put it is the larger the number of members, the larger the value of the network. But it's not just that every new member boosts the value one notch. With every addition of one new member, the value of the entire network increases exponentially.

Take a town that has never had telephones installed. A telephone company sets up shop in town and gives only one person a phone. That phone is useless because there's no one else to talk to on it. Then the company wires together two people in town. That's marginally useful. Then another two people get wired together on the other side of town. That's slightly better. Now two telephone relationships can thrive. Then the company ties together the two isolated pairs, and suddenly the situation gets much better. Instead of being able to contact only one other person, anyone in that expanded network can now contact three. Yet the company had to string only one more telephone line to triple the value to the network members. And that logic will continue to play out as more connections are added. The expense of adding one more person will be less than the overall value gained by the network, so there's an incentive to keep expanding the network. In that hypothetical town, everyone on the network benefits from the addition of every new member, and everyone will benefit most by having everyone wired.

The same logic applies to the Internet of today. There's a strong incentive to get everyone into this emerging new network—not just the top quarter of the population, who fit the knowledge worker profile. Getting everyone on the Net is not just some philanthropic urge to be nice to all people. It makes good business sense. You want to sell your products over the Internet? The first step is getting every potential customer into that network to begin with. You want to streamline costs by doing away with employee paperwork? Then all your employees have to be able to tie in on-line. Expand the network. It's in everyone's interest to do so.

The logic of networks does not apply just to technological networks. The New Economy is not called a *networked economy* just because it is based on networked computer technologies. Networks have become the central metaphor of how we organize work— whether it's through technology or face-to-face. Networking is the key economic activity that we engage in, whether glad-handing at conferences, schmoozing at the office, working the phones, or sending e-mail. But even in this broader economic context, the new rules of network logic apply: Expand the network. And how do we expand the network of the New Economy? Through education. With a new economy driven by knowledge workers in an era called the Information Age, education has never been more important. You might say we've always expanded economic opportunity through education. True, but this time the stakes are even higher. This time we're in the midst of a transformation of the economy from one characterized by brawn to one characterized by brains.

Production as Learning

Economic change always precedes educational change. Historically, we've constantly seen examples of how the economy quickly adapts to a new technology or a new method—and only later, sometimes quite a bit later, does the educational establishment scramble to catch up. This lag shows up in relatively minor ways, such as the recent shortage of computer programmers in the United States. The digital revolution exploded in the United States in the mid-1990s, and high-growth regions soon had sucked every available coder into the economy and were desperately looking for the kids coming out of school. They didn't find nearly enough. In 1996 and 1997, Silicon Valley had 100,000 job openings at any given time. Other high-tech regions, like Minneapolis, became so desperate that they mounted advertising campaigns to woo established coders from the strapped Valley itself.

This educational lag time works on a deeper level as well. Occasionally the economy changes in such a fundamental way that the traditional educational system gets badly out of sync with it—prompting the need for radical systemwide reform. This happened in the epoch-changing transition from an agricultural economy to an industrial one more than a century ago. Once the economy had become more industrial, business leaders realized that the educational system was not adequately preparing young people to become productive workers. What industry needed was a workforce that was literate, could do basic math, and implicitly understood the large-scale factory system that the economy was heading toward. As Alvin Toffler argued in *The Third Wave*, the educational system itself evolved to resemble the factory system of that economy. We mass-produced workers by taking young children and feeding them into an assembly line educational system. We sorted kids into classes, had them memorize uniform lessons, and tested and graded them in an eerie kind of quality control before passing them onto the next teacher one grade up. At the end of the line, there popped out a productive worker. At the time, that's just what that mass industrial society needed.

Today the U.S. educational system is in a severe disconnect from the emerging New Economy. Since the 1980s, the economy has raced ahead and the educational system has lagged behind. There's been some haphazard success in sending young people into a roaring economy, but not so much because of the educational system as despite it. In fact, the widespread public perception is that the educational system is failing our children. The concern had mounted to such a degree by the 1998 elections that education had emerged as the most important issue on the voters' minds according to many polls and the many candidates championing the issue. The business community—particularly those tied into the New Economy sectors—has taken the lead in pushing for more resources and greater reform. For example, Sun Microsystems sponsors "Netday," an annual push to get volunteers to wire up schools. Frankly, these businesses are not motivated purely by the desire to expand the minds of young children. They fear that we're not turning out productive workers. Again, they're driven by cold, hard economic reality. Pure and simple. Something must be done.

We're in one of those epoch-making transitions. As in the shift from agricultural to industrial work, the nature of work is changing, and changes in education can't be far behind. *Production is learning.* What's really a mindbender is that work itself has become learning. In other words, the best productive processes are emulating the best learning processes, and the best companies are acting like the best schools. How? Good managers today take nothing for granted. They question everything—every strategy, every process, every figure. That's the same kind of probing open-mindedness a good teacher imparts to his or her students. Increasingly companies are trying to establish a highly decentralized system of management that empowers all employees to think for themselves, to experiment and innovate. Creativity is encouraged and rewarded as it is in good schools. And good companies today are relentless in promoting this process of learning and growing—occasionally making the radical breakthrough but more constantly refining every day.

The new form of education that must emerge is not about technology. Certainly young people coming up through the elementary and high school systems need to be fully exposed to the new networked computer technologies, which will increasingly permeate their work environments and all aspects of their lives. But the future is not about mastering new technologies. If anything, computer technology will become increasingly easier to use. The new form of education will have much more to do with preparing young people with successful work habits for the New Economy. Young people will have to become veritable learning animals. They will need to become adaptable, innovative people who can move confidently within an economic environment that is constantly in flux. Bill Gross, the entrepreneurial founder of Knowledge Adventure, one of the largest makers of kid's educational software in the United States, has an apt way of putting it: Learning is nothing more than getting stuck and unstuck. You're cruising along until you run into a problem that blocks your way forward, then you keep at it, perhaps asking help from others, until you figure out a way around it. This, in essence, is how we learn. Gross also argues that this is a process that will continue throughout one's work life in the New Economy. The generic job will be constant problem solving, getting stuck and figuring out a way to get unstuck.

The educational system, then, will need to place a premium on producing people who can master those challenges and thrive in that environment. But in the new networked environment, they will also need to be able to work within teams and on projects that include people on the other side of the world. We need a more globally oriented, networked-oriented educational system that fosters constant innovation. That's even more important because many workers must relearn whole new careers over the course of their lives and must constantly re-create themselves. It's commonly said that people today will typically move through five different careers in the course of their lives. What they learned in high school or college will date quickly as the pace of change in the economy continues. We have almost no idea what specifics a knowledge worker will need to know even ten years down the road.

For this reason, we shouldn't even be using the term *education*. It immediately conjures up an image of educational institutions geared to children in kindergarten through twelfth grade or young people coming out of colleges and universities. We need to create a much more comprehensive *learning society*. Obviously we still need to channel an immense amount of attention and resources into transforming what we now know as K–12 education. We need to get young people started out right. At this level, U.S. education does not have high enough standards, social discipline, or parental involvement. And the current system of higher education needs to be substantially reoriented—just not as radically as the lower grades. In the United States, higher education provides many assets going into the twenty-first century—at its best creating some very innovative and brilliant leaders in all fields. But at its worst, it is an inefficient bureaucracy of tenured professors, which resists change. There's much room for improvement.

And if learning is to be the central activity in the New Economy, then society's support of learning can't stop when an individual reaches age twenty-one, or even when a person reaches the top of an organization. A learning infrastructure must evolve that supports constant exploration and advancement throughout an individual's life. This kind of support is in everybody's interest.

Investment in the new infrastructure for the new learning society will be the way we end up "expanding the network" and keep growing the New Economy. It's a way of ensuring the inclusiveness of the economic system without resorting to redistribution through handouts to people who still would not find themselves productive or fulfilled. Communism and the welfare states tried handouts and found they ultimately debilitated the recipients, the very people they were meant to benefit, and sapped the vigor of the overall economy as well. Rather, investing in a learning infrastructure that empowers individuals to sustain themselves is better for them and for the overall economic system. This learning infrastructure will help create the context for a meritocracy of intellectual excellence that will benefit individuals as well as the society as a whole. No society can invest too much in assuring access to knowledge right now. Those millions and billions of brains are our future. And we have a lot of problems to solve.

Twenty-first Century Choices: The Making of a Long Boom

Part Four: "Learning Innovation"

Salma Aboulahoud here again. Welcome back to our series. The explosion of activity around learning that happened in the first two decades of the twenty-first century is something that every young child studies in history today. All the characteristics of what we in 2050 take for granted as the Learning Society were roughed out in an atmosphere of wild experimentation back then.

However, the changes are even more dramatic when contrasted with the state of education in the preceding two decades, the 1980s and 1990s. The big story of learning started with educational systems in real distress, as evidenced in the United States. The elementary and secondary systems of education in the United States at that time were caught in an intergenerational struggle. As the World War II generation retired into static incomes, they began a tax revolt, starting with a cap on property taxes in California in 1978. Ronald Reagan rode the popularity of tax cuts to political prominence, and this movement soon spread around the United States with all forms of tax reduction.

The public education system—and the younger generation—was one of the main casualties because it was totally dependent on shrinking tax funds. This was particularly true of school districts in inner cities, where the property values were in decline.

By the end of the 1980s, the results were catastrophic. Classrooms were overcrowded, the physical infrastructure was deteriorating, and because of poor conditions and low salaries for teachers, not enough talented people were attracted to teaching. Young people were turning to drugs, forming gangs, and bringing weapons to school. Affluent families were pulling their children en masse from the public systems.

Only when the economic boom gained momentum in the late 1990s did the lean tax rates begin to generate enough resources to counter those disturbing trends. Classroom sizes began dropping, teacher-to-student ratios improved, the infrastructure started to get repaired, and it became possible to move beyond the basics to the reinvention of education itself.

Right around the turn of the century, changes in technology and the New Economy forced everyone to reexamine how young people needed to prepare for work and for life. It soon became obvious that education was the key to success in the future, that well-trained minds were the most essential asset for any company, any institution, and any society functioning in a knowledge economy.

The concept of education itself was undergoing a paradigm shift. Education was no longer just learning how to do something that had already been discovered and laid out. It was more about learning what to do next. It was about gaining the skills to navigate the New Economy and the world. It was about adaptable, future-oriented thinking. It was about stimulating innovation and creativity. In short, education was about producing curious, creative, expressive learners for life.

The breakthrough came in 2002 with the update of an educational innovation that had greatly benefited the World War II generation and stimulated the

economic boom that it had enjoyed. The GI Bill had granted returning veterans the money to use for their higher education at any institution, public or
private. The GL bill, the Global Learning Bill of 2002, made a similar commitment of immense resources to all young people and their families to pay for a
wide range of learning experiences in lower and higher education—with the
requirement that a portion of the higher education be accomplished abroad.

The federal commitment of new funds with little centralized control stimulated a flood of other funds from business and private sources and set loose a
wave of innovation that created what we know as the Learning Society. The
new environment of abundant resources helped blur the previously rigid lines
between private and public education, between formal schooling and continuing education. Anything that helped people learn more was considered
good.

The private schools that had proliferated with the deterioration of public
schooling were in the best position to move quickly into experimentation.
Many affluent families had paid the extra money and moved their children into
those systems because they were more adaptable and were already trying out
new educational models.

Beginning around 2001, the public schools were revitalized through the
widespread initiation of charter schools, giving parents and educational innovators far more choices as to how to educate their children. A rapid expansion
of new schools—both private and public—was spurred by an entrepreneurial
market for education reminiscent of the can-do ethos of Silicon Valley.

Many of the brightest young minds coming out of college were drawn to the
wide-open possibilities in the education field—starting new schools, creating
new curricula, devising new teaching methods. They were inspired by the idea
that they were succeeding by helping others succeed, and by building the
twenty-first century paradigm for learning.

The excitement spread far beyond private schools, which were teaching
about 20 percent of all students by 2010. Charter schools acted in a symbiotic relationship with the private schools and quickly adopted many of the new
models developed there, but they also did their own experimenting, which the
private schools adopted in turn. The competition was healthy, not cutthroat.
Good schools were rewarded, and good ideas spread.

By 2008, about 35 percent of all public schools were charter schools. The
new models spread to the more traditional public schools with a slight lag
time, ensuring that all sectors of society benefited from educational innovation.

ONE OF THE KEYS TO THIS SUCCESS WAS THE DROP IN VIOLENCE AND DRUG USE IN schools, which CAME FOR SEVERAL REASONS. THE boom HAd improved THE financial conditions ANd THUS lessened THE STRAIN OF HOME life FOR MANY POOR FAMILIES. PARENTS BECAME MUCH MORE ENGAGED IN THEIR CHILDREN'S EDUCATION BECAUSE THE STAKES IN THE knowledge ECONOMY WERE NOW SO HIGH. THE YOUNGER GENERATION ALSO MADE THEIR OWN choices AFTER WATCHING THE devASTATION OF THEIR OLDER BROTHERS ANd sisters who HAd TURNED TO GANGS ANd drugs. This WAS INTERGENERATIONAL learning, AS IMPORTANT AS ANY OF THE OTHER FORMS.

LEARNING Nodes

Today WE KNOW THAT THE EducATIONAL SYSTEM IS ONLY HALF THE EQUATION THAT GOES INTO A LEARNING SOCIETY. To build A full LEARNING SOCIETY, THE EducATIONAL ENVIRONMENT MUST BE INEXTRICABLY ENMESHED WITH THE WORK ENVIRONMENT.

This shifT did NOT COME EASILY. EducATION HAd ALWAYS BEEN THOUGHT OF AS A PREPARATION FOR WORK. AduLT EducATION WAS ALSO THOUGHT OF simply AS A TEMPORARY RETURN TO school TO LEARN A NEW skill BEFORE WORKING AGAIN.

AROUND THE TURN OF THE CENTURY, LEARNING WAS RECOGNIZED AS ONE OF THE CORE ACTIVITIES OF knowledge WORK, SO THE WORK ENVIRONMENT ITSELF BEGAN TO EMULATE good LEARNING ENVIRONMENTS. A NEW infrastructure EVOLVED OUTSIDE THE TRADITIONAL school SYSTEMS THAT SUPPORTED THIS ECONOMIC ACTIVITY. By 2005, NEW public SPACES CALLED *nodes* WERE BEING CONSTRUCTED WHERE COLLABORATIVE LEARNING TOOK PLACE AT ANY TIME OF THE day OR NIGHT, DEPENDING ON WHEN PEOPLE felT CREATIVE.

Since LEARNING ANd discovery TOOK PLACE EVERYWHERE, PEOPLE OUTSIDE FORMAL ACADEMIA FREQUENTLY WENT BACK TO COLLEGES ANd UNIVERSITIES TO TEACH ANd collABORATE ON RESEARCH ANd MENTOR OTHERS. THE WALLS OF ACADEMIA CRUMBLED ANd THE LEARNING NETWORK SPREAD OUT EVERYWHERE.

This devoLUTION IN THE LEARNING infrastructure WAS SPURRED by THE INCREASINGLY PERVASIVE SPREAD OF THE NEW TECHNOLOGIES. By 2005, MOST YOUNG STUdENTS IN THE United STATES HAd ACCESS TO good COMPUTERS WITH full ANd free ACCESS TO THE INTERNET. By 2010, ESSENTIALLY EVERY child IN THE United STATES HAd POWERFUL TECHNOLOGICAL devices AT his OR HER disposal ANd, OF COURSE, could SPEAK TO THEM.

A big boost TO LEARNING CAME WITH THE USE OF VIRTUAL REALITY simULATORS, which HAd BECOME VERY EFFECTIVE by 2009. A child could EXPERIENTIALLY EXPLORE ALMOST ANY SET OF ideas, OR ANY TIME IN history, OR ANY PLACE IN THE UNIVERSE. ONE could see the world of the dinosaurs, or walk on Venus, or travel on the bottom of the oceans, or visit Renaissance Venice.

The devices could take abstract ideas in mathematics or philosophy and depict them symbolically in virtual reality space. Virtual Reality transformed education by letting children experience the things that previously could only have been described.

The Web became the universal knowledge tool. It was assumed that virtually all information and knowledge were always accessible. Kids grew up reaching into that infinitely large encyclopedia of human knowledge and retrieved what they needed anytime, anywhere. By 2004, the Web was sufficiently developed so that everything of use to a child could be found there.

To provide for all adults, the Web's content had to approach the level of libraries. In 2001, a major step toward that objective came when Project Gutenberg completed the task of putting 10,000 books on-line. Many of the world's leading universities focused on their key specialties and committed themselves to getting electronic versions of all books and written material in those areas on-line. By 2005, almost all new books were being published in electronic form. By 2015, relatively complete cyberspace libraries were up and running.

Everyone Learns

Americans were very good at adaptation and innovation. Their outlook was well suited to revolutionizing education and building the Learning Society far beyond school walls. But the recognition of the importance of education was a universal phenomenon. The demand for high-quality education exploded all over the world.

The increasing use of satellite communication created a whole new group of world-class lecturers. Professors from all over the world who were known for giving the very best lectures on Aristotle or quantum theory or genetic coding were more widely available, and students all over the world tuned in to these world-class lectures.

As early as 2003, there was a constantly available on-line university environment providing some of the best instruction anywhere in the world. By 2020, this was universally available and being used by hundreds of millions of people throughout the world. A truly global educational revolution had taken place.

4

THE NEW
EUROPEAN RENAISSANCE

Europe is creating a new model of economic and political integra-
tion that much of the rest of the world may follow. The European
Union and its latest financial integration are transforming the rules
of sovereignty among highly developed nations. Latin America, a
cultural kin to Europe, has also begun a developing-world version of
the economic and political transformation toward the new rules of
the global game.

THE NEXT REGION HEADING toward the New Economy is Europe.
Europe, with a slight stutter step, is going through many of the
same changes that Americans went through in the early to middle
1990s. European businesses and households have been quickly
adopting new computer technologies and getting wired up to the Internet. They have been incorporating many of the same financial innovations: starting a mass migration of individuals to stocks and
mutual funds, taking to initial public offerings, and nurturing new
venture capital practices. The fundamental restructuring of the economy is proceeding more slowly but still steadily in the right direction. By the late 1990s, Europeans were finally pushing through with
privatizations (e.g., of their public telecommunications companies),

going through with corporate restructuring, and deregulating the
economy so that smaller entrepreneurial firms could begin creating
growth and jobs.

And so by the late 1990s, the European economy had begun to
awaken from its slumber and pick up its growth rates—just as the
United States had earlier. The European gross domestic product
(GDP) grew a modest 1.5 percent in 1996, a much better 2.5 percent
in 1997, and 2.9 percent in 1998—a year when much of the world
was in economic turmoil. That's the aggregate of all eleven countries
participating in the European Monetary Union. More than half the
countries in the even larger European Union showed growth of more
than 3 percent in 1997. Some, like Ireland, were growing at 8 percent.
Other economic indicators were similarly positive. The European
Stock Index actually outperformed the Dow Jones Industrial Average
for 1997 and 1998. Government budget deficits as a percentage of
GDP dropped quite dramatically from 4.2 percent in 1996 to 2.4 percent in 1998. The rate of inflation kept coming down from a very
healthy 2.2 percent in 1996 to an even better 1.2 percent in 1998.
Even unemployment, that bugaboo that has haunted Europe for
decades, showed signs in the late 1990s that it had topped off at (a
still alarming) 11 percent.

The transition has by no means been uniform across Europe. In
general, the transition has been working its way down from early
adopter cultures in the north to the Mediterranean cultures in the
south. The British have been the innovators—even though they declined first-round participation in the European Monetary Union.
They have essentially been in lockstep with changes in the United
States from the beginning of the Long Boom era. That Anglo-Ameri-
can bond runs deep—from the friendship between Margaret Thatcher
and Ronald Reagan to the one between Bill Clinton and Tony Blair.
Given the cultural affinities between the two nations, it makes sense
that their economic progress would be roughly in sync. Yet the
British put a particularly European twist on their version of the New
Economy.

The transition next began in the northernmost countries surrounding Great Britain—starting with the smaller ones. In the 1980s, the
Dutch brokered a deal between unions and government that set them

on the path of the New Economy early. The Nordic countries quickly began a high rate of technology adoption, though they continued to struggle with the political transition out of a welfare system. By the late 1990s, Germany appeared committed to shifting forward. All the key economic actors in Germany seemed to "get it"—that the globalized economy was forcing changes that Germany could not ignore anymore. Even the Social Democrats, the left-of-center political party that, after sixteen years, regained power in 1998 said they understood. The Germans, as well as the other northern European cultures, are pragmatists. They see the world as it is and eventually adapt.

The French and the southern European cultures are another story— they are romantics. Many French intellectuals like to construct their own elaborate interpretations of the world, which tend to place France smack in the center. This is particularly true of the political and economic elite, who still try to run everything from the center of the nation, Paris. But the French people—particularly the young people—are much more entrepreneurial, more susceptible to being drawn to the New Economy and the out-of-control principles of the Long Boom. Many of them are congregating in London and the other more freewheeling cities of Europe because they want to break out of the constrictions on their home turf and innovate. The same goes for the Italians and other Mediterranean cultures. They lag in making the transition now but have the potential to be adept participants soon.

EUROPE'S CONTRIBUTIONS TO THE WORLD

The Europeans collectively will play a very key role in the global transition through the politics of the Long Boom. With the United States, they will act as a bastion to hold out against further deterioration of the global economy and to help move the world through the inevitable anxieties and occasional downturns. The Europeans taken as a whole are equal partners with the Americans. Those key eleven countries integrating their currencies have a combined population of more than 290 million, compared with more than 270 million for the United States. They constitute 19 percent of world gross domestic product, compared with 20 percent for the United States. They are involved in 19 percent of world trade, compared with 17 percent for the United States. Their wealthy class, defined as those people with investable assets greater than $1 million, have $5.5 trillion to steer around the world, compared with $4.7 trillion coming from the U.S. rich. The sheer economic heft of Europe is indisputable. But the Europeans have more to contribute than that. From a global perspective, the Europeans are part of that innovator culture—Western civilization. They can be expected to be key creators of the new twenty-first century system being born. And they will be in countless ways. But already they are embarked on several critical projects. Three huge contributions stand out.

One, there's been an intriguing shift in the politics of Europe, starting in the mid-1990s. In country after country, political control has shifted from the right to the left, from conservatives to social democrats. Broadly speaking, political control shifted to—for want of a better phrase—"parties of the people." They were the parties associated with the average worker rather than the business class, with labor rather than capital. In Britain the shift came in the spring of 1997 with the transition from John Major's Tories to Tony Blair's Labour Party. By that summer in France, Lionel Jospin's Socialists had swept out the center-right government led by the Gaullist Party. By the fall of 1998 in Germany, Gerhard Schroeder was leading the Social Democrats and Greens to power by ousting Helmut Kohl and the conservative Christian Democrats. Italy even followed the trend that fall when a government was formed by Massimo D'Alema, head of the former Communist Party, now renamed the Democrats of the Left.

One way to think about this shift has to do with the European sense of solidarity. Europeans generally have a deep concern for all members of their society, so it makes sense that they would quickly start counting the casualties of the New Economy. From a global perspective, that's just great. We need a lot of people thinking through how to make this economic transition much gentler. Some of the Europeans groping toward this new formula call their approach the "third way," or some variation on that theme. Britain's Blair uses the "third way," Germany's Schroeder calls it the "new middle." These phrases are political slogans in search of an overarching vision—a vision like the Long Boom. But they all carry the same core message: We do need to change over our economy in this global transition, but we also need to ensure that everyone will make it to the other side. That's a message that needs to be heard and dealt with for the good of people all over the world who are facing transitions of their own.

If the Europeans can put that sentiment into practice, they will have made a great contribution to the world. However, they have to stay locked on Schroeder's middle or Blair's third way. They can't drop back into the old leftist ideology that will unravel the economic progress achieved so far and prompt an eventual rightist backlash and destructive ideological war. A crucial test case is Germany, where many powerful Social Democrats still appear caught in the old leftist ways. Germans need to let go of that ideological baggage and adopt the Long Boom mind-set. They must adopt the rigorous new economy policies and then build on that framework while finding ways to mitigate the social damage that powerful economic change will inevitably bring. They must stay centered all the time.

Contribution 2: From a historical point of view, Europeans also have been involved in a process of economic, financial, and perhaps political integration that will have long-term repercussions for the rest of the world. Since the fall of the Berlin Wall in 1989, Europe has been going through a massive east-west reintegration. The European Union, now numbering fifteen nations, is well on its way to expanding the economic community by as many as ten eastern and central European nations by 2003. Certainly half of them, including the key nations of Poland, Hungary, and the Czech Republic, will be accepted by that time. In slightly more than a decade, Europe will have taken two sides of a highly divided world and fused them together into a workable whole. It will have shown how to successfully integrate peoples with backgrounds in both communism and capitalism. The symbol of this process will be Berlin, the new capital of a united Germany. After massive reinvestment and a comprehensive face-lift on its eastern side, the city harmonizes the legacies of two very different pasts.

Europe has been integrating internally as well. The western European countries have been taking economic integration to higher and higher levels ever since the Treaty of Rome established the European Economic Community in the late 1950s. But within our Long Boom time frame, particularly in the 1990s, the integration shifted into high gear. By 1993, the European Union had established a single market, so that products can essentially ignore borders. By 1999, most members had adopted a single currency, the Euro. This is a very big deal. The Euro becomes the mechanism for forcing changes that countries and companies can't seem to make on their own. The Euro pushes the European economy to a level of integration that spurs needed growth, helps create jobs, softens the transition, and finally begins to take on the structural unemployment problem. Those that can't summon the will to change or take responsibility for painful decisions can blame the Euro—it is better to work under that cover than to have no change at all. But the true global significance of the Euro has more to do with the example it provides.

The Europeans are embarking on a process of integration that many other regions of the world, particularly in Asia, may need to go through, too. How do you take a dozen countries with different languages, habits, histories, cultures and currencies, and tie them together as one single economic entity? How do you create brand-new transnational institutions to overlay the existing national institutions in heavily populated countries with long, proud traditions? Americans don't have much to contribute to that end. They built most of the core institutions for the United States decades—indeed, a couple hundred years—ago, long before the population filled out. Everyone speaks the same language and shares the same general culture. What do Americans know about achieving this kind of integration? The Europeans are the ones to watch. The world is much closer to Europe writ large. What happens in the monetary and economic integration front in Europe in the next few years will have a large bearing on what happens in the rest of the world soon after.

Contribution 3: Although some may have thought that the path of increasing European unity would lead toward a kind of "United States of Europe," Europe actually seems to be heading more toward a "United Cultures of Europe," with the distinction between cultures cutting very fine indeed. It's not just Spanish culture, but Basque culture; not just French, but Provençal or Parisian; not just British, but Welsh or Scottish. Identity in Europe appears to be devolving into regional and local subcultures and simultaneously aggregating at the top into a new kind of European identity vis-à-vis the world. The

identities that seem to be suffering in the long run are the ones related to the nation-states that fall in between.

The nation-states are now getting their just deserts. Over the centuries, national identities have often been foisted on the local subcultures and regions of Europe. In a forced march toward greater
centralization, the core cities of Europe literally conquered the surrounding countryside. Those core cities—Rome, Paris, London,
Berlin—became the capitals of the new nation-states and controlled
the activities of almost everything around them. Now, as they respond to the global forces that are prompting a reorganization of the
world, Europeans are both returning to their local identities and redefining themselves as a larger culture, a European one. The national
identity is less useful to them.

Once again, the Europeans are blazing a trail that will be followed
by the rest of the world. This two-dimensional identity is the future
for all of us: We will all increasingly identify with the very small and
the very large—in the parlance of today, thinking globally, living locally. We will each have to live on some particular plot of the planet,
and so we will tend to relish the peculiarities found around us and
identify with them. But we will still need to operate in an increasingly globalized world. In this, the newly transforming Europeans
will have much to teach us.

Latin American Revival

From the long-term, Long Boom perspective, the influence of Latin
America's cultural ties to Europe warrant grouping Latin America here
rather than, say, with other developing countries. Because of these
ties, Latin Americans have some strategic cultural advantages going
into the transition to the New Economy and are therefore well situated to embrace it. Developing regions coming out of communism
have to start with the basics of building civil institutions based on the
rule of law and the logic of financial markets, whereas the Latin
Americans can build on a long tradition of working within the institutions of capitalism. What's more, they have already gone through
much of the pain of financial restructuring that the Asian economies
are facing up to only now. Latin American countries had their debt

crisis in the 1980s, after becoming hooked on borrowing easy money—mostly U.S. dollar loans from multinational sources—and then realizing too late that they were over their heads in debt. They spent the 1980s in a painful retrenchment of governmental policy and broad economic restructuring. The Latin American governments slashed much of the fat in their budgets and shifted to more austere economic policies, and the financial sectors began the long, hard road of reform toward the necessary standards of accounting.

The approach, which was the developing world's version of what Reagan and Thatcher had begun in the United States and Britain just a few years before, became known as the *Washington consensus,* referring to the policies encouraged by global institutions like the World Bank and IMF (International Monetary Fund), which are based in Washington. The program called for privatization of state-run monopolies, deregulation of governmental control over business, lower trade barriers, lower barriers to foreign investment, reform of the tax systems, a focus on fiscal and monetary policies for fighting inflation, and the maintenance of a competitive foreign exchange rate. The Latin Americans had bitten the bullet on this approach by the late 1980s, but following the Washington consensus was a very difficult process, so difficult, in fact, that the Latin Americans call the period the "lost decade." For example, the per capita income in Latin America in 1990 was less than that in 1980. However, despite the pain, in many countries the restructuring effort achieved its purpose. By the late 1990s, when Asia and much of the developing world was succumbing to a near financial meltdown, Latin America was able to hold back disaster indefinitely. Brazil, by far the largest economy in the region, was the key player in holding the line in the chain reaction of currency collapses. It had made enough financial reforms to placate the governments of the developed economies, which came to Brazil's rescue with $41.5 billion in emergency loans. And with time, Brazil satisfied the global financial investors, which had initially misjudged the situation and lumped Brazil and all of Latin America with other troubled developing regions. As of 1999, the upturn had begun.

Latin America spent those same couple of decades, the first half of the Long Boom, going through another equally significant transition—a political one toward democracy. At the start of 1980, the vast majority of Latin American governments were authoritarian—if not flat-out military dictatorships. At that time you could go to the tip of South America and find the junta of Argentina and the iron grip of Chile's General Augusto Pinochet. You could go to the broad belly of the continent and find Brazil run by the military; go to Central America and find either brutal right-wing strongmen or, in Nicaragua, a left-wing version; and go all the way to the north and find Mexico's only political party in full control. By the middle of the 1990s, though, almost every Latin American country had a democratically elected government. If not perfect, democracy clearly had taken hold. This democratization was also underappreciated by investors, which tended to lump Latin America with the faltering Southeast Asian countries. Democratization is a very difficult process in any context and takes a great amount of time and society's energy to pull off. The transition is frequently messy, with violent outbursts and missteps before there's a final settling down. It's a good process to have behind you, rather than ahead. Asians still have much of it ahead of them. Because the Latin Americans have much of it behind, they can concentrate on the next wave of reforms, those that will enable them to fully participate in the Long Boom.

The historical migration from Europe to the Americas was not uniform. Immigrants from northern Europe generally headed to North America, and those from southern Europe generally headed to South and Central America. The colonial powers also split that way: the British and French in the north and the Spanish and Portuguese in the south. Clearly these lines were not rigid. The Spanish initially colonized large parts of western North America, and northern Europeans from places like Germany migrated to Argentina and parts south. But by and large, the north-south cultural split of Europe replicated itself in the two Americas. This arrangement continues to play itself out through the early stages of the Long Boom. If the people of southern Europe are moving slower toward the New Economy than the people in northern Europe, the same lag time is happening in the Americas. In North America, the United States and Canada are moving more quickly through the transition—quicker even than Europe—and the South Americans are taking the slower boat to the same place. They'll get there, but not in a rush.

On an even deeper level, the cultural split between north and south is rooted in the Protestant and Catholic divide that bedeviled Europe for much of its history. Since the time of Max Weber's classic nineteenth century analysis of religion's impact on economic development, *The Protestant Ethic and the Spirit of Capitalism,* many have studied the phenomenon. The most recent is David Landes, a Harvard historian and the author of *The Wealth and Poverty of Nations,* who clearly sees the differences between people within the two religious cultures as playing a big part in their lopsided developmental success. The Catholic culture of South America, be it the Spanish or Portuguese variety, tended to reinforce more hierarchical social organizations than the more individualistic Protestant culture of North America. This difference in culture has had a subtle but pervasive influence on the mental habits of the workers over generations, and those mental habits nurtured in a more rigid, hierarchical environment are not the ones best suited to the more innovative, freewheeling environment of the New Economy. The more hierarchical culture also tended to create big inequalities in wealth. In most South American societies, a tiny elite has traditionally held the vast majority of wealth, and the majority has been a huge mass of impoverished peasants. Industrialization began to change some of that distortion, but the gross inequalities remain. There's no better example than Brazil, which still has among the most severe income disparities in the world. Of all major nations, Brazil has the highest rating—30—on the "Gini index," which economists use to measure the distribution of wealth. This means that in Brazil the average income of the wealthiest 20 percent is roughly thirty times that of the lowest 20 percent. (The index rating is roughly 4 in Japan, 10 in the United States, and 15 in Mexico.) And those inequalities are perpetuating themselves through access to good education. Again in Brazil, only 17 percent of the population receives some high school education, compared to 43 percent of Mexicans and 91 percent of people in the United States. And this is happening as the world heads into an information age, an era that increasingly values education and knowledge.

But the southern European legacy has its assets as well. The Latin Americans have a very resilient social fabric and a tradition of strong families that will act as flexible, adaptable units going into our more fluid age. Thus they have much to teach their northern counterparts, who are struggling with deteriorating family life and a frayed social fabric that's partly a consequence of the more individualistic northern culture. The Latin Americans, like the southern Europeans, also have a burgeoning, entrepreneurial culture that will serve them well in the years ahead. Even the poor people in the barrios display a remarkable ability to make the best of scarce resources. For example, the shantytowns of São Paulo and Rio de Janeiro in Brazil, called *favelas*, spring up overnight on abandoned land and steep hillsides. The government does nothing to encourage them, yet somehow electrical lines are strung, water pipes are connected, community centers are organized—all out of sheer human energy, creativity, and will.

Another big contribution that the Latin Americans will make to the world is having a truly multicultural and multiracial society. There are no other regions or even countries where the races blend together so seamlessly. Only a handful, like the United States, have such a diversity of cultures. This characteristic is partly a function of the immigrant history of the Americas, but it's also partly a legacy of the upside of Latin America's pervasively Catholic culture. Catholicism is a universalistic religion, driven by a desire to convert everyone to the true faith. The upside is that all human beings are considered God's children and worthy of salvation—and, by slight extension, marriage. The Catholic immigrants from southern Europe were much more apt to intermarry with the Native Americans than the Protestant immigrants to North America, who often massacred them. So today Latin America is peopled by numerous mestizos, a blend of European and Native American stock. On the eastern side of the continent, you can add to that mix the Africans originally imported as slaves. So in Brazil, a large portion of the population has some African blood, and the Brazilian culture is a delightful mix of influences from three continents. This mixing of races and cultures gives Brazil a vitality that's unmistakable by anyone who visits there. It will give Brazil, and other countries of Latin America, a leg up on the future.

In the twenty-first century, the blending of cultures will be inevitable with the advance of globalization. All the world's cultures that have remained separated for centuries will continue to become exposed to all. A great cross-fertilization of ideas will accelerate with the ubiquity of global communications and media. Regions of the world, like Latin America, that have a proven ability to meld cultures and diverse ideas will have a great advantage. In the future, diversity will spur creativity, which will translate into value and, ultimately, wealth. In a global economy, diversity will be both a means to an end and an end in itself—a better place to be.

Twenty-First Century Choices: The Making of a Long Boom

Part Five: "The Inclusive Community"

At the turn of the twenty-first century, the Americans acted as if they were in the tip of a great rocket lifting through the atmosphere. They were blazing a path through the New Economy and focusing on what lay ahead. They seemed to love the white heat of change.

At that same time, the Europeans acted as if they were situated in the middle of the rocket, partly pulled along. Their focus was more on what happened in the wake of the trajectory. They had deep concerns for anyone blown away by the blast and for those left far behind.

The Americans and the Europeans had complementary concerns and skills that turned out to be very valuable in the tumultuous period from 2000 to 2020. Both groups exhibited true global leadership and took on responsibilities far beyond the call of duty. And both groups were highly innovative, each in its own very different way.

In essence, the Americans focused on efficiency, while the Europeans focused on equity.

The Americans were preoccupied with finding the best way to use the new technologies and make a more productive economy. They were fascinated by cutting-edge ideas and very comfortable with the highly competent people who could quickly execute them. The Europeans were preoccupied with helping all workers in their societies make the economic transition and with finally trying to reduce the gross inequalities that had left the majority of people in the world desperately poor. They took the lead in applying the concepts of the New Economy to everyone.

These two global leaders had other complementary characteristics: The Americans were more bold but also more abrasive. The European leadership

STYLE WAS MUCH MORE diplomatic, growing out of subtle and sophisticated interaction among the disparate European cultures.

The Americans were more drawn to market solutions to social and political problems than the Europeans, who had a long history of wrestling with the philosophy and responsibility of the state.

The Americans emphasized the primacy of the individual, the Europeans emphasized the value of the group and harbored a deep sense of solidarity that led to one of their greatest contributions, the Social Transition Funds.

The Marginalized at Home

Low job creation and persistent high unemployment in Europe in the first decade of the new century made it increasingly clear that the lingering social welfare system was exactly the opposite of what was needed in the New Economy.

The old system discouraged risk and enshrined the rigid status quo. Businesses found it difficult to get rid of workers, so they refrained from hiring new ones. Workers were reluctant to let go of old jobs and learn new skills because they did not see clear opportunities. European society was deadlocked over the issue of labor flexibility.

Both the business community and the workers in the first years of the century came to understand the need to create globally competitive companies that could afford to hire ever more people because their output was growing as they succeeded in the global markets.

U.S. companies were globally competitive partly because they were able to shed labor easily. The Americans believed society's obligation was to provide a good education and abundant work opportunities, and to eliminate barriers like discrimination. After that, it was up to the individual. The able and hardworking did well; the lazy and inept did not. And those who were helpless needed some minimum social safety net. As a result, the United States created many more new wealthy people than Europe, but also many were very poor. In addition to the terrible plight of those inflicted by poverty, this resulted in higher social costs, like crime.

The Europeans were more comfortable with lower highs and higher lows. In other words, they wanted fewer poor people and accepted fewer wealthy as a result. Their values were different, and the Social Transition Funds (STFs) were the new mechanism that reflected those values and liberated the European economic system from its quandary. Instead of paying unemployment taxes, companies were required to invest in the STFs.

These funds provided social support and a limited income for employees who lost their jobs because of the necessary changes in their companies. More important, the funds invested heavily in the education of workers and facilitated the transition to new work. Because of the funds, companies, now freed of unnecessary workers and able to maintain globally competitive wages, could grow and create new jobs. The workers were supported and provided with learning opportunities but were obligated to embrace the corporate changes.

The funds also became important sources of investment in nascent sectors of the European economy, acting in a role similar to that of pension funds in the United States. The STFs ensured higher growth and flexibility in the European economy without putting all of the burden on the worker, on business, or on society.

By 2006, the European economy was roaring, and unemployment was so low that many countries were actually encouraging immigration. The funds were a Pan-European phenomenon, facilitating the continuous economic transition to a knowledge society.

The Pan-European community by that time included countries far to the east of what had been the twentieth century's Western Europe. The STFs extended the community's reach from the heart of western Europe to eastern Europe, then to the former European republics of the Soviet Union, and eventually to Russia. By 2020, all of eastern Europe and all of Russia were within the European economic zone. Greater Europe went from Dublin to Vladivostok—and all members of the economy based their transactions on the Euro, by then the most powerful currency in the world.

The newer parts of Europe were all interlinked with the old in an extremely effective network of communication and transportation that got more complex and efficient all the time.

This infrastructure had facilitated the enormous expansion of available workers and available consumers, which boosted the European growth rates and sustained the twenty-year boom—all the while preserving solidarity.

Helping the Poor of the World

The most intractable problem in the world at that time was the gut-wrenching, bone-chilling poverty in which about half the global population remained trapped.

The images of turn-of-the century villages are shocking to us now: the houses with dirt floors, the open sewage systems, the rivers used for drinking water and bathing, the children in rags and bare feet, the emaciated bodies of people caught in famines. Yet these were very common sights in those times. In fact, they were so common and seemed so immense and so permanent that most people in the developed countries found ways to ignore and forget about them—that is, until the Europeans decided to engage the problem.

The Europeans put resolving global inequities back on the world agenda and took the lead in trying to solve this massive problem once and for all. Some of the early prodding came from the Scandinavian countries, with their long traditions of conscientious introspection and social activism. Some prodding came from those carrying on the legacy of the European socialist movements. But in the end, what moved the Europeans to action was accepting that the most troubled regions of the world had only recently been their colonies.

For most of the twentieth century, the vast majority of the lands in the Middle East and Africa had been under European colonial control. Most African nations had been given their independence as late as the 1960s. By the end of the century, these were the most impoverished.

The colonial legacy, however, was not all negative. The Europeans had a deep understanding of these regions and could build on ties that went far back—in some cases, centuries. There were myriad personal and business relationships that could be leveraged to help these countries. Many Europeans had relatives, close friends, or business associates in places like Nigeria, the Ivory Coast, the Congo, Zimbabwe, Pakistan, Jordan, or Indonesia. Those relationships helped deepen the sense of concern that kept the Europeans motivated.

The first step the Europeans took was to initiate technology and telecommunications deals that were highly advantageous to these developing regions. As the new global telecommunications infrastructure was built, the Europeans brokered generous cross-subsidies, with the affluent paying more so the poor could pay little to nothing. This was a formula that had worked in the previous century in building telephone and electricity infrastructures that eventually connected everyone.

This twenty-first century effort met with the same success, starting with the giant satellite projects like Teledesic. That company needed to get the approval of virtually every country in the world through the World Radio Conference, which allocated satellite parking spots. With European backing, the poor countries got great terms.

The big break came in 2008 with the establishment of the Global Equity Funds. By this time, most of the developed world had long enjoyed an economic boom. THE people with the top 10 percent of incomes were getting extremely wealthy—and the top entrepreneurs were making almost obscene amounts of money. THE affluent classes that made up the next highest 30 percent of incomes were feeling really prosperous. Capital was becoming so productive that the moneyed classes were consistently getting historically high returns. Even people with middle incomes, the next 30 percent, felt financially secure and also confident about the prospects of their children.

THE public, both in Europe and the United States, was open to a new form of taxes to invest in less fortunate parts of the world. THE middle class knew its investments would lead to impoverished people's becoming consumers and thereby expanding global markets. A global capital gains tax was initiated to fund the Global Equity Funds. However, the majority of the funds came from a different source.

By that time, what had been called electronic commerce, or e-commerce, was long past its experimental phase, which had warranted a hands-off approach. A large portion of the world's commerce now took place on-line. THE Europeans proposed that a slight fee, one that would barely be noticed, be added to most on-line transactions. E-commerce had dropped the costs in many retail and service sectors dramatically, so even with the addition of small taxes, people found the prices much lower than before the turn of the century—and so they found the new microtax palatable.

However, those slight fees from all electronic transactions added up to great sums that could be applied to developing the most disadvantaged parts of the world. By 2009, one year after being set up, the Global Equity Funds had amassed $300 billion.

THESE funds were not used for flat-out redistribution to poor countries and peoples. THAT had been the static model of social welfare that hadn't worked. THE funds were instead deployed on three levels:

THEY acted as grants to purchase fundamental computer technology and telecommunications equipment. THOSE industries often offered the equipment at cost as part of a long-term investment to get more people using their products.

THE funds also acted as venture capital investors that funded essential infrastructure or promising economic sectors and companies.

And third, the funds made their way to entrepreneurial individuals in the form of microloans. INFORMATION technology allowed the micromanagement of tiny pieces of capital, as little as fifty dollars. THESE microloans could be tracked and eventually, in the aggregate, yielded a meaningful return.

These microloans made a huge difference to poor people trapped in the poverty circle. For example, a woman with a stall selling oranges at a village market could take a microloan and build up a week's inventory that allowed her to squeeze out a profit beyond the subsistence income she had made day to day.

The Global Equity Funds consciously directed capital to what had traditionally been considered high-risk regions. Within several years, however, most of the funds had proven to be well spent and were bringing decent returns, which were immediately reinvested.

Success of the Global Equity Funds paved the way for the investment of private capital, which by 2010 had grown to immense levels and of course dwarfed the public funds. The private funds were constantly looking for new high-growth opportunities and were running out of virgin investment turf. The private managers needed little persuading after seeing the results of the Global Equity Funds. By 2015, ten times as much private capital as capital from the Global Equity Funds was moving into these targeted regions.

That strong, steady investment over the next twenty years went a long way toward rectifying the great imbalances in wealth and poverty that had always been the norm. The gross inequities had been mitigated over time by a rise in the floor of incomes worldwide.

Poor people around the world felt much better about their prospects and their future. The rise in their living conditions and the economic activity in their regions did much to lessen resentments and to bolster hope.

5

ASIA RISES AGAIN

The many economic virtues of Asia drove a high-growth economy since the 1980s. The failure of politics to keep up with economics led to the crisis that started in 1997. The solution is to build the transparent institutions of political democracy and good government that will allow those pent-up economic forces to take off again. Once that happens, Asia can leverage immense human resources and take its rightful place in helping lead the world.

FOR MOST OF WORLD HISTORY, what we now know as the West and the East operated in completely separate spheres, in almost total ignorance of each other. There were some vague skirmishes along the borders of the two spheres and a bit of overland trade, but by and large they were two worlds, two megacivilizations, completely isolated. Certainly there were other civilizations that sprouted up in different regions of the world and made significant contributions to the advance of humanity. But from a historical perspective, world power has settled in two key centers: the cradle of Western civilization in Europe and Eastern civilization in China. They have been the two areas of political ballast in the world over the long haul, and if long-term geopolitical stability is to be maintained, somehow those ancient power centers must come to terms. The twenty-first century will see more power sharing between these two civilizations and, ultimately, a fusion of the best contributions of both. Therefore, it's worth going back and thinking about how the two civilizations have interacted up to now. Where were the points of cross-fertilization?

The West impregnated the East first. The first real breakthroughs in connecting the isolated cultures came from the Western explorers of the fifteenth and sixteenth centuries. Though the West had initiated the contacts and had some great advantages in weaponry, those early trading contacts were more like mutually beneficial cross-fertilizations. By the seventeenth and eighteenth centuries, though, the power relationship had gone out of whack, and the transfer of ideas was decidedly one-way. The West had grown increasingly powerful through the invention and development of capitalism and industrialization—two incredibly dynamic forces that overpowered any competing systems, including the traditional systems of the East. As the West rode those twin forces to world power, it also spread those systems to other parts of the world, along with the core ideas and the practical know-how to replicate these economic successes. The transfer took place in different ways in different parts of Asia—also depending on which European power acted as the conduit. In China, the transfer took place in quarantined cities like Hong Kong and Shanghai. In India, the transfer took place through a colonial system that covered the entire country. In Japan, the transfer came later, in the nineteenth century, and then only when forced on the Japanese. Setting aside for the moment all the violence and subjugation that accompanied this transfer, from a long-term historical perspective the system of capitalism and the process of industrialization advanced as global systems and global phenomena.

That was Act I. The twentieth century brought Act II. The twentieth century saw a great global struggle between two competing sets of ideas. One set belonged to the members of the communist camp and included various watered-down versions of socialism and variants that were intellectually rooted in Marxism. These roughly believed that the economy should be run through central planning and state control, and that political decisions should be made by a central party acting in the interests of the mass of people. The other set of ideas was held by what could be called the capitalist camp, but it was Capitalism 2.0, the updated version of capitalism that had evolved from the raw version spread in the prior era. This camp basically believed that the economy is best organized as a free market, and that political decisions are best made through democratic processes. It took the entire century to work out the debate between these two camps, but by the 1990s, the winning combination was clear. Free markets and democracy overwhelmingly won out.

Why free markets and democracy? Understanding this question is absolutely essential to understanding the basic dynamic of the Long Boom and the key formula for the future. Set aside all the distracting analysis about how the capitalist West outmaneuvered the communist world. Set aside all the baggage about what particular form of democracy we're talking about. Think about the basic systems of markets and democracy. Think about them in their essence, in the abstract. The reason that markets and democracy turned out triumphant is that in their essence they are *self-correcting systems*. There's nothing morally superior about them. They are just the best systems yet devised by humans. They can change directions relatively quickly and right themselves over time. They can tolerate temporary mistakes and misdirections because the systems themselves are designed to gather feedback and regularly adjust course. In the case of markets, this adjustment can be almost instantaneous—maximizing economic efficiency. In the case of democracies, the adjustment is less frequent but is institutionalized. Periodically the system is forced to contemplate changing course. This was not the case with the communist system. The economy had almost no feedback mechanism and an excruciatingly slow method of adjusting course. And the body politic had only one option. Which brings us to "the rule of twos."

The Rule of Twos

The rule of twos is simply an observation of healthy systems. Healthy systems always have two good options to choose from, and even better, three. This rule works out in economics and politics alike. When you have just one big telephone monopoly, over time service tends to suffer. When you have a healthy competitor, the service of both companies improves. More than two is even better. This basic rule-of-twos formula plays out in almost all healthy industries or sectors of the economy. For example, in long-distance telephone service in the United States, there are AT&T, MCI, and Sprint. For every Coke, there is a Pepsi, and probably some RC Cola scrambling for a little bit of market share to stay alive.

Scott McNealy, the chief executive officer of Sun Microsystems, has a slightly different way of articulating the formula: Every healthy market roughly breaks down into 60/30/10 percent shares. The dominant player will hold 60 percent of the market, the credible alternative will hold 30 percent, and the scrappy dark horse will hang onto 10 percent. If those percentages get too distorted, that market becomes unhealthy. So from McNealy's point of view, the computer software industry runs into trouble when Microsoft grabs 90 percent of the market for operating systems. There's little room for a healthy competitor to build a credible alternative that everyone can switch to if the industry leader stops innovating or jacks up prices.

The rule of twos similarly plays out in politics. The healthiest political systems always have a couple of options. The U.S. political system has shown a remarkable resiliency for a couple of centuries mostly because it has a two-party democracy, and neither of the parties ever gets too dominant. And there's always a third party potentially out there in the grass roots. There's nothing magical about two policy options. The world doesn't always break down neatly into two ways to solve every problem. In fact, theoretically, every problem could be solved in an infinite number of ways. But two-party democracies always have at least one other option at all times.

The parliamentary democracies of Europe in effect replicate this rule of twos despite technically having a bunch of smaller parties. There are usually just two credible parties or de facto metaparties, which to the voter are coalitions of smaller parties that actually act as factions, so power shifts in Great Britain from the conservative Tory Party to the Labour Party; in Germany from the Social Democratic to the Christian Democratic coalition; in France from the Gaullists to the Socialists. If anything, Europe displays more of the rule-of-threes phenomenon than the United States. It has the political version of McNealy's economic win/place/show distribution. The plethora of smaller parties creates an opportunity for a third alternative that might get locked out in the United States. Nevertheless, the overall result is the same.

Not so with one-party states of all kinds—even those that claim to be democracies and periodically poll the people. If there aren't two healthy choices, then elections are a moot point. In Africa, single-party states are the rule rather than the exception, and the system's defenders argue that Africans traditionally organize their communities this way: The chief heads the tribal village, and the national leader heads the nation. Elections are more about validating this authority than about choosing between alternatives. But the rule of twos is not about preserving cultures. It is about effectiveness, about facilitating change in a world that's quickly changing by the day. Those cultures that find ways to establish self-correcting political systems will be able to move into the fluid future with relative ease. Those that don't will find themselves increasingly ineffective and at some point paralyzed.

Which brings us to transparency. Self-correcting systems also work best when all the moving parts of the system can be seen by all. The more exposed the system, the earlier problems can be detected and the more people can suggest solutions. Working democracies attempt to institutionalize political transparency. That's why Western democracies are fixated on a free press. A free press will burrow into the guts of government and business to expose what's really happening. The same holds for freedom-of-information laws and the guarantee of free speech. They are the means to keep the self-correcting system healthy.

The transparency rule holds in the economic world as well. Markets work better when more players have more and better information. That's part of the secret of the productivity of the New Economy. Computer technologies are raising the amount and quality of information available to markets of every kind, and that information is boosting their efficiency. Financial systems work better with more transparency. If banks or investors have better information about where to lend money, that money will be more productive. If individuals have more information about the performance of financial institutions, they will steer their money to those that function best. No matter how you look at it, transparency makes an economic system work better, period. It locates the most effective actors. It highlights the most successful methods so they can be emulated by others. It points out inefficiencies. It finds bottlenecks. It exposes corruption. Transparency is good.

The world must not slide back into the old ways of thinking about these concepts. Talk about transparency can devolve into very emotional discussions of free speech that can cut along East-West lines. Talk about the rule of twos can turn into loaded arguments about competition. We have to think instead about what we will need for the future. Shorn of all ideological overtones, stripped down to its essence, we will need this: *adaptable units, working in self-correcting systems, moving into a flexible future.* And right now, the systems that come closest to that ideal are the market economies and democracies, operating in as transparent ways as possible, and striving to maintain a healthy rule of twos.

The countries and cultures rooted in Asian civilization ran into trouble in the late 1990s largely because they ran afoul of these principles. For starters, they tried to run their economies and societies with too little transparency. During the economic boom of the 1980s and early 1990s, that deficiency didn't seem to matter. The pent-up forces driving toward economic development overwhelmed the need for careful attention to financial details and the access to good information. As a result, the Asian financial systems—even those in the most developed country, Japan—simply did not have the standards of transparency found in the United States and Europe. Companies did not have to report nearly the same amount of information to the government, let alone to shareholders. The press rarely delved for controversial information on business and government. Outsiders, particularly from the West, contributed to the problem by abandoning the standards they would have insisted on if investing in their home markets.

In this context, any culture is ripe for corruption. There was a lot of money sloshing through the system, a lot of places that money could hide, and very little oversight, so it was understandable that corruption began to spread through many parts of Asia. Good information was not circulating, and without it, those inside the system could not isolate problems as they arose. On top of that, the Japanese lending sources, which had been contributing half the capital throughout Asia, dried up because of Japan's continuing domestic problems. So, in July 1997, the international investors began to pull their money out. First, the currency traders hit the overvalued Thai baht and started a stampede out of that economy. But there was nothing unique about Thailand, and soon the electronic herd of global financiers began to pull out of the entire region.

In retrospect, it seems astounding that a region could go from boom to bust almost overnight, that savvy businesspeople and global investors could have been so blind to the mounting problems. Frank Lutz, one of those global investors who worked in Southeast Asia for four years from a base in Jakarta, explains that the investors were like players caught in a Ponzi game. Everyone realized the murkiness of the financial environment and understood that it violated the basic investment standards of the West, but those who had risked investing in the region consistently reaped huge returns throughout the boom times. In the highly competitive world of global finance, more prudent investment managers had trouble convincing their investors to settle for the lower returns of the safer investments, and eventually they threw caution to the winds. Also, those who invested early continued to make big money as long as newcomers kept entering the region and investing behind them. But once the last guy on the pile backed off, that started a chain reaction: No new players were coming, and some smart players were going home. Game over. Time to run.

If that weren't bad enough, most Asian countries had never really heeded the rule of twos. So, in the economic crisis, there was no credible political force ready with alternative plans. The Liberal Democratic Party has run Japan for its entire post–World War II history—with one two-year aberration. So faced with making an upgrade of its system software to prepare for the New Economy, Japan instead stagnated for the entire decade of the 1990s and went from the most dynamic industrial economy in the world in the 1980s, to one reminiscent of a deer caught frozen in the headlights of an onrushing car. And there was no alternative political opposition to lead the country with a fresh set of ideas.

The Chinese have managed great economic success during the Long Boom years, even though they have not followed the rule of twos in the political sphere. They may not continue to be so lucky in the future. In 1978, Deng Xiaoping was able to broker a political succession out of the Mao era and fundamentally change the direction of economic policy. Due to Deng, China did have a credible alternative that time around, but the communist system has no institutional way of replicating that kind of succession again. Any credible alternative must grow furtively within the monolithic culture of Communist Party politics. The Chinese challenge will be to allow the same kind of maturity in their political system that they have allowed in their economic system. They may not be at a point where they will throw open their political system to the democratic impulses of a billion peasants, but they need to allow a healthy development of choices, one that fosters the rule of twos.

Southeast Asian countries provide a great example of what happens when your political system doesn't evolve, when the system won't allow clear political choices. When faced with the Asian financial meltdown of 1997, Indonesians had no means of establishing a succession to the Suharto regime save rioting in the streets—and you can't depend on mass looting and social breakdown to prompt a change in policy. Much better to set up a democratic system that heeds the rule of twos. Malaysia is the next country likely to experience social breakdown because—you guessed it—there is no mechanism for the succession to Prime Minister Mahathir Mohamad. For years, Mahathir groomed his own designated successor, who, as soon as he displayed independent thinking, found himself in jail. Mahathir can justifiably argue that he brought great modernization and endeared himself to the citizenry by spurring stunning growth rates for much of his eighteen-year rule. Again, that's great. But the rule of twos is not about judging a regime's past. It's about ensuring a quick, smooth, healthy succession to the next big thing. It's about the future. It's about ensuring the Long Boom.

Waiting for the Textbooks

Don't dwell on the bad news about Asia. That's largely about mistakes in the past and the legacy of old habits that die hard but nevertheless are dying. The good news about Asia is that the region is filled with incredibly quick learners. In fact, they're just waiting to forge ahead in a new direction. That's how Anthony Mitchell, a British businessman based on the Korean peninsula for the last ten years, analyzed the current situation in Asia and the crisis the Asians face. He said that when faced with a radically changing global economy, Asians did not know what to do. Winging it is not part of their repertoire. And at this stage of change in the global economy, no one really has the new formula nailed down. In short, Mitchell says, the Asians are waiting for the textbooks to be written and MBA courses to be designed. They are fantastic at absorbing new methods and mastering set courses—far better than their Western counterparts, who lack their discipline and sustained focus. Point them in the right direction, hand them the class syllabus, and watch them learn. Fortunately for them, the world is just about at the point right now where the new formulas are being cracked. The books are just coming out. The New Economy courses are starting to enter the business schools. The Asians are ready to rock and roll.

The Asian cultures generally revere learning, and so they have very high levels of literacy and education, a huge asset going into the Knowledge Age. No one has to convince people who grew up influenced by Confucianism that learning is to be valued, that the learned are to be respected, and that everyone should strive to be taught more. They are also extremely hard workers and have a penchant for saving. These are both cultural qualities that are extremely useful in fueling a capitalist economy but that are very difficult to get people to acquire. The Chinese in mainland China—communist China, mind you—maintain a savings rate of almost 40 percent of their earnings. Americans save less than 5 percent. The Japanese have saved *$9 trillion*, mostly in government savings accounts with a return of less than 2 percent. Americans are upset if their mutual funds don't return 20 percent. If anything, the Japanese save too much. The government cuts taxes to stimulate the sluggish economy, and instead of spending this tax money, the citizens squirrel the money away. But from the Long Boom perspective, think of the capital resources ready to be put to use across Asia. And think about leveraging that propensity to save for the future and invest for generations to come.

Given these rock-solid fundamentals in Asia, it's no wonder that the region boomed through the 1980s and most of the 1990s—and will inevitably do so again. Japan went from complete devastation in 1945 to a $5-trillion economy in 1995—second only to the U.S. gross domestic product of $7 trillion. Compared to Germany, which started from an equally devastated point in 1945, Japan has more than twice the economic heft. (Germany's GDP was slightly more than $2 trillion.) And per capita income in Japan was almost twice that of the United States: $40,000 to $26,800. China started the 1980s with a GDP of about $300 billion. By the late 1980s China's growth had roughly reached rates of 9 percent and it ended the late 1990s with an $817-billion economy. And that level of development has just whetted the appetite of the nascent Chinese middle class, which is at a stage comparable to where the Japanese were in the late 1960s and early 1970s, before the real takeoff. South Korea, it is said, accomplished in 20 years what the United States took 200 years to develop. Once the Asian societies figured out the formula for industrialization, they took off on a tear. There's good reason to believe they will soon do the same in the next wave of capitalism, the move to the knowledge economy.

But don't think that the Asians will just take from the world community and not contribute. The Asians have plenty of contributions to make. They may not be innovators of the grand plan, the overarching system, but they are innovators all the same. Fumio Kodama, author of *Emerging Patterns of Innovation: Sources of Japan's Technological Edge* and a professor at the University of Tokyo, makes the point that the Japanese, as well as other Asians, are good at incremental innovation. They take the big idea and then significantly refine it. So Americans invent the VCR player, but the Japanese refine the technology and the industrial process and end up with a much better product. You can find hundreds of these examples, from refining the organizational management principles of W. Edwards Deming, the American management theorist who became a guru in Japan, to figuring out a way to make better, cheaper memory chips. This ability to refine ideas will become increasingly apparent in the coming decades as the Asians fully engage the Digital Age.

There's one huge—both figuratively and literally—contribution that the Asians will make. Think 1 billion people. What does anyone in the West know about organizing 1 billion people? Americans, despite all their entrepreneurial genius, would have absolutely no clue how to live in a society of 1 billion people. Yet thinking in terms of billions of people is the future. The planet is packed with 6 billion people and counting. If we must live as one planet of billions of people, how are we to proceed? The Asians are the ones to look to for guidance. They have experience in dealing with billions. They have the only two contiguous societies—China and India—that operate with those numbers. Going into the future, Asia will have plenty to contribute. Asians, as much as anyone, will help create the future of the world.

THE JAPANESE REALISTS

The Japanese are an island people. They can be thought of as the British of Asia. Both of these countries are just far enough away from the action on the mainlands so that they can remain protected and relatively secure. This position often gives them the liberty to take what they like of value from the continents and devise their own original interpretation of it. Yet this distance can lead to isolation that can get problematic at times.

The Japanese endured centuries of isolation that stagnated their traditional society right up into modern times. A kind of time warp perpetuated their very static feudal society, which not only ignored but actively shut out the outside world. That all began to change in 1853, when Admiral Perry sailed a small U.S. naval force into Tokyo (then called Edo) Bay and literally forced open the door. The stunned Japanese emerged blinking into the world and very quickly realized they had a lot of catching up to do. So began what was called the Meiji Restoration, which, despite the deceptive name, was much more like a revolution. The Japanese people exploded in a frenzy of modernization that soon made theirs a powerful nation that had to be reckoned with by the beginning of the twentieth century.

This was how Japan was introduced to capitalism and other Western ideas. It was a peculiarly Japanese way to proceed: Resist change at all costs for as long as possible, and then adopt new ideas wholesale and apply them to everything. This was also the pattern after

World War II. The Japanese had got stuck on the vision of an imperial Japan until they were hit with not one atomic bomb, but two. They then adopted a radically new set of political and economic ideas foisted on them by the Americans. They made the changes they needed and as a result pulled off the transition—although with a lot of turmoil.

The pattern emerged again at the waning of the twentieth century. The Japanese rode the post–World War II economic model to unimagined heights until the late 1980s, when they got stuck on autopilot and kept moving in the same direction while the rest of the world was steering a new course. The Japanese economy stalled and continued to stagnate—seemingly waiting for some outside force to give it the shove it needed. Despite a severe recession that lasted the entire decade of the 1990s, the poorly performing economy remained a problem essentially within its own borders. Even the financial crisis of all of Asia and its spread to other developing markets and threat to the entire global economy have made little impact on most Japanese. The major crisis lies just ahead. When the insolvency of many of Japan's leading financial institutions can no longer be ignored because the average Japanese family's precious life savings are finally threatened, the Japanese people will force fundamental reform on both their political and their financial systems. The outcome will be a more open and transparent and less bureaucratic system.

From a global perspective, when Japan upgrades its financial system to world-class standards, many other countries stand to benefit. The Japanese are sitting on gobs of capital that has wasted away for way too long. Think of what will happen when the Japanese put *trillions* of dollars to work in an efficient way. The Japanese have almost $10 trillion in low-performing savings accounts. Today banks are sitting on a trillion dollars in nonperforming loans that were lent to those who squandered it. Soon they will clean up that mess and be in a position to lend money to companies that can squeeze every bit of productivity out of it—both in Japan and abroad.

The coming financial crisis will help clean up the old mess and make possible an evolution away from a small number of very large export-oriented manufacturing companies and toward an economy of many small and medium-sized service-oriented firms participating in the global knowledge economy. Stronger, healthier financial institutions will again be able to invest in the rest of Asia. Once they come to accept the new rules of the game, the Japanese will be ready to enter the global economy wholesale and to begin the frenzied process of applying the new ideas everywhere, refining them along the way.

Japanese companies are slowly moving toward the corporate restructuring that's going on in other parts of the developed world. This is an even more painful process than in the West because the Japanese postwar miracle was built partly on the practice of providing lifelong employment in exchange for employee dedication. Breaking up that bargain is hard to do, but the leading Japanese companies are already doing so. Sony and Toyota are top-flight global companies that have kept up much more with the times. Other Japanese companies simply need to leap into this New Economy. The models, both inside and outside Japan, are already there. All they have to do now is shift the focus to the next generation of products, the Digital Age products that are quickly becoming mass commodities.

Ah, generations. We mentioned the transition to a new generation of products. The Japanese really need to make a transition between generations, that is, to transfer power between generations of people. In the first half of the Long Boom, there was a generational power shift in the West. The Baby Boom generation, those born in the wake of World War II, took power from the generation that had grown up in the Great Depression and fought the war. The power transfer has happened in all fields, from business and the media to education and politics. Some key political moments symbolize that overall change. In the United States, you could say it came in 1992, when George Bush, the former World War II fighter pilot and sitting president, lost to Bill Clinton, the Baby Boomer who opposed the Vietnam War. In Europe, the wave of handovers happened a few years later, starting with Boomer Tony Blair in England and ending with Gerhard Schroeder in Germany, who at fifty-four was technically not a Boomer, but who campaigned on making a generational change and beat the old war horse Helmut Kohl, age sixty-eight. This kind of generational change simply has not begun in Japan. The government and business worlds are still monopolized by people trapped in the post–World War II mentality. When the ruling Liberal Democratic

Party chose a new prime minister and overhauled the cabinet in the summer of 1998, it filled the key position of finance minister with Ki-ichi Miyazawa, a seventy-eight-year old elder statesman who had been a fixture of Japanese-U.S. relations for four decades.

The problem here is not that old people can't lead countries and companies. The problem is that the differences between the so-called Boomer generation and the World War II generation are extremely relevant right now. For example, the Boomers are a media-savvy generation, having grown up with television and remain fascinated by new forms of media. This is a handy attribute to have when heading into the fast-paced Information Age. The Japanese of that Baby Boomer age are also largely media-savvy in the same way. Many of the Boomer and younger Japanese are extremely adept at software and new media. They produce most of the world's best video games. Who is better at games than Nintendo and Sony Playstation? They are the world leaders in animation. They have a large number of multimedia artists who are pushing the boundaries of technology and art. The problem is that all the people who understand those fields are young, and when you are young in Japan, you are relatively powerless.

Older people can exploit a cultural principle that age confirms wisdom and that elders are best positioned to lead. This built-in bias surfaces in many cultures around the world, but it's extreme in Asian cultures, including the Japanese. The inexorable aging of the Japanese population complicates the situation because the electorate's perceived personal interests will coincide with that bias. Elders may be best suited to lead in *static* societies. Traditional societies never changed much, so the cultural ethos that arose enshrined the oldest as the wisest. The oldest had watched the same game played the longest. They had the experience to make the best call. But in dynamic societies that are constantly changing, the older generations tend to lose touch with the front edge of change. The younger generations increasingly take on importance because they truly understand the new developments. They see the emerging future best. The most future-ready societies will find ways to utilize the insights of their young people and shift the balance of power, at the very least downplaying the power of people who best understand the past.

The next few years will see the inevitable retirement of the earlier generation of leaders in Japan and the ascendancy of a new group of leaders. Young people in Japan tend to be more influenced by the United States than the older generations. Starting with Admiral Perry, the Japanese, more than any other region of Asia, came under the influence of the United States. Other European nations barely touched the country. And then with the U.S. occupation after World War II, the Japanese got a crash course in being American—from instituting a U.S.-style constitution to watching U.S. movies. This postwar experience partly accounts for the extraordinary economic performance of Japan vis-à-vis the rest of Asia in that era. Certainly most of the credit goes to the core strengths of the Japanese—but do not underestimate the importance of Japan's strong interactions with the United States. The result was a complex mix of historical Japanese values with the new American institutional models. Generationally speaking, the Japanese Boomers, who grew up during that period, tend to have more American attributes. In the even younger generation that came after them, this U.S. influence is even more pronounced. These young people today, partly because of their increasing affluence, have often studied in the United States or traveled widely. And the march of U.S. influence in Japan proper has only increased.

To grab a glimpse of the future of Japan, go to the United States and study Japanese-Americans. They have fused together parts of the two cultures and are thriving, compared to both the Japanese in the homeland and other American groups. Japanese-Americans are extremely adept at new technologies, very creative, and very entrepreneurial. In other words, they are perfectly well suited to succeeding in the New Economy, and to moving confidently into the future. And the same can be said of this generation back in Japan. The Japanese are in transition right now. They need some time. But just give them two, three, at most five years, and we'll be watching the Japanese miracle, Take 2.

The Chinese Networkers

To grab a glimpse of the future of all China, simply go to Hong Kong. There you'll find the most advanced version of the Chinese East-West fusion. That's where, long ago, the British first brought the seeds of capitalism and planted them on that inhospitable little rocky island. The Chinese had their own way of dealing with the intrusion of the Westerners. As an ancient power center and a humongous country that defied outside control, China could keep the Westerners quarantined in a few port cities. Those cities then turned into hothouses where the two cultures could cross-fertilize and mutate. In the case of Hong Kong, that method certainly bore fruit. If anyone ever had any question about whether the Chinese people are suited to capitalism, a visit to Hong Kong would provide the answer. The Chinese harbor all the attributes needed for success in the capitalist economy, whether the old version or the new. They have the general Asian attributes in spades: the hard work and discipline, the fanatical savings and desire to invest, and the deep reverence for learning. But they are even more endowed: They are highly curious and creative, and they have very high energy levels.

These are not attributes that blossomed only in Hong Kong. Go up the coast to Shanghai, another quarantined port city that sprang out of the West's imposition of the opium trade, but one that never had the distortions of colonialism. This is a true Chinese city that has swelled from internal migration and now houses a good 15 million people—many more than Hong Kong. Shanghai is like New York City—on speed. Every single person is like a charged particle that's zapping around the city with no regard for street lights or traffic management—yet miraculously accidents are avoided and order emerges from the chaos. This is a society that operates beautifully when out of control. Despite the image of a society ruled top-down by a cabal of communists, the reality is that the Chinese are almost self-organizing and are perfectly suited to a market-based economy and, with time, decentralized democracy. For the future, this is a very good asset indeed.

Asian culture in general is coherent and distinct compared to that of the rest of the world. But within Asia, the cultures break down further and have very clear distinctions—particularly between the cultures of Japan and China. One big distinction has to do with the fundamental way they organize their societies. The Japanese have a very corporatist society, organized in very large units. The Japanese, it can be said, think of their entire people as one unit, one great big family. This kind of organization makes change very difficult because the Japanese need to achieve almost complete national consensus before moving along. As Kenichi Ohmae, a Japanese entrepreneur and intellectual leader, says, "If you ask a question of 1,000 Japanese, you will get one opinion. If you ask a question of 1,000 Chinese, you will get 1,000 opinions."

Even the subunits of Japan play out this way. Take industries. Japan is famous for the convoy system, where all the companies within an industry move in the same direction at the same time. They collaborate almost as if the entire industry were one organization. This has happened in the banking industry, with the healthy banks carrying the bad ones indefinitely, refusing to let them fail. Then a massive crisis of the entire banking industry finally forces a shakeout of the losers. Or take corporations, which feel obliged to take care of all their employees for life. Needless to say, this is not an economic environment that's conducive to change.

The Chinese, on the other hand, are organized by families. These are not necessarily nuclear families in the Western sense, but extended families that creep up to the level of clans. These family loyalties are more fundamental than loyalty to the nation or any organization in between. So, compared to Japan, China is much more decentralized, much more flexible, and more ready to move into the future. To be sure, the imposition of communism for the four decades after World War II tried to supersede that familial organizational principle with one that took the mass of all people as the basic unit. The state ran whole industries and the lives of all employees within them. State-run companies provided housing as well as education for employees' kids. But that massive effort never shifted the core loyalties of the Chinese people. Their default mode remains set on families. So as the vestiges of communism get stripped away from the economy and society, the family unit will come back to the fore. Family-run businesses are driving much of the entrepreneurial energy of the booming economies of the coasts. And families are taking over providing for the welfare and security of their family members. Thus the Chinese can take more radical steps to restructure their economy, which, compared to that of the Japanese, has a much longer path to modernization. But that versatile dynamic puts them on the fast track.

The problem with organizing an economy by families is that families don't scale up very well. They work great when creating small businesses and building success up to a point. But eventually those companies reach the size where the family members can't continue to fill the key posts. When a company reaches the stage of becoming a truly global competitor, key positions need to be filled by people drawn from a larger gene pool than one family. One family can't be expected to consistently produce world-class managers, accountants, engineers, lawyers, and strategists. The company needs to start drawing diverse talent from outside sources. The scaling problems also coincide with succession problems. The first-generation entrepreneur who built up the business does not always produce an equally adept second-generation successor. The luck-of-the-draw method for selecting leaders usually brings more bad luck than good. The meritocracy of democracies proved to be a much better way to pass the power of the state. The same holds true today of corporations in a global economy. The more meritocratic the method of finding leadership and talent, the better. Corporate monarchies are doomed.

Organizing an economy by families also has a tendency toward corruption. Just as you run into problems trying to find the best people within your family, you also run into problems trying to provide for the worst. Family loyalties toward the least capable family members can distort the economic decisions that the family company makes. This kind of emotional overlay in economic decisions leads to both inefficiencies and often corruption. At some point, you'll cover the tracks of your family. After all, family ties supersede all. This is why the Chinese characteristic of organizing themselves by families is both a blessing and a curse. The lack of scalability is one of the prime reasons that most people would be hard-pressed to name one global company with a Chinese name. Chinese companies don't go global—at least, they haven't yet. And corruption has plagued almost all the Chinese-dominated economies of Asia, with the exception of those of Singapore and Hong Kong. This family-based organizational principle is one reason corruption is, if not exactly inevitable, endemic throughout Southeast Asia and mainland China. But the lack of scalability and even the corruption, though big problems, can be solved by putting more meritocratic and transparent systems in place. Overall, the historical reliance on families as the basic organizational unit tabs up as an asset. Over time, this convention has engendered deep-seated habits that are as valuable as they are difficult to teach.

The Chinese are the ultimate networkers. They have been working at this game of networking for a long, long time, sending out their spidery networks of traders across Asia and the world for centuries. Almost any small city in the United States and Europe is sure to have a beachhead of a Chinese network in the form of a Chinese restaurant or laundry or small shop of some sort. Behind each storefront is a vast network of family members that might stretch all the way back to Asia itself. The immediate nuclear family, including all the family members, parents and children alike, work from the front end in apparent self-supporting autonomy. But other behind-the-scenes family members might provide the startup financing, or ongoing services, or advice and support in a pinch. They might be located in the next town down the road, or another region, or another country. These networks, channeling money and workers and support, spread like capillaries throughout Asia and the West. The networks run so dense that they defy untangling by outsiders.

The economy of the future, the New Economy, is a networked economy. Sure, the networked economy is about networked computers. These are the key tools that allow new ways to organize. But let's not lose sight of the fact that the technology simply helps people organize themselves better, through networks. The technology is the facilitator of this superior means of organization. The West, having come to networking through the technology, and being partial to gadgets in the first place, has remained focused on the technology. The Chinese have long thrived on building these human networks and mastering the skills that make them work well. They've done it almost completely without technology up to this point. But the technology is completely in sync with what they already do. Information technologies are essentially relationship technologies, and the Chinese are masters at relationships. Where other peoples will need to go through transitional struggles to reorganize around the new technology, the Chinese will slip right into the model of the networked economy.

The Chinese networks are so dense and economically influential throughout Asia that one can almost analyze Asia's progress toward the networked economy by studying the Chinese. More than 55 million ethnic Chinese live in Asia outside mainland China and run many of the economies—particularly in Southeast Asia. Chinese people who represent more than 4 percent of the Indonesian population, own more than 70 percent of the Indonesian economy. That's partly why indigenous Indonesians lynched Chinese during the collapse of the Suharto regime and the ensuing economic crash. They were frustrated by the success of the Chinese, many of whom had lived in Indonesia for generations and had even taken local names. The Malaysian government decreed that indigenous Malaysians, the Bumiputras, must hold 50 percent of the economy. If that decree had not forced equality, the Chinese would have gobbled the vast majority of that economy, too. The Chinese ran outright and were the majority population of three of the four vaunted Asian tigers that stunned the world with their torrid growth in the 1980s and 1990s: Hong Kong, Taiwan, and Singapore. The fourth, South Korea, was the only one to collapse in the Asian financial crisis. Taiwan, the one that most closely compares with Korea in size and output, actually thrived during the crisis due to the much more decentralized, entrepreneurial nature of its economy, which also is decidedly high-tech, and due to its robust democracy. And Singapore has been a model for all Asian countries in making the transition to a higher value service economy and, ultimately, a knowledge economy. The tiny city-state had no natural resources to speak of save brainpower—which it is leveraging quite well.

The offshore outposts of Taiwan and Singapore, like Hong Kong, confidently point to what a China shorn of its communist legacy can mean to the world. These are countries that have incubated a Chinese brand of capitalism longer than the mainland and have succeeded famously. Taiwan is little more than an experiment in transporting millions of mainland Chinese from places like Shanghai and letting them go in relative freedom. They boom. Singapore has a longer legacy of British colonial grooming and has shown an even greater propensity for high growth. And what we've seen from the mainland since the early 1980s augurs well for its growth in the future. Since Deng came to power in 1978, mainland China has produced perhaps the greatest reduction in poverty that the world has ever seen. The

GDP has grown, on average, 9 percent a year. Income per person has grown by 6 percent a year. Driven by this fevered pace, China's share of the world's GDP has doubled to 10 percent. And its GDP per person has risen from a quarter to half the world average. Looking ahead, Angus Maddison, an economic historian, estimates that even if Chinese GDP growth slows to 5.5 percent a year, which seems reasonable given other Asian countries' growth at comparable stages of development, China will match the GDP of the United States by 2015. The Chinese economy will then compose 17 percent of the world's GDP, and income per person—all billion-plus of them— would match the world average. And that's just crunching the numbers. Straight mathematics. You need to factor in how an increasingly well-adjusted China would thrive in a burgeoning global economy. As China becomes more open and more integrated into the world community, the economic juices will start to really flow. Once the market economy and even a rudimentary form of self-correcting democracy take hold, the Chinese will really thrive. The last twenty years have been merely a prelude to the takeoff. The next twenty years will be the real eye-openers. That's the Long Boom scenario. That's the twenty years yet to come.

The Indian Entrepreneurs

The city of Bombay is built back from the point on a peninsula where stands a triumphal arch called the Gateway to India. The British built the arch as a monument to themselves, celebrating the point of contact where West meets East. It's aptly named. The British used Bombay and other coastal cities like it as portals into the vast Indian hinterland. In India, as opposed to China, the British tried another sort of experiment that spread Western ideas of capitalism and industrialization in very different ways. This was the saturation method. The British over time established a comprehensive colonial administration that spread across more than half of what is now known as India, and its influence spread further still.

One unusual way to think of India is as Britain's other big colony. In the eighteenth century, the English headed to North America and formed the American colonies. Everyone understands the cultural transfer that jumped the Atlantic that way. But people forget that the Brits also headed to Asia and invested a large part of their time and resources in the Indian subcontinent. The cultural transfer happened there, too. The British built both a physical and, more important, a *cultural* infrastructure that lives on in India to this day. Compared to other Asian cultures, India has really absorbed many of the cultural institutions that have proved to be so successful for people rooted in Western civilization. Unlike many other Asians, the Indians have left the painful transition to democracy behind them and have a functioning liberal democracy, their own self-correcting political mechanism. The Indians also inherited many of the less obvious economic prerequisites for a well-functioning capitalist economy. They have a long tradition of abiding by the rule of law, complete with a vast system of judges and lawyers well trained in applying that law and negotiating fair settlements. This is not at all a common understanding in Asia. In many Asian countries, an individual or company with a grievance has no means of rectifying the wrong save supplication toward—or worse, bribery of—someone in power. Unlike in India, Asian business deals are often done by handshake, with no paper trail of carefully crafted contracts. India also has the oldest stock markets in Asia—dating back more than 150 years. They have had successive generations of people experienced in making markets work and connecting capital to worthy companies. On the other hand, many Indian graduate students learned socialist economics at the London School of Economics and came home to take prominent positions in their overly bureaucratic government. They kept applying these socialist principles long after they were discredited around the globe.

India also has picked up an intangible asset virtually by osmosis. Part of the British colonial legacy was that English became the national language uniting the diverse Indian peoples, who also speak a wealth of local languages. True, English was imposed on the Indians, but as alien as the language was, it proved so useful that the Indians themselves retained it as their national language long after the British left. To this day, the affairs of state and key media are all in English. And in the future, the Indians will be in a more advantageous position to interact in the global context because, like it or not, English has become the global language. You can complain about the historical circumstances that led to its ascendance, and you can rail about the unfairness of the benefits to English-speaking people, but it's just a fact: The world absolutely needs a global language in which to conduct the increasing amount of traffic in global business and world affairs, and English has become that global language.

These assets are one key reason, among several, why India might become the dark horse economy to contribute yet another booster to the Long Boom by 2020. People tend to think of the economic firepower of Asia residing in Japan, China, and the quasi-Chinese archipelago of Southeast Asia. To those same people, the stereotypical image of India is of a countryside filled with frail people roaming around with begging bowls. But in actuality, there are several Indias. One, indeed, is made up of large numbers of peasants still living in an agrarian age. Nearly 40 percent of its population is too poor to afford an adequate diet. Another sector, though, is made up of an educated, relatively affluent middle class. This is not a tiny group of elites living at the very apex of the social pyramid. This is a class that numbers about *300 million people*. That's 300 million people who live a life that roughly approximates the middle-class lifestyles enjoyed in the West. That number of people is more than the total number of all Americans, rich and poor, who number about 270 million. In a nation of almost a billion people, this number might get lost in the swell of the poor, but their absolute numbers are actually very significant and can make a big impact on the world. These middle-class Indians possess many of the attributes that allow a people to thrive in the global economy. The Indians, like the Chinese, have strong extended families that formed vast networks throughout Asia and the world. Like the Chinese in Southeast Asia, the Indians run much of the commerce in eastern and southern Africa. And Indian immigrants surface throughout the United States and Great Britain, often running their own family businesses. These are very entrepreneurial people who value enterprise, autonomy, and hard work.

Middle-class Indians have all the habits that will allow them to thrive in the Long Boom. They place a premium on education, and their educational system, another legacy of the British, turns out students who often go on to graduate work in the West. The Indians have extremely good schools for engineering and technical training, which produce large numbers of people well skilled in software development. However, those people generally earn only one-third the salary of an American with comparable skills. So India has formed some top-notch high-tech centers like that in Bangalore, a former British colonial resort town in the mountains, which now attracts global multinationals looking for skilled talent. Bangalore thrives by providing the world with very capable software engineers who speak English and can complete software projects that might be designed in hubs like Silicon Valley. The Bangalore engineers have not yet emerged with the same creative design talent, but they are the workhorses, who, among other things, are cranking out the code to solve the world's Y2K problem. Bangalore is a thriving middle-class oasis that's more the norm in India than outsiders think. It's also more about the future, a future in which India helps the world boom.

India and all of Asia could provide the key to long-term global economic growth. A potential global economic juggernaut could be built based on an alignment of the countries within the two metacivilizations of East and West behind the new model of the networked economy. Those within Western civilization are already most of the way through the transition, and those within Asian civilization show many of the characteristics that instill confidence that they will shortly do the same. If Asians get the politics right, and if they put in place the necessary political institutions, then all the other ingredients are there for an economic recovery. And once the Asians show the way back on track, other less endowed developing regions can follow their lead.

6

The Global Challenges

There are three great challenges from three regions that potentially stand in the way of the Long Boom. Russia, in the short term, and the Middle East, in the medium term, must reinvent themselves politically and become more highly integrated into the global economy. The long-term challenge is what to do about the desperate poverty that traps Africa. With the coming prosperity of the Long Boom, such human misery can't be allowed to continue.

THE WORLD FACES A NUMBER of huge challenges that fall outside the realm of pure economics but that could have a boomerang effect on the potential global growth juggernaut. Tensions between the United States and China could ratchet up to such an extent that the world ends up with a new Cold War, nudging toward a hot one. Crime and terrorism could spread so much that the world would recoil in fear. People who constantly worry about being blown up or ripped off are not about to open up and connect with others. A major ecological crisis could get out of hand much quicker than anticipated and the world would need to devote an extraordinary amount of resources and attention to fixing it. The cumulative effects of pollution could begin to dramatically effect the health of individuals, putting extreme stress on our systems of medical care. A social and political backlash against globalization and the changes brought by the New

Economy could greatly undercut the path of progress. People have to choose to move forward—and they just might not.

Out of all the potential scenario spoilers out there, three stand out as key long-term, medium-term, and short-term challenges that ultimately need to be solved by the politics of the Long Boom. These three challenges arise out of three regions that are not yet on the trajectory of the Long Boom and that have greater obstacles to getting there. However, the people of these regions do have assets that they can use to make the transition and thrive in the long run. But they will need help at this point. It's in the interests of the more prosperous regions to provide that support as soon as possible, particularly in the case of the short-term challenge, Russia. Failure to meet this challenge, as well as the other challenges, will truly be a disaster.

The Russian Rebound

Believe it or not, Russia is one of those economies that doesn't really matter in the grand scheme of the global economy. It barely breaks the top twenty, with a gross domestic product before its most recent crisis of about $300 billion, about the same size as Argentina or Taiwan or, for that matter, the state of Illinois. Russia could check out of the global economy, and, in effect, few would even notice. However, Russia does have one thing that really, really matters. It has 23,000 nuclear bombs.

You have to hand it to the Russians. With great courage, they abandoned the Cold War and the effort to spread communism worldwide. The West had spent forty years girding for a battle to the death with the evil empire, and then one day on CNN we found out that the whole effort was no longer necessary. The Russians unilaterally called, "Game over," and jumped wholeheartedly into capitalism and democracy. Jumped might be an understatement. The Russians came barreling out of the hothouse of communism and dove head first into the ice-cold lake. They completely scrapped both their economic and their political systems and entered the chaos of wide-open gangster capitalism and raw power politics. Obviously, the Chinese took a different approach. The Chinese avoided political reform and mostly opened up the economy at a measured pace. And this more conservative tack came from a people much more naturally suited to take to capitalism. The Chinese merely had to peel back the structures of communism and let the natural inclinations of the Chinese come to the fore. The Russians, on the other hand, were starting from scratch. They had no long history of trading and establishing networked businesses. They didn't have much of a history of initiative or enterprise or even hard work. So the Russians soon found that they needed to do some serious work on establishing the civil institutions a society needs for a market economy and a democracy to take hold and ultimately thrive. In the heady days of the dissolution of the Soviet Union, people talked about a new Russia rising within the decade. As the 1990s dragged on, and as the economic and political problems of Russia mounted, the reality sank in that the difficult transition would take longer. But Russians are beginning to understand they lost out badly by their inaction in the early 1990s, by their failure to understand the importance of the rule of law and a sound court system. Building the necessary institutions takes time and lots of sustained effort. You can't just think out one year or two. Cut Russia some slack. Give them another ten years.

The Russians need more than just time. They need a serious commitment of investment, financial aid, and even food. They need that support from their former nemesis, the United States, the country that now needs to show that it's a true global leader. The Russians did their part to end the Cold War. Now the Americans need to do their part to clean it up. The noblest way to frame the project would be a post–Cold War equivalent of the Marshall Plan, which helped rebuild Europe after World War II, including building the remains of Nazi Germany into a long-term ally. The parallel is so obvious that it's puzzling that U.S. leaders can't get the public to respond. This is clearly the right thing to do. And a hard-nosed budgetary case can be made. Ten years after the end of the Cold War, the U.S. military budget has been trimmed by only $60 billion a year, from $330 billion to $270 billion.

The major reason we have not been able to capture a bigger "peace dividend" is that our military strategy continues to require that the United States be ready to fight two separate major ground wars at the same time. This policy, which made sense when the Soviet Union was a threatening nuclear superpower and China was a looming antagonist, no longer addresses the security threats faced by the United States, the only superpower in the world today. We are overprepared to fight wars unlikely to occur and underprepared to respond to more pressing localized conflicts like those in the Balkans and more probable terrorist attacks. With a new twenty-first-century military strategy, the United States could become better prepared to protect its national security interests at the same time as it reduces the cost of its military preparedness. This new strategy would allow additional cuts in the military budget, while maintaining security in a world that poses different threats. Of course, closing some of the unnecessary army bases that are kept open only because Congress continues to play pork barrel politics would also save money.

Americans could take 10 percent of the existing military budget and channel the funds to Russia in the form of targeted aid that supports Russian efforts to build the infrastructure necessary to operate a fully functioning democracy. Roughly $25 billion dollars a year for a decade would be decisive in helping Russia though its transition and would be money well spent. It would reduce the fears of the Russian people about the West. It would buy the security that will be jeopardized if conditions get worse in Russia and nationalists take power and rearm. If that happens, the West will spend the next decade pouring much more money into defense rather than building the Long Boom, and generations will look back on our stupidity. Americans can't construct a civil society within Russia or build the market economy. They can help provide the funds to see the Russians through their trauma, to buy them time. Ten more years. Give them the time. Give them the help they need.

The Russians have some marvelous assets going into this transition, not the least of which is their remarkable capacity for suffering. They have shown that they can put up with immense levels of trauma. They lost 20 million lives defending their country in World War II and suffered through seventy years of communism, with all its purges and gulags and shortages. They are fully capable of making it through the next 10 years of a difficult transition. And once through, they will have much to contribute to the global economy. They have some of the world's most abundant natural resources, including oil and natural gas, their cash cow for the time being. The Soviet Union might not have delivered the goods for a consumer economy but it did provide a very good education for almost everyone, and Russia has a highly educated populace and large percentages who have received higher education. This human capital takes decades to build up, but it also takes decades to waste away. Right now the brainpower is simply in a holding pattern, and in some fields—like mathematics or rocketry or even some software design—the Russians are world-class. A transitioned Russia will have much to contribute to the world. They could tie into an expanded Europe. They could act as a bridge stretching to Asia. And by permanently neutralizing their nukes, they will allow everyone on the planet to breathe easier.

The Middle East Middle Road

Jerusalem challenges our idea that diversity is an asset in the modern world. Here, where three great religions share a common ground, conflict, not innovation, is the norm. The differences among Muslims, Christians, and Jews have not been a strength, but a profound weakness. Even within their own faiths, sectarian conflicts are the rule. It would be foolish to imagine that we authors could identify the clear way forward for the Middle East when so many experts have failed. However, it is hard to imagine a better future for the world that does not address some of the explosive conflicts of this region, particularly the threats posed by small nations using weapons of terror. The specter of terrorism is one of the most worrisome threats to a global economic expansion. After the pressing Russian challenge, international terrorism presents the most compelling medium-term challenge facing the world. People living in constant fear of being blown up will pull inward and cut themselves off from others. They will erect defensive barriers and trust only people exactly like themselves. This is truly a disaster scenario for the future. It's not good for any region in the world, and certainly not good for the Middle East.

The struggles in the Middle East today are not primarily a clash of civilizations or religions. They are not fundamentally theological in origin. Many of the conflicts have familial and tribal roots, and others are cultural. The Hashmites, who rule Jordan, have warred with the Saud family for generations. The Persians, who dominate Iran, have fought with the Arabs in the Gulf region for even longer. For most of this century, the Kurds have fought for their own country against the Turks and the Iraqis. These struggles have nothing to do with Arabs versus Jews or Christians versus Muslims. However, the legacy of Western colonialism in the Middle East has colored all of these local struggles. Most Islamic societies were dominated first by European colonial powers and often later by Western companies— and these intruders often displayed a disrespect for local culture. The local people then equated modernization with Westernization. To modernize was to become like Europe or the United States, and they clearly had mixed feelings about that. In the postcolonial era, many nations of the region have developed internal struggles between the modernists, now considered secularists, and the traditionalists, who are increasingly the religious fundamentalists. In the near future, in both the Arab countries and Israel, the internal struggles between the secularists and the religious fundamentalists could lead to even greater instability in the region. The Long Boom for the Middle East and the world depends on the secularists' retaining or gaining power in matters of state. The religious fundamentalists' desire for closed, intolerant societies is decidedly inconsistent with the Long Boom.

Oil. You would think the discovery of oil in the Middle East would have been an across-the-board positive development. Oil was the key commodity fueling the Industrial Age, and the people of the Middle East sit on top of the planet's largest reservoirs. In fact, oil in the Middle East has proven to be a great tragedy. The oil initially drew the Western colonial powers, which exploited the region and generated hatred that's still seething. But even after the West left, the oil created a small oligarchy of powerful indigenous rulers who were able to distort the development trajectory of their nations. The oil oligarchies did not take the money and invest in developing an industrial base and educational infrastructure for their nations. They mostly squandered it on themselves and on luxurious but irrelevant public projects, or on unproductive handouts to citizens. On top of that, huge bureaucratic states arose that drew their lifeblood from the oil money but now suck the lifeblood out of the citizenry. During the heyday of OPEC in the 1970s, the money was flowing freely, and so bureaucratic extravagance could be overlooked. In the 1980s, with the global oil glut, the money slowed down and the situation turned more dire. By the 1990s, with prices still dropping, it was getting intolerable. While much of the world boomed and moved toward a new global economy, the Middle East stagnated under the weight of bureaucratic states, unable to change and with few economic resources to leverage. On top of that, despite occasional price spikes, the future appeared even worse as oil was expected to decrease in importance with the advance of alternative energy technologies and more diverse energy sources.

The fundamentalist brand of Islam arose in reaction to the great oil tragedy and as a backlash to exploitation by the West and its so-called modernization. But in a deeper sense, it arose in reaction to the injustices of the unresponsive oil oligarchies and the presumed bleakness of the undefined future. And that pessimism about the future only compounds the region's tragedy. But Islamic fundamentalism is not Islam. Islam originally birthed a culture that exploded with intellectual curiosity and new discoveries. From the seventh to the twelfth centuries, Muslim societies were extremely dynamic, and the civilization emerged as a world power and a cradle of scientific innovation. That was a brand of Islam that was much more tolerant and open-minded—much more future-friendly. And that's a brand of Islam that is still alive and growing today.

The missing ingredient in the Middle East has been the middle class—at least until now. It hasn't thrived or greatly expanded in numbers as in Asia. But it has inexorably grown. Caught in the reality of their respective nations' bipolar politics, members of the middle class have switched their allegiance between elites and religious leaders—or simply laid low. Though still small today, the middle class is growing in numbers and influence and is poised to make an impact on the politics of the Middle East in the first decades of the twenty-first century. These people are like middle-class people everywhere. They want to establish a growing economy and enjoy the benefits of spreading prosperity. They want to open trade with the world and be able to purchase basic consumer items—the classic washing machine, television set, and car. They want to educate their children so their children's lives will be better than their own. They want to be able to speak their mind. Like middle-class people through history, they tend to be more tolerant and moderate—and their religious beliefs reflect that tendency.

And in the end, they want democracy. These are the people who will increase in importance in the coming decades and will help shift the politics of the Middle East toward the global norm. They will be the leading actors who, with the help of other countries in the world community, will build their region—they will take it from tragedy to triumph. These middle-class people will be the constituency of the Long Boom.

THE AFRICAN PROMISE

One of the key long-term global challenges concerns Africa, the most poverty-stricken and least developed portion of the world. In recent years, most attention directed to Africa has gone to the middle of the continent, where horrific ethnic and tribal wars have terrorized the populace and depressed hopes for a better future. But Africa has other, more positive, but less visible developments, particularly in the south. It's easy to lose sight of the incredible strides taken in South Africa just since the 1980s. That country has gone from seemingly unresolvable guerrilla warfare over apartheid to a functioning democracy that balances the rights of whites and blacks. It is critically important that South Africa's example of embracing democracy spreads to the rest of the continent. South Africa's most prominent political prisoner, Nelson Mandela, became one of the most respected national leaders in the world. Instead of a riot of violent retribution, the country has engaged in a formal process of reconciliation. This is one of the most impressive displays in the world of trying to dissipate violence and hatred through dialogue. Africans have a deep belief in the value of forgiveness. That ability to forgive is one of the foundations of the healing process going on in South Africa, and it could be a key to rapid progress for all of Africa in the future.

Africa can also ride some very fortuitous global technological trends. The newest generations of the best technology often cost less than the old ones, and Africans can get the newest, best, cheapest technology at the same time as people in the developed world, thus leapfrogging stages of development. Also, technologies are becoming much more decentralized, so that much less up-front investment is required to set up elaborate infrastructures. In telecommunications, wireless phone systems are much cheaper and quicker to install than was running land lines through crowded cities. And new generations of solar power or even hydrogen fuel cell power will allow African villages to get reliable electricity without stringing cables from huge hydroelectric dams or oil-burning power stations. Africans can also piggyback on infrastructure that the developed nations are setting up anyway. The West is launching several vast satellite systems for phone and Internet service that can be reached from every foot of the planet. These systems will allow pockets of tech-savvy middle-class Africans to access the global economy despite being surrounded by a sea of abject poverty. That access will be good for those individuals and good for a world that until now has benefited insufficiently from the creative contributions of Africans.

Africa will also stand to benefit from overall global growth as other peoples in other regions trade up the economic food chain. There was a time when tennis shoes were made in the United States. Then production moved to Japan, then to Korea, then to Malaysia, now to China and Indochina. Each time production migrated, the original host country traded up to creating higher-value-added products. That migration will continue, and those at the lower end today will move to greener pastures, leaving opportunities for developing countries in Africa to begin the long path of upwardly mobile development.

One obvious economic opportunity for Africa is in textiles and fashion. The many cultural regions of Africa have distinct styles of art and distinct design traditions, as well as a long history of creating fabrics. A thriving textile and fashion industry could be built around distinct clusters scattered across the continent. Each African cluster would be known globally for its particular offerings of textiles or clothing. And with the new decentralized but interconnected technologies, they could integrate into the mainstream global economy quite quickly. These clusters would not necessarily be limited to apparel industries. Clusters could develop in any area in which a region excels.

Africa has always been valued for its natural resources. In fact, the attraction of those resources was behind the colonial occupations of the nineteenth and the first half of the twentieth centuries. By the time Africans controlled their own countries, many of the resources were commodities subject to the vagaries of world markets, with very thin profit margins. However, Africa has one natural resource that is now almost unique in the world: It has the most unspoiled natural rain forests on the planet. The rain forests in Latin America and Southeast Asia have been rapidly developed over the last several decades. The trees are being lumbered, and the land is being cleared. In terms of rain forests, the early development stage of Africa is a plus. The rain forests are becoming the biological laboratories of the world, where important new molecules are being discovered. These are being used by the pharmaceutical companies to develop new forms of drugs and other biotechnology products. Africa could become a vital link in the new biotech industries of the future.

Everyone can benefit when the world booms. That will become increasingly true the longer the Long Boom can be sustained. As the world becomes richer, the sense of obligation to the less fortunate regions will become greater. Until now, the world has been able to almost ignore the plight of Africans. But if the Long Boom were able to sustain global growth rates of between 4 and 6 percent a year, the world's wealth would more than double by 2020. That level of prosperity enjoyed in many places around the world would make the contrast with the poverty in Africa nothing short of obscene. At some point, the world community would be forced to act—if not out of genuine compassion and generosity, then out of utter shame. Africa clearly has the potential to develop, but the challenges are so great that any successful effort will take time. The really long-term solution to the African challenge will fall to the Long Boom generation, our children. These are the people who will come to power in the twenty-first century. They will redress the historical injustice of Africa. Then that region will thrive, too.

To: corelist@zing.com
Subject: Anxiety
Date: Friday, 17 Dec 1999, 12:20:15 –0800
   I was thinking about you guys late this afternoon as I was driving into San Francisco across the Bay Bridge and could see the sun setting far out in the

Pacific Ocean behind the other bridge, the graceful Golden Gate. Those beautiful ocean sunsets never fail to touch me, at least momentarily, even on a day such as this. I was stuck in a massive traffic jam on the bridge—all five lanes were stalled. At one point, nobody budged for a full thirty minutes. Of course, I was already late on my way home for dinner, and this jam made me more outrageously late. This week was horrible at work. I was being pulled in five directions, with two major projects hitting final deadline and a year's cleanup to do before the holidays. I had clients in several countries calling me at all hours of the day and night. Two people on my projects walked out for better opportunities elsewhere. I looked around me on that bridge, trying to locate the idiots who had started honking for absolutely no reason except to vent their frustration and drive all the rest of us insane. Half the people in the cars had their windows rolled up and were jabbering on cell phones. I remembered how I once thought those phones pretentious and a waste of money. And just as I remembered that, my own cell phone started to ring yet again.

This whole situation seems like a metaphor for my life. In the midst of great beauty and opportunity, I feel trapped and anxious. On the one hand, I'm at ground zero in the digital revolution. This is the center of the planet when it comes to computers and the Internet. They say the future is being born right around me, and for that I am ecstatic. The romantic in me always wanted to be in the center of some kind of revolution, and I now got it, though not in the way I expected. The pragmatic in me also appreciates that the economy of this area is booming and I am well positioned to reap the benefits. It turns out my skills are in high demand. The times are bursting with possibilities and seething with changes. We're on a roller coaster ride that's pumping our adrenaline as we get whipped around all over the place while hanging on for dear life. This is either the greatest moment to be alive—and we are having a blast—or this is a moment of extreme anxiety. I'll tell you—I swing from one to the other every day.

I am anxious about everything. And I'm not alone. Everyone in the world seems anxious about everything. Everything in the world appears anxiety-provoking right now. The computers are doing it. In what seems like just a few years, computers have gone from these machines that no one was really thinking about to machines that are running the world. What happens if these computers completely crash on January 1 and all pandemonium breaks loose? What if the Y2K crazies holed up in the hills are right? How much faster can this global economy keep accelerating? We're taking billions of dollars and swooshing them into countries and then snatching them away. The whole economy in Asia imploded. That's the same Asia I was talking about ten years ago. They were taking over the world, the future was there. And now they are face down on the mat.

Forget the world, I'm anxious about me. Mol, my partner, my lover, my wife—I love her to death, but I'm slowly killing her. My marriage of ten years is being strained so badly that it's about to snap. That's enough of a tragedy, but now I've also got a kid. I love Amy to death, too. She is an amazing kid, and I'd like nothing better than to be there for her. She's now five years old and at that age when she's just fascinated by everything in the world around her. But she also has so much to teach me about the wonder of life and how to look freshly at things. I love them, yet I have no time to be with them because my work life is insanity. It's pulling me in so many directions that I've got to work all the time just to keep up. I've got to respond to e-mail, phone calls, faxes, memos, sticker notes over every surface of my cubicle. I've got to be in meetings, I've got to attend conferences, I've got to travel across the country and sometimes the world. And then everybody expects everything from me immediately because no one has established any boundaries.

It used to be that I'd be sucking down cigarettes to calm my nerves. But nobody smokes in California, including me. It's kind of amazing how that happened so quickly. People said, "Smoking is stupid. Why are we doing this?" And then they cut it out. They cut it out everywhere—restaurants, planes, offices, airports, buildings. In California they've even cut it out of bars. The mentality is that if you want to kill yourself by smoking, fine, but don't do it around other patrons or the person serving you beer. Some of this came from legislation backed by broad public support, but most of it came from peer pressure. None of my friends around here smoke; none of you smoke, even though most of us did ten years ago. This shift in social norms happened quite unexpectedly and is in the process of wiping out a huge health problem. Lung cancer is going to be dropping here, whereas in China 80 percent of the people smoke, and they are dropping like flies with lung disease. It shows how societies, just lots of regular people, can change their ways almost overnight.

Anyhow, I never see you guys; we are all working like maniacs; we only communicate briefly in these e-mails. At the end of the year, I pump out this one long e-mail to you—my annual deal. I miss you guys and the times we once shared. I wouldn't want to go back to our old miseries, but I sure would like to find more time to enjoy those other sides of life that now seem lost. That's why I was thinking of you as I sat staring at that beautiful sunset through my windshield this evening—blocking out the blaring horns. We spent so many hours watching sunsets turn to moonrises as we discussed everything and nothing at the same time. But just as I relaxed into that reminiscent reverie, my cell phone bleeped and I had to snap back to the work world. And then soon after, the traffic began to move, and I slowly negotiated my way home, apologized profusely to Mol, got my twenty minutes with Amy, and only now, with both of them asleep, do I get a few minutes to write an e-mail to you. So I'm now pushing the send button with my finger. If I wait another couple more minutes, it might be my forehead as my face hits the keyboard and I'm fast asleep.

PART THREE
The Engines
of
the Twenty-first
Century

THE ONLY WAY TO KEEP the Long Boom going is to figure out a way to slow and eventually eradicate damage to the environment. There is no other option. The environment is already strained to the breaking point, global warming is starting to seriously affect the climate, and many people in the world's megacities are choking to death. A global boom until 2020 would put us all over the edge—unless we do something dramatic right now.

Section III lays out the coming waves of technologies that will allow us to grow rapidly while actually lowering the strain on the environment. These are not pie-in-the-sky technologies but practical ones, many of which are far along in development and ready for commercial use. We talk about how the impending shift to new fuel cell energy technologies could eliminate dependence on oil and promote hydrogen as our primary fuel source—one that has virtually no

by-products but water. We show how the revolution in biotechnology
not only will rework our treatment of the human body but could be
used to overhaul our industrial and agricultural processes and greatly
reduce pollution. And we hail the arrival of nanotechnology, which
will eventually provide the long-term pollution solution. If you think
the future is just about computer technology, you're in for a jolt. An
average life span of 120 years? Machines the size of molecules?
They're both in the works—along with much more.

We end Section III with our notion of wild science, the probability
that some major scientific breakthrough will soon come along and really blow our minds. We now have millions of scientists pushing the
boundaries of human knowledge in all directions, from the sub-
atomic to the distant reaches of outer space. By no means are we at
the end of scientific discovery. It's more like we've just begun. Expect
the unexpected. It's coming any day.

7

Saving the Planet

Climate change is a truly global challenge that will increasingly affect the entire world community. The high rates of economic growth that will come with the Long Boom make it imperative that we shift toward more ecologically benign technologies and move rapidly away from fossil fuels. Creating a prosperous global economy in balance with nature is totally feasible and practical. Nothing stands in our way.

AND THEN THE WEATHER started getting weird. Not that we hadn't had strange weather before. Every decade had some strange event, like the Dust Bowl in the 1930s, when drought, combined with incessant high winds, picked up a foot of topsoil in the middle of the United States and dumped it like snow in places like Chicago. That was weird. But by the 1990s, the weather was getting *really* weird. And it seemed to be happening all over the planet at about the same time. At least it sure seemed that way to an awful lot of people, people who began to worry, a little bit more each year . . .

Why, you may ask, are we now talking about the weather? Well, it turns out that we have dealt with only about half of the great challenge facing the world. The more intractable and long-term problem, the one bound up with the global environment, is still to come. And for that matter, we've really explored only about half the technology that will emerge in our Long Boom era. So the story gets worse, because this new problem is much more complicated and difficult to master, and better, because we have a lot more resources at our disposal than most people would think. It all depends on how you frame the situation, with a positive or a negative spin. Either way, though, we have to go back to contemplating the weather, because that's where the message began to sink in.

A few people began noticing what seemed like an increase in severe weather in the 1980s, but the real action started in the 1990s. One of the first big events to draw attention was Hurricane Andrew, which struck the coast of Florida and ravaged areas from the Louisiana coast to the North Carolina mountains in 1992. Every winter the southern and eastern coasts of North America get whacked by hurricanes, but Hurricane Andrew was something different—more ferocious and the most damaging one so far. That storm caused more material damage than any other natural event in the history of the United States to date. Not that the United States has any monopoly on humongous hurricanes. One of the biggest hurricanes ever recorded hit Central America in 1998. Hurricane Mitch was not only huge, but unique, which is partly why it was so destructive. Normally hurricanes move across the Atlantic toward the United States, but Mitch came to Central America and just sat in the same spot for four days, unleashing relentless winds of 180 miles an hour and dumping as much as fifty to seventy-five inches of rain. No one had ever seen a storm anything like it, and so no one was remotely prepared. As a result, more than 11,000 people died, with thousands more missing. When it was over, Nicaragua, Honduras, El Salvador, and Guatemala were devastated, and their developmental clocks had been set back twenty years. The president of Honduras, Carlos Flores Facusse, actually said the storm destroyed fifty years of progress.

Then there were the floods. The Mississippi River swelled like never before in 1993, causing the most flood damage in U.S. history. This natural disaster was exacerbated by an accumulation of bad engineering decisions, which had repeatedly dammed up the river and developed on what had been the natural floodplain. When the waters exceeded the engineers' worst-case scenario, the river tore up much that had been built from Minneapolis to New Orleans. But the Americans had no monopoly on boneheaded environmental engineering decisions. The Chinese suffered through the worst floods in their modern history in the summer of 1998, partly because of their past policies on deforestation. The extreme rains caused so much damage, affecting more than 250 million people, that the Chinese reversed their policy and began replanting. Then there were the fires. In 1997, the Indonesians lived for months in a fog, so to speak, when a severe drought led to massive fires in the rain forest, which, by definition, is supposed to be wet. The smoke hung over not only Indonesia but Malaysia and other parts of Southeast Asia—causing widespread respiratory problems as millions of people sucked in smoke day after day. The following year, 1998, Brazil had equally damaging fires in its rain forest, and Mexico had blazes that kept smoke hanging for weeks over both Mexico and the United States.

The big events were scary enough, but it was the more regional weather problems that really hit home. On the local level, all of us seemed to have our own weird weather stories. Take one year in the United States, say, 1998. There was a deluge of rain in California, including the relatively dry south, like the city of Santa Barbara, which had twenty-one inches of rain in February—an event that happens once every 1,000 years or so. Northern Californians had massive mud slides when the earth simply could not absorb any more water. Texans withered through weeks of summer temperatures of 100 degrees and above. Florida translated that heat into wildfires, which caused hundreds of millions of dollars in damage to more than 700 square miles of land. New York City had extremely unseasonable temperatures, for example, 86 degrees Fahrenheit at the end of March, only nine days after snow fell in Central Park. Lake Erie never even froze in the winter of 1997–1998, something that had happened only two times before. But snow it did in South Dakota on March 1, a full thirty-two inches, which is almost double the normal amount for the entire month. And snow was still falling in the mountains of Idaho in mid-June, only five days before the official start of summer. There was no break in the weirdness. In the first month of 1999, the United States experienced the most tornadoes it had ever recorded.

At the time, the most common explanation for all the weirdness was El Niño, the extensive pool of warm water that develops in the tropical Pacific Ocean from time to time and disrupts normal global

weather patterns. That was the pop analysis, which came from everyone from the TV weather announcer to your Aunt Ida. El Niño certainly played a part, but the more informed analysis began to shift to
a different, more disturbing set of facts. The average surface temperature on Earth in 1998 was the highest ever recorded since people began using thermometers in the mid-nineteenth century. The 1998
number easily beat out the next highest year, which was the previous one, 1997. In fact, seven of the ten warmest years on record
since the mid-nineteenth century occurred in the 1990s—and the
three other top temperatures occurred in the 1980s. Some scientists,
using techniques like studying the rings of trees, argued that 1998
was not only the hottest year on record, but the hottest in the millennium, stretching back to the times of the Holy Roman Empire.
The record-breaking average world temperature, about 58 degrees in
1998, was a full degree higher than what scientists call the recent
long-term average, which is the average for the thirty years from
1961 to 1990. And 1998 was the twentieth year in a row that the
earth's average temperature had been higher than that recent long-
term average.

   The first big public explanation of the concept of global warming
had come ten years before in the dramatic congressional testimony
of James Hansen, a climatologist and head of NASA's Goddard Institute for Space Studies. Hansen just happened to face Congress in the
midst of a summer heat wave that was scorching Washington—and
that punctuated his message. He carefully argued to Congress and
the national media that strong evidence supported the idea that human emissions were creating a greenhouse effect and warming the
planet. When fossil fuels like oil, coal, and natural gas are burned,
they emit carbon dioxide, which remains in the atmosphere and
helps trap heat—much as the panes of glass in a greenhouse do.
With the increasing industrial development of the late twentieth
century, the amount of carbon dioxide that humans had created had
begun to make a demonstrable difference. Hansen was lambasted by
many skeptics as being too premature in his analysis. But by 1995,
the Intergovernmental Panel on Climate Change, a United Nations
group of scientists, had reached the same conclusion. And the temperatures of the late 1990s did nothing to undermine the claim.

The facts will continue to come in, and there's a very good chance, a high probability, that they will continue to overwhelmingly support the notion that we're in the middle of a global warming and that human beings are mostly at fault. There might be some natural causes beyond our control, but we're the ones tipping the balance. We don't have to tip the balance much. The world's temperature today is only five to nine degrees warmer than in the middle of the last Ice Age. And mainstream scientists project that we will warm the planet another two to six degrees in the next century if carbon dioxide emissions and other greenhouse gases are not reduced. In the twentieth century alone, we appear to have raised the world temperature one and a quarter degrees, and for most of that century, most of the world was not industrializing. If the temperature continues to rise at the projected rate—let alone accelerate—we could be heading into a wild ride of rising sea levels, shifting climatic zones, mass migration away from coastal areas, and a lot more of that weird weather. William Calvin, a professor at the University of Washington who has researched the linkage between evolution and climate change, speculates that global warming will actually quickly boomerang back into a far more catastrophic global cooling, which will bring on another Ice Age. The way that would work is that global warming could trigger melts of northern ice that flush freshwater into the oceans, changing the flow of warm ocean currents. Those currents have been warming Europe and other parts of the Northern Hemisphere, but their absence could plunge the North into permanent cold.

The Coming Environmental Crisis

The threat of severe climate change is the crisis that will drive us through the next decade. This environmental crisis will not dissipate after the turn of the century. For that matter, the public perception of this as a full-blown crisis will not even fully materialize by then. But little by little, with more facts, more public discussion, and more mass experience of unusual weather, people around the world will shift from their preoccupation with the millennial transition, which could be solved in relatively short order, to this more long-term problem. This emerging crisis will create the impetus to change. After all, everyone could be affected, and in the worst-case scenario, large portions of humanity might not survive at all. This is the dual nature of crises: They are both bad and good. They cause an extreme amount of fear and disruption, but they also get people geared up for action. In the case of this environmental crisis, the response requires both rapid technological advances and increasing global regulatory harmonization, two key elements that will accelerate the Long Boom.

More than any other person, Paul Ehrlich, author of the 1969 book *The Population Bomb*, got the world thinking about how we might be destroying Spaceship Earth. Ehrlich came up with the basic equation that defines the environmental impact of humans:

Environmental impact = Population × Affluence × Technology.

In other words, population, affluence, and technology are the three variables that determine how severe people's impact on the environment will be. If the population goes up and the other two variables hold steady, the environment will be more stressed. If the population goes down in the same situation, the environment will be better off.

Ehrlich spent the bulk of his book pointing out that the population of the planet as of 1970 was soaring, and he projected more of the same. If that trend continued, he argued, the planet was heading into a catastrophe. Luckily, the trend did not continue, and population increase was quickly reined in in many parts of the world. Some methods were Draconian, like China's one-child-per-family rule, but much of the progress came not from conscious policies, but as a by-product of development and affluence. People who migrate to urban areas—and middle-class people in general—have fewer kids. Most of all, educated women tend to have fewer kids. Virtually every industrialized country has seen its fertility rate plunge below the point where the population can replicate itself. All Europe, the United States, and Japan, as well as developing Asian countries like South Korea, Thailand, and China, have fertility rates below the 2.1-children-per-woman replacement level.

This shift has been stunning. In 1975, only 18 percent of the world's population lived in countries with a fertility rate below replacement levels. By 1997, that ratio had more than doubled to 44 percent of the world's population living in such countries. The United Nations has projected that by 2015, a full 67 percent of the world's population will live in countries with negative population growth. This projection accounts for a radical reappraisal of the world's projected population figures. In 1975, the total population was 4.08 billion. By 1997, that number had grown, though more slowly than many expected, to 5.85 billion. By 2015, the revised total is now expected to be 7.29 billion, and by 2050, 9.4 billion. That's still a lot of people, but far fewer than projected in the 1970s. And that's just the mainstream projections based on current trends. Those numbers do not take into account new initiatives to promote birth control in the next fifty years. And they certainly do not factor in the effects of a Long Boom, which would greatly expand the middle class and raise educational levels around the world. The point is that population now does not seem to be the variable that will blow out Ehrlich's equation on environmental impact. If anything, the more pressing concern of global demographers is what to do with too *few* young people supporting too many old people.

Affluence, the second part of Ehrlich's equation, needs to go up for most people in the world. Some environmentalists argue that the only way to save the planet is to consume much less, live much simpler lives, and adopt a slow- or no-growth global economy. This has been a losing proposition from Day One. There is virtually no political support for that approach in any country and never has been since ecoactivists first articulated the idea in the 1960s. People want to live well: People in the developed world who already live well will not give up their standard of living; people in the developing world will not give up the dream of living well no matter what they are told; and any basic sense of justice would prevent the developed world from denying the developing world that aspiration. In addition, because a growing number of people live in democracies, the no-growth movement is essentially dead. Population growth seems to be slowing. We can't rein in affluence. But that's okay. We can

solve the global environmental problem by focusing almost exclu-
sively on the equation's third variable: technology.

Technology, in the long view, has a pretty good track record of becoming environmentally cleaner with successive generations. In the
middle of the nineteenth century, London was a horrible place to
live. The air was foul, and all the buildings were covered with soot,
mostly because the entire economy was run on crude technology and
the energy source was coal. As they moved up the technology ladder
and the energy chain to oil, natural gas, and nuclear power, London-
ers began to breath fresh air again, and the blackened city soon
brightened up. This sequence has played out over the years and
around the world again and again—and will continue to do so.

The other point is that pollution is not permanent. Most people
think that once the air or water is polluted, it is ruined forever. That's
not true. Newer technologies can not only be pollution-free, but they
can even go back and clean up. Bodies of water like Boston Harbor
and the Hudson River were so polluted by the 1970s that people were
warned not to touch them. The Cuyahoga River, which flows into
Lake Erie, caught fire in 1969. Now all of those waterways are clean.
Los Angeles was notorious in the 1970s for smog that accumulated
from its freeways. Today, the air quality is dramatically better. New
technologies like catalytic converters, partly spurred by good government regulations, made the difference. And the technology does not
have to be expensive or on the cutting edge. Water use per person in
the United States dropped by about 20 percent from 1980, the highest year ever, to 1995. Much of the conservation came from the widespread use of more efficient technologies, including simple advances
like smaller toilet cisterns that flush less water.

The world needs to go through a massive shift to new, more environmentally benign technologies. Most of the technologies are already here, already fully developed, and getting competitively priced.
We're not waiting for some scientific breakthrough—let alone a miracle to solve the world's energy needs. But what we do need is the serious and sustained migration toward these new technologies,
preferably as fast as possible. In other words, the entire world needs
to change over its capital stock, which means employing new equipment, machinery, hardware, and facilities. In the past, we usually

waited for wars to prompt that changeover. After World War II, the defeated Japan and Germany literally started from scratch with all their old industries and technologies sitting in rubble. As they rebuilt, they used the newest technology and—what do you know?—their economies became the most productive and efficient of the postwar era, and incidentally, their environments are among the cleanest in the industrialized world. New technology is more productive, which is why business adopts it in the first place. New technology is more efficient, which helps boost the productivity and also leads to less waste and so less pollution.

The developed world, the postindustrial regions like North America, Europe, and Japan, have the resources to make this kind of concerted technology changeover—all they lack is the political will. The harder part concerns the developing world, which does not really have the resources and is potentially the biggest environmental problem from this point on because they are industrializing faster and have the greater numbers of people. The two sides—the developed and the developing worlds—have been tussling over this for the entire decade of the 1990s as the world community figures out who to blame for the pollution problem and who will be responsible for cleaning it up. This was the main debate in the Earth Summit in Rio de Janeiro in 1992 and the United Nations Conference on Climate Change held in Kyoto in late 1997. Let's cut through the rhetoric and lay out the real situation: The developed world has done the bulk of industrializing up to this point, and so they have used the most energy, done the most polluting, and put the bulk of carbon dioxide into the air. However, they have now advanced their economies and technologies to the point where their energy and pollution levels are beginning to stabilize if not come down. The developing world, on the other hand, is just moving up through this same developmental trajectory, and it constitutes a lot more countries coming through the pipeline. This is where all the growth in energy use and pollution will come from going forward. Those are the facts. We just need to figure out a solution and deal with this together.

Those in the developing world have an extremely high incentive for reining in pollution. They live smack in the middle of the worst of it now. We were just describing how horrible it was to live in nine-

teenth-century London. Well, you can journey into the past by traveling to any of fifteen or so megacities in the developing world today.
Five of the ten most air-polluted cities are in China, where one in
every four deaths is caused by lung disease. The source is no mystery:
China still gets more than 75 percent of its energy from coal—the
same fuel that polluted Charles Dickens's London. The developed
world has an extremely high incentive to help the developing world
clean up because the air that's hanging over China—or Bombay or
Jakarta or Bangkok or São Paulo or Mexico City—is all simply a part
of that relatively thin, fragile atmosphere that wraps around the
planet. What goes up into the air from Shanghai will eventually affect a person in Paris or Moscow or Chicago or some little town in
Patagonia or Hudson Bay. Although this is an obvious point, not
enough people seriously think about it now—but that may change
very soon because the developing world is exploding economically,
and if it follows the historical pattern, it will explode in filth, too. For
example, China is expected to triple its coal consumption by 2025
and will then be by far the world's biggest producer of greenhouse
gases, all by itself dooming the rest of the world's efforts to reduce
carbon dioxide emissions by the recommended 60 to 80 percent.

We need to break the historical pattern of development. The old
model was to let every country slowly make its way up the technology food chain. That roughly meant that every country had to tough
it out through all the awfulness that accompanied that crude technology and industry. So you had to choke on coal for a while, you
poisoned your water with chemicals, you drove cars built on 1950s
technology even though the developed world drove Acuras or Sat-
urns. The new model of development is informed by the new global
awareness that increasingly will infuse everything. We're all parts of
the same entity. We're part of the same highly integrated global economy. We're ultimately part of the same global society. We're certainly
all part of the same environmental ecosystem. We need to work together. We need to coordinate our efforts. We need to transfer know-
how and technology. It's a big leap to make after a long history of
hatred and warfare, hostility and bitter competition. The old developmental model was much better suited to that framework. It was actually in a nation's interest to keep potential competing nations in a
lower technological track. But now it's in every nation's interest to

bring every other nation along. Those in the developing world get a jump start into a higher standard of living. Those in the developed world will sell much of the technology and capital equipment—and will get a nice return on their investments. This shift to environmentally clean technology is in the self-interest of every single individual on the planet. We're all breathing the same air.

ONE PLANET

There was a time, not very long ago, when people had never seen a photograph of the whole earth. By the mid-1960s, we had sent rockets into space and had many satellites winging around the planet, but the general public had never seen what the earth actually looks like. Stewart Brand, a young iconoclast and freethinker, started mounting a campaign to get NASA to release the image. It turned out NASA was not withholding the image from the public. No one had bothered to take the picture in the first place. For whatever reason, NASA just hadn't thought of it—that is, until Brand came along. So in relatively short order, NASA did take the picture and made it public, and it ended up on the cover of the premier issue of Brand's *Whole Earth Catalog* in the fall of 1968. The now-familiar image was stunning at the time. There we saw our living planet against the stark black backdrop of space. We saw the greens and browns of the landmasses contrasted with the blues of the oceans, and all that enveloped in the soft white swirls of the clouds. There were no lines drawn to delineate nations. There was no sign of human beings at all. But it was clear that the planet was alive with life.

That image really made people stop and think, and many credit it with giving birth to the environmental movement worldwide. First of all, the image was astonishingly beautiful. Who in the world would want to alter that kind of beauty? Second, the image showed how vulnerable we all are. If we screw up this planet, there's no other place to move to and nobody around to help us out. We're just this little speck of life in the universe, and we could very easily turn into a lifeless piece of rock. Third, the image drove home our interconnectedness. The clouds stretch all the way across oceans and link continents. One cloud vortex spins off a tendril that moves north, while another one spins off and reaches south. You can almost feel the movement in the photograph as this living thing slowly breathes in and out. Somewhere, underneath those clouds, about 4 billion human beings lived, mostly oblivious to the fact that they were simply one very small part of the whole.

Only two years later, in 1970, the first Earth Day was held. Most of the activity took place in the developed countries, particularly the United States and Europe, which held the bulk of the world's middle class at that time. Middle-class people have the luxury to think beyond sheer survival. This applies in double doses to the children of middle-class families, who are liberated by their affluence to think about anything they want to and are encouraged to think big. By 1970, the developed countries were swarming with affluent Baby Boomers. The early Boomer cohort was moving through its final stages of college education and, predictably, was ready to latch onto a noble cause such as protecting Mother Earth. To this day, most Baby Boomers consider themselves environmentalists no matter what political party they identify with.

The young people coming after the Boomers slipped right into the same environmental preoccupations. The children of the Boomers, what we call the Long Boom Generation, are being raised by environmentalists, taught by environmentalists, and bombarded by environmentally sensitive media. This environmental sensibility has become so pervasive that it has spread beyond the boundaries of class and gone completely global. Global Business Network conducted an international survey of teenagers in 1988, asking them what was the number one issue on their minds. The astonishing result was that, no matter what country or socioeconomic class they came from, all of them talked about the environment. And that bodes well for the future because the post-1970 generations are now taking over positions of power all around the world and becoming the political majority. Their rise is none too soon.

Thinking of the planet's environment as one highly interdependent ecosystem is a no-brainer. At least it's a no-brainer today, thirty years after we started staring at that beautiful photo of earth suspended in space. Our awareness of that environmental interdependence brings with it an awareness of our interdependence in other spheres. Solutions to global problems can be found only in working together, in understanding and exploiting our interdependence. We need to exploit our truly global community of scientists and our truly global media. We need to begin to figure out better ways to broker difficult political deals in a global context, as we did in the treaty that stopped the production of chlorofluorocarbons, which had been destroying the ozone layer. In Long Boom terms, the environmental crisis is a catalyst that will increase global interdependence over time. In another 30 years, we'll laugh about how fractured we feel now.

The Story of Oil

The last great global economic boom, the post–World War II boom, ended in the oil shock of 1973. Oil, that lifeblood of the industrial economy, shot up in price by a factor of 4, going from just $3 a barrel to $13 in the dollars of the day. That hike was bad enough, but then came the shock of 1979, which nearly quadrupled the price again, from $13 to $45. Almost all forecasts at that time told the world to brace for another big price hike in the late 1980s, to $100 a barrel. Nearly everyone believed the conventional wisdom that we were heading into a grim future of soaring energy costs. Instead, the price of oil never rose beyond that $45, dribbled downward for a few years to about $34, and then in 1986 plunged to $16, drifted around in that price range for a decade, and in the late 1990s even touched $10—costing, in inflation-adjusted dollars, less than before the price increase of 1973. In the U.S., gasoline now costs less than bottled mineral water. In fact, cheap oil has been helping propel global growth in the early stages of the Long Boom. What happened? The story of oil is a great story of the adaptability and ingenuity of human beings, how people react to a dire situation and promptly solve it.

First of all, the oil price signals of the 1970s stimulated the supply side of the equation. If oil was going to bring top prices, a lot more players were going to hustle to find oil or squeeze it out of the currently available sources. This economic incentive encouraged massive investment in oil platforms in the treacherous North Sea and in Alaskan oil fields that were less accessible than those in the Middle East. The U.S. oil companies went back to the old oil fields of the previous era, which were more difficult to drain completely but could still be sucked dry. The higher prices also drove a great wave of technological innovation in the oil industry that stimulated the discovery of new oil fields. For example, high-powered computers were able to amass a continuous flow of data to map the fields more accurately and enhance oil recovery.

Just before the first oil shock, in 1972, the Club of Rome, an organization of intellectuals from around the world concerned about global problems, came up with its extremely influential book, *The Limits to Growth,* which warned that the world, given the rates of consumption at that time, had about thirty more years worth of oil. The actual reserves of oil were much larger. In the late 1990s, about thirty years later, we still have enough oil to last until at least 2030.

Second, the high oil prices also stimulated the development of much more efficient uses of energy, most dramatically in three areas of heavy energy use: manufacturing, transport, and real estate building management. All three of these major industries had economic reasons to channel big money into saving energy. At first, most engineers in those fields figured they could improve energy efficiency a few percentage points with better technology. In fact, from 1975 to 1985, the United States improved the country's overall energy efficiency by 40 percent, as measured by the amount of energy used per unit of GDP. The auto industry did even better: From 1973 to 1986, the average new car in the United States became twice as fuel-efficient, going from thirteen to twenty-seven miles per gallon. Granted, after that time, with the lowered cost of gasoline in the United States, the incentive weakened, and so did the drive to efficiency. However, most of Europe and Japan maintained relatively high gas prices, and so the incentives remained, and the efficiencies kept going up. And in other industries, the drive for efficiency maintained its momentum even after the raw price of energy began to decline due to competition in the market. Efficient energy use has become a selling point. So today you can't even buy an inefficient refrigerator or furnace for your home.

However, there is so much more we can do if properly motivated to pursue energy-efficient technologies. The book *Factor Four: Doubling Wealth, Halving Resource Use,* commissioned by the Club of Rome, argues that the world could increase the efficient use of the planet's resources by a factor of four by using readily available current technologies. In other words, we could quadruple the amount of wealth created at our current level of using resources. Or we could halve the use of resources while doubling the wealth. Cars could be made of superlight carbon composite materials rather than steel frames. Or houses could be designed to retain heat or stay cool, depending on the climate. Or electronic books, rather than paper catalogs, could be used to display products. Or videoconferencing could help reduce some kinds of travel. These are not gee-whiz technologies or unique suggestions—and that's just the point. They could be adopted immediately and have a big impact on lessening the human degradation of the environment.

The third way the signals of high-priced oil played out was in stimulating the development of alternative energies. The 1970s oil crisis gave the nascent solar energy industry a big boost. Many small, innovative companies started up only to come upon harder times when the oil prices dropped in the 1980s and undercut their competitiveness. However, some survived and only now are getting to the point where their products, like solar panels, are being manufactured in large enough quantities to make solar energy competitive with other energy sources. Solar energy is particularly competitive in places that are not on the cheap electric grid—like an emergency telephone on an isolated highway, or in a village in a developing country.

Governments in the developed countries saw the end of oil in sight in the 1970s and moved big funds into researching energy sources to replace it. Unfortunately, some of the largest chunks of public funds in the United States were badly misplaced—particularly in the futile search for the secret to nuclear fusion. Alas, nuclear fusion, the release of energy through a nuclear reaction where atoms fuse rather than break apart and create waste, is one of those goals that has been permanently within our grasp in just twenty-five years. Twenty-five years ago scientists were giving that projection and they still say the same thing today. The governments of France and Japan, having no natural energy resources to speak of and so having long been enamored of developing nuclear energy, put much research into successive generations of nuclear technology that produced less waste and were much safer. Those countries, and others like them, are moving toward the use of what some call *green nukes*. They still produce radioactive waste, though in less quantities, but they don't have much other environmental impact—including no contribution to global warming. They don't create carbon dioxide when they produce their electricity. That may be something to consider in the future, a trade-off between the problems of nuclear waste and those of carbon emissions.

It helps to put that decision, or the story of oil for that matter, in the larger context of the story of energy. The world has gone through successive waves in the rise and fall of the predominant form of energy—each new one more potent yet cleaner than the last. All of the major energy sources so far have been hydrocarbons, and the cleanliness has to do with how much carbon is in the energy source compared to how much hydrogen. Carbon is bad. Hydrogen is good. The world started out using wood as the predominant energy source. We burned wood to release energy. However, wood has a very high carbon content compared to its hydrogen content—and so it is a very dirty fuel. With the early industrial revolution, coal rose up as the predominant energy source, and wood declined in relative importance. Coal has less carbon content than wood, but it still produces a lot of emissions and pollution. Oil took off in the late nineteenth century, helping power the later industrial revolution and eclipsing coal as the predominant fuel source by the second half of the twentieth century. Oil had less carbon and more hydrogen content than coal. Natural gas, however, has even less carbon content than oil and has steadily increased in use throughout the twentieth century and is on a trajectory to surpass oil as the world's major energy source right about now. So the world has migrated through four major energy sources in the space of about 200 years. We've gone from relying primarily on wood, the dirtiest, to natural gas, the cleanest, by upgrading our technologies each time. But there is absolutely no reason why history will stop in its tracks with natural gas. The obvious next move is to migrate to technologies that are powered on pure hydrogen.

A very strong case can be made that we are already in the beginning stages of a major shift to a hydrogen-powered economy. This shift is so huge that it is difficult to perceive while trapped in the moment. But if the twentieth century was seen as the era of oil and hydrocarbons in general, then it is extremely likely that the twenty-first century will be seen as the Hydrogen Age. And the first couple decades of the next century, the second half of the Long Boom, will be seen as the dawn of that Hydrogen Age. This kind of monumental transition in the fundamental energy source for the planet can't happen completely within decades. It might well take the entire first half of the twenty-first century to fully achieve. And its achievement will bring widespread repercussions, such as a geopolitical rearrangement as Middle Eastern oil declines in importance. But the main consequence will involve the environment because hydrogen is much more environmentally benign than its predecessors. An economy ultimately powered on pure hydrogen can essentially eliminate emissions. No carbon. No carbon dioxide contributing to global warming. But also no other pollutants. No carbon monoxide, no sulfur dioxide, no nitrogen oxides. For that matter, no acid rain. But that's getting ahead of the story. Because before we consider the environmental wonders of this new fuel source, we must understand the technology that enables us to use it. A new technology of the fuel cell is being developed that will soon eclipse the internal combustion engine—and help save the planet in the process.

TWENTY-FIRST CENTURY CHOICES: THE MAKING OF A LONG BOOM

PART SIX: "GROWING TOGETHER"

THE YEAR 2010 WAS AN UNFORGETTABLE ONE IN GEOPOLITICS—THE YEAR OF THE CASPIAN SEA CRISIS. IT WAS THE LAST TIME THAT THE WORLD NEARLY WENT TO GLOBAL WAR, A WAR THAT MIGHT HAVE INVOLVED ALL THE GREAT POWERS AND LAUNCHED NUCLEAR WEAPONS. IT WAS THE YEAR THAT THE MIDDLE EAST, EUROPE, RUSSIA, AND CHINA FINALLY CAME TO TERMS WITH THE GROWING TENSIONS IN THAT TROUBLED REGION. AND IT INTRODUCED A SURPRISING NEW WORLD PLAYER.

Oil HAD OFTEN BEEN THE CAUSE OF WAR, AND IT PLAYED THAT ROLE AGAIN IN 2010. THE DEMISE OF THE TWENTIETH CENTURY'S COLD WAR HAD OPENED UP THE GEOGRAPHIC SOURCE OF OIL AND NATURAL GAS RESERVES THAT STRETCHED FROM SAUDI ARABIA ALL THE WAY TO SIBERIA. THE HALF OF THE REGION THAT HAD BEEN UNDER THE CONTROL OF THE SOVIET UNION HAD BEEN ONLY PARTLY EXPLOITED DUE TO THE LACK OF GOOD TECHNOLOGY THAT COULD REACH DEEP RESERVES AND EFFICIENTLY MOVE THE RESOURCES OUT OF THE REGION.

BY THE TURN OF THE CENTURY, THE LIBERATED REGION WAS SWARMING WITH WESTERN OIL COMPANIES, PARTICULARLY FROM THE UNITED STATES, WHOSE RESERVES HAD been drying up at home. And the region was full of foreign capital waiting to exploit some of the best oil fields left on the planet.

Add to the situation new nations that were eager to quickly develop their one resource and move out of centuries of stagnation. These new countries—Kazakhstan, Turkmenistan, Georgia, Azerbaijan, and Armenia—had some Muslim roots, some European roots, and a very complex cultural, ethnic, and religious mix.

The difficult challenge of getting oil and gas out of that region had been addressed in the early part of the new century by a major pipeline built across Azerbaijan and Turkey to the Mediterranean, one across Azerbaijan and Georgia to the Black Sea, a refurbished one up into Russia, and one across to China.

Caspian Sea oil and natural gas were increasingly important to many great powers on the periphery—Europe, Russia, and China: China needed to use the oil and natural gas to begin to replace its dirty coal, Russia needed oil to feed its ravenous appetite for outside income, and Europe's booming economy was partly based on the cheaper oil coming out of the Caspian region.

A bustling oil market began to develop around the Caspian Sea. Great fortunes were made, and an economic boom was well under way by the end of that first decade. That is partly what led to the problems.

The Islamic Backlash

The politics of the Persian Gulf had taken a strange twist in 2005, when the House of Saud was overthrown and replaced by a radical Islamic fundamentalist regime. Saudi Arabia became simply Arabia—and decidedly anti-Western.

An unanticipated anti-Western alliance developed around the Persian Gulf among Iran, Iraq, and the new Arabia. Kuwait and the other smaller nations could do nothing in the face of the power of these three oil giants, and these giants started looking north to the Caspian Sea.

They feared the alternative oil and gas marketplace that was developing in the Caspian region was undercutting their clout. The new reserves were depressing oil prices and strategically acing them out of their central role in world oil production. They also bristled at the heavy Western influence in those new, relatively secular nations.

Many of the societies of the Caspian Sea region, like the societies of the Persian Gulf, had very traditional Muslim elements that were not in control of the secular governments, did not welcome the consequences of abundant wealth, and objected to the increasing connection with the West. These resentments spawned radical fundamentalist movements that were aligned with and secretly supplied by the Gulf Triad. They began to initiate terrorist acts and build underground militias.

The war of terror against Western companies and the secular governments of that region prompted an internal crackdown. The Gulf Triad took that as a persecution of their Muslim brothers and began preparing for an invasion. They were heavily armed with the latest weapons. They had long-range missiles and large air forces. And it was unclear whether they had chemical and biological weapons of mass destruction.

The situation came down to this: A primarily Christian Europe and a secular Russia and China were being challenged by a relatively unified front of the Gulf powers. The Gulf forces were using the defense of Islam as the excuse for a drive to control the entire oil- and natural-gas-producing region.

The military forces began to line up. To the north, the Russians amassed troops right on the shore of the Caspian Sea. To the east, the Chinese moved mobile units through friendly Kazakhstan. The Europeans had their long-range air squadrons on high alert. And the Americans, locked out of any land access to the region, had carriers in the Mediterranean and Arabian Seas.

War seemed imminent in early August. It was as if the beginning of the twentieth century was playing itself out again. Like World Wars I and II, this was a war that no one wanted but no one seemed able to prevent. The Guns of August were about to rumble again.

The Broker between Civilizations

The resolution of the crisis came as a surprise because it was not the military might of Russia and China that prevailed. It was not the religious fervor of the Persian Gulf nations and their Islamic allies that prevailed either. It was not the diplomacy of the Europeans or even the might of the Americans. Rather, the solution came from a nation that most people had stopped thinking about: Turkey.

When we look back from our perspective, Turkey was the perfect nation to face up to this challenge because of its status as a hybrid Muslim European nation. The Turks defined themselves as European, not Middle Eastern, though they had been consistently denied formal acceptance into the European Union. However, the Turks were regarded by Middle Eastern countries as Muslims, though not radical ones.

Turkey's secular society had tolerant traditions, with large Christian communities and a variety of different Christian and Islamic sects. Turkey had also been a world power in the Ottoman era and understood the responsibilities that role entails.

Before the armies could march, before planes could fly, before missiles could be launched, the Turkish military inserted itself between the Islamic forces to the south and the secular forces to the north. Turkey then went to the United Nations and asked for a peacekeeping role in forestalling this war.

The Security Council—the Russians, the Chinese, the Americans, the Europeans—and the nations of the Persian Gulf and of the Caspian region did not quickly accept the Turkish proposal, arguing for two tense weeks. They then entered even more protracted negotiations to see whether a permanent accord could be reached.

Every time the war threats began to mount, Turkey committed more forces and resources. It also stepped up its diplomacy: Its diplomats went to the Europeans and said you can trust us because we, too, are Europeans with long, enlightened traditions. They went to Russia and China and said we are a modern secular state that honors the rule of international law. And they went to the Muslim nations and said you can trust us because we are brothers—we will look out for you, too. And they assured the United States that they were loyal allies in NATO.

The strategy worked in the end. As the war was delayed, global opinion built fervently against the showdown, and the vast majority of people around the world used every democratic mechanism and media outlet to voice their strong disapproval.

After many months of negotiation and a stare-down on the battlefield, war was avoided, and the Caspian Sea Accord was signed by all parties in Ankara on December 13.

The accord set up a peacekeeping mechanism around the Caspian that Turkey supervised. It laid out how the oil and gas reserves were to be managed, how production would be coordinated, and how an integrated distribution system would be established.

Iran was supported to build another pipeline out of the Caspian region to tie into the facilities on the Persian Gulf. This pipeline helped create one market that shared the burdens and the benefits of the energy boom.

Arrangements were made to increase the travel and immigration of people between the Gulf and Caspian regions. And the new countries around the

Caspian Sea made guarantees of full religious tolerance while getting guarantees that the militias would demobilize.

The Caspian Sea Accord turned out to be a critical agreement for the world. The consequence was a deeper understanding between the Islamic and European countries. The ancient divide between Christian and Muslim, between Arabs and the West, began to heal through the day-to-day practical interaction that took place. The accord gave all parties something to manage together.

The accord was also critical because it signaled that the global community would simply no longer accept large-scale war or even the posturing leading up to it. As we know, this accord set the tone for other accords in regional conflicts. Again and again, mechanisms were found to negotiate differences and balance interests rather than fight them out.

The Caspian Sea Crisis had tested the mettle of the new global order. Unlike in August 1916, this time the world community held firm and dispassionately worked out the disagreements. Conflict was avoided, and the Long Boom continued.

8

Dawn of
the Hydrogen Age

The key issue in solving our environmental problems is changing our energy source. We need to end our dependence on fossil fuels. Fortunately, an array of alternative energy technologies are coming on-line that will make possible abundant, cheap, clean energy. Fuel cells hold the potential to supersede the internal combustion engine in the next two decades. The fuel cell's clean energy source, hydrogen, could soon replace oil.

THE INTERNAL COMBUSTION engine has had a long history and a full reign as the king of technological beasts. Developed in Germany in the last few decades of the nineteenth century, it was a great advance at the time—far better than engines powered by steam and the like. Daimler-Benz can claim the lion's share of the initial innovation, but many different companies modified the engine in the early days. The technology improved by leaps and bounds in the first two of decades of the twentieth century. But from that point on, most improvements were essentially tweaks. People made small improvements in the efficiency and upgraded the materials and, in the latter part of the century, added on electronic gadgets that enhanced a particular function, like fuel injection systems, but the core technology, the basic way the engine worked, remained the same. Essentially, gasoline is squirted into a cylinder with a bit of air and blown up. The explosion moves a piston, which helps crank a drive that moves the wheels and thus the car. Today, between four and eight cylinders make a lot of explosions very fast—like thousands of them per minute. Every car zinging past on the freeway is virtually a mini explosives factory; what we've done is contain those explosions and channel them in very productive ways. However, with those explosions come some unwanted by-products, like heat and emissions. No matter how hard people try to reduce emissions—for instance, by adding catalytic converters—they can't be eliminated from the process. There's got to be a better way. As it turns out, there is.

Enter the fuel cell. Actually, the fuel cell entered the picture even before the internal combustion engine's advent in the 1870s. William Grove, a physicist who later switched careers and became a judge, first conceived of the principle of the fuel cell in 1839. He observed, as many high school students can easily do today, that when an electrical charge is put into a beaker of water, the hydrogen molecules and the oxygen molecules in good old H_2O separate. Grove figured out that the process would also work in reverse. Hydrogen molecules could be combined with oxygen molecules to produce an electrical charge. Wouldn't it be great to find a way to cheaply and easily combine those two extremely abundant molecules and generate the power to meet all our power needs? And an additional benefit is that the only by-product of combining these two molecules is water that is perfectly safe to drink. The concept was great, and potentially revolutionary, but the practical application has eluded everyone ever since. In fact, playing around with what became known as fuel cells was nothing more than a laboratory curiosity until NASA finally used hydrogen-powered fuel cells in spacecraft in the 1960s and 1970s. In space, fuel cells provided both electricity and drinking water. But NASA could get over the kind of hurdles that had stopped progress on the ground, namely, exorbitant costs. In recent years, however, the fuel cell has been making a comeback after a series of technological improvements brought the cost down. And so larger numbers of people began seeing the feasibility of this technology and turned their attention and resources to it.

The fuel cell is such an elegant technology, such a perfect fit for the twenty-first century. Unlike the internal combustion engine, the fuel cell works more like biological organisms. It does not explode things or create much heat. It does not work by producing high pressure. Instead, it creates energy through chemical reactions much like those in the human body. Our bodies take in oxygen and fuel in the form of food, change its form, and pass the result through membranes to oxygenate the blood, which supplies the energy to all the cells of the body. In the process, the body creates relatively low levels of heat and some waste that can be recycled into our environment. The way fuel cells work is basically the way all nature works, by changing the energy states of substances very gently and very efficiently. Simply put, hydrogen is fed into the fuel cell, and a catalyst induces the gas to separate into protons and electrons. The protons pass through a membrane and combine on the other side with oxygen molecules from the air to form water. The electrons, however, which can't pass through the membrane, are rechanneled and used to power an electric motor. The fuel cell itself has no moving parts and is two to three times more efficient than an internal combustion engine. Again, the only by-products of this process are electricity, water, and a low level of heat.

The one catch to the fuel cell is the source of the hydrogen. The production of hydrogen can have its own environmental impact, depending on what source is used. For example, hydrogen can come from hydrocarbons. Some fuel cell engines being developed can be run off ordinary gasoline but then they do produce some waste by-products, including carbon dioxide. Hydrogen is one of the most abundant atoms in the universe and can be extracted from many sources, including renewable ones, which have no adverse environmental effects. One renewable fuel is the methanol gas that comes from biomass, which is decaying organic material ranging from lawn grass to sewage. The great dream of fuel cell proponents is to produce hydrogen from completely renewable energy sources like solar energy or wind power, which can be used to initiate the process of electrolysis in water. This would eliminate all greenhouse gases and pollutants from the process and could supply our energy needs forever. Sadly, the practical development of this sunny scenario is probably decades away, but in the meantime, less perfect sources of hydrogen could start us on that trajectory.

The use of fuel cells to supply our power needs may sound too good to be true, but as they say in the journalism business, follow the money. Take a good long look at the amount of money being invested in fuel cell development and at the players behind that money. Start by looking at Ballard Power Systems Inc. in Vancouver, which wants to become the Intel of fuel cells. Just as Intel produces the basic microprocessors that are the brains of most personal computers and increasingly other kinds of products, so Ballard wants to produce fuel cells of various forms that can be used in a variety of products. It has made much progress in boosting the power of fuel cells in recent years and is generally considered the leading fuel cell company, though not by much. Others are nipping at Ballard's heels. However, the success of the company has begun attracting big money from major multinational corporations. In 1997, Daimler-Benz invested $320 million to acquire a quarter of the company and to jointly develop fuel cell systems for cars and buses, promising that it would mass-produce 100,000 fuel cell cars by 2004. This is Daimler-Benz, the same company that kicked off the whole era of the internal combustion engine and is considered among the most conservative in the auto industry, which is a pretty conservative bunch to start with.

And Daimler-Benz is not alone. More than half of the sixteen largest auto companies in the world are now working on fuel cell programs. Far from trying to squelch fuel cell development and protect their internal combustion engine market, they see themselves as transportation companies that need to evolve with the times and the technology. This is an example of how the Long Boom works. If you want to change the world, you can't hope that a few revolutionary companies alone will overturn the old order. That approach will provoke a severe backlash from the old order, which will dig in its heels and lash out to destroy the challenge. Far better to lure the old order in the new direction and get it to contribute its immense resources and brainpower. Doing something about global warming requires engaging the $1-trillion-a-year global auto industry. But altruism will go only so far. They need to see how they can profit from the emerging new order as well as be good guys. On the other hand, sheer financial gain is not the only motivator. Most people working for the global auto industry, from the top leadership to people on the assembly lines, want to believe that they are doing the right thing, trying to preserve the earth for future generations. The development of the fuel cell provides that kind of win-win opportunity.

The first decade of the twenty-first century is likely to see a technological free-for-all as the competing auto companies and some savvy newcomers like Ballard scramble to find the secret formula that will become the standard for cars. This scramble will closely resemble what happened 100 years ago in the early years of the horseless carriage. In 1900, three credible versions of the horseless carriage were vying to emerge supreme. Engines powered by electric batteries controlled about 40 percent of the small emerging market. Engines powered by steam cornered another 40 percent. And the remaining 20 percent went to the internal combustion engine (ICE) powered by gasoline. Over the next twenty years of fierce competition, the ICE won. We face that same craziness today. Each company or combination of companies is betting on a different technological alternative. Some are starting out with hybrid electric vehicles, which use very efficient ICEs to power the electric generators that then drive the wheels. These vehicles avoid the pitfalls of battery-operated cars, which can run out of juice after only seventy-five miles or so, and they also don't use nearly as much fuel as straight ICE cars. Toyota mass-produces such a hybrid car and has sold it in Japan—and now, in the United States. This hybrid gets sixty-six miles to the gallon, about twice the mileage of a Corolla of similar size, and cuts carbon dioxide emissions in half, while reducing hydrocarbons and nitrogen oxides by 90 percent. Other manufacturers may develop cars driven by gas turbines that run on natural gas, a cleaner fuel than gasoline. Neither of these models involve fuel cells, but they are currently more realizable and perform better and pollute much less than full ICE cars.

When it comes to fuel cell cars, many options exist. Chrysler, before merging with Daimler-Benz, announced that it was working on its own fuel cell car that runs on a variety of fuels, including gasoline. It doesn't want to wait for someone to develop an alternative fuel infrastructure. Rather, it wants fuel cell cars to be able to extract hydrogen from the gasoline found at any existing pump. However, this approach grates on environmentalists, who point out that this car won't reduce emissions nearly enough. They would rather back a company like Ford, which is designing a fuel cell car that carries around hydrogen gas in tanks. But critics of this approach warn of safety concerns. Ever since the *Hindenburg* airship explosion in 1937, hydrogen gas has tended to scare the public.

Which brings us back to the oil industry. You can't talk about transforming the global auto industry without talking about a concomitant transformation of the industry that supplies auto fuel. Lucky for the Long Boom, the oil industry is emulating the auto industry and showing a great interest in fuel cells. Oil companies think of themselves as energy companies that will evolve with the future forms of energy. Many of the big players in this industry are also devoting significant resources to research on fuel cells and the development of hydrogen. For example, in 1997, Exxon and ARCO initiated a multimillion-dollar research alliance with Delphi Energy & Engine Management Systems, a former division of General Motors, to develop a processor to extract hydrogen from fossil fuels such as gasoline and methanol.

Changing our current energy infrastructure from supplying oil to supplying hydrogen won't be easy. One approach to building a new hydrogen infrastructure is to take advantage of the existing infrastructure. We have already figured out how to get gasoline to nearly every neighborhood in the world. The first fuel cells could extract hydrogen from gasoline and get our transport system moving in the right direction on the right technology. That extraction could either happen at gas stations or on board the cars, though that would be a harder engineering challenge. Right now creating hydrogen from gasoline, or several other substances for that matter, takes a rather large machine. It might make sense to start them out as stationary processors at a neighborhood station and later migrate smaller versions onto the cars themselves. Another approach is to jump-start into pure hydrogen fuels that immediately maximize the environmental benefit. We could convert current gasoline stations into hydrogen-creating stations that don't draw off gasoline, but something cleaner, like natural gas. We could then put the pure hydrogen gas right into the car. A variation of that approach is to bypass the current energy infrastructure completely. Researchers at Northeastern University in Boston have claimed that they used graphite nanofibers to inexpensively increase current hydrogen storage capabilities by a factor of 10. If true, then enough hydrogen could be packed into a single cartridge that would allow you to drive a car for 5,000 miles or more, compared to 450 miles at most with today's gasoline vehicles. The empty cartridge could then be refilled and shipped via existing package delivery systems like United Parcel Service. Each car would only need to "fill-up" with one or two cartridges a year.

These pure hydrogen gas options, more than the others, bring up the specter of dangerous explosions in car crashes. It's the *Hindenburg* syndrome again. However, hydrogen is actually no more dangerous than gasoline, which we seem to live with just fine. Gasoline fires follow the liquid on the ground. Hydrogen flames burn upward with the gas, so that hydrogen may actually be safer in the open air, but more dangerous in contained spaces like mechanics' garages. Hydrogen is also a clear, odorless gas that burns relatively coolly and is hard even to detect. That means that we might have to add color or smell to the gas as safety features, just as we add smell, for example, to the natural gas used in homes. We seem to be able to maintain peace of mind with every car on the freeway hauling around twenty gallons of explosive gasoline, and with explosive natural gas running through lines in every neighborhood. We have learned to live with that minimal risk. The same will be true of hydrogen.

One expectation in the energy field is that nearly all energy will eventually be provided as electricity. Hydrogen may become the main carrier of energy, but when we want to use that energy, we will convert it to electricity. All this talk about the diverse options for powering automobiles in the first decade of the twenty-first century obscures the fact that electric motors will ultimately drive the wheels. The debate is about the kind of fuel source or initial technology that will provide the electricity. A battery vehicle will get recharged by electricity that originates in a utilities power plant, whatever form that plant takes. A hybrid vehicle will depend on gasoline and an internal combustion engine. A fuel cell vehicle will be powered by hydrogen from some source. However, the ultimate power for all of these vehicles will be electricity.

The vast utilities industry won't be immune from these energy trends. Whatever its use, nearly all energy will ultimately move into the form of electricity. Thus some great synergies will occur across all energy fields. Developments in how to cleanly produce electricity for mobile transport can also apply to producing electricity for everything else. And sure enough, fuel cell work is proceeding in the utilities industry as well. Some of the work on providing stationary power actually may be ahead of the car-related work. International Fuel Cells, a Connecticut company subsidized by the U.S. Defense Department, had already installed 90 fuel cell generators by 1997, powering buildings ranging from hospitals to casinos to jails. The Japanese government is sponsoring a consortium of Toshiba, Fuji, and Mitsubishi that wants to develop 100 fuel cell generators ranging from fifty kilowatts to eleven megawatts by 2001. For the first time ever, a fuel cell powered a suburban New Jersey home in a 1998 project closely watched in many quarters, including the U.S. Department of Energy. Plug Power, the company behind the project, claims it can commercialize fuel cells for houses by the year 2000, with each unit costing between $3,000 and $5,000 each. Detroit Edison, a part owner of Power Plug, plans to buy between 30,000 and 50,000 units.

Power to the Periphery

The utilities industry may end up driving the development of fuel cells more than it follows, partly because of the second trend in the overall energy field: decentralization. That trend plays out in several ways, not the least of which is ownership. The utilities industry around the world is just beginning to go through the process of deregulation that has already shaken up other vital industries like telecommunications. We've seen how that played out first in the United States and then in Europe and other parts of the world. The huge national telecommunications firms that had been heavily regulated by government were suddenly broken up or privatized, and the whole field was thrown open to competition. The result was an ex-

plosion of innovation and entrepreneurial activity. That's just starting to happen now with electric utilities. This time Europe, particularly Britain and Scandinavia, have led the way in allowing a wide
array of energy producers to sell directly to consumers. California
started down this path in the United States, and other states have
quickly followed. This competitive environment allows a small company that wants to produce clean energy from wind in the Great
Plains, or from solar power in the deserts of Arizona, to contribute its
electricity to the national grid and charge a green-minded consumer
who draws from the grid in California. It also opens up big opportunities otherwise not available for innovative firms that want to develop fuel cells and produce electricity that way. Let a thousand new
companies bloom. Out of that profusion of innovation, progress will
move at a healthy pace.

The decentralization trend also applies more literally. The generation of power will move increasingly closer to the user. That's not to
say that centralized power plants in densely populated cities will go
away. However, the era of consolidating and centralizing power generation is over. In the future, the tendency will be to build power generators of the needed size as close as possible to where the power is
needed. The power system will increasingly look much the way computer systems now look. We used to have all the computer power at
the center in a mainframe. Now we place a computer chip with
enough power to do the required task right where it's needed. We
don't do away with the computer network, the equivalent of the electric grid, but we distribute a lot of computer power—just as we will
increasingly distribute a lot of electric power. Allied Signal is selling
microturbines that are based on the same technology as jet engines
and can run on a variety of fuels, including natural gas, methane, or
gasoline. They are a low-cost, extremely quiet source of thirty kilowatts of energy, which is enough to power a convenience store. These
turbines also produce virtually no pollutants compared to their
larger competitors and do away with the need for power lines. So a
new suburb or new town might use a series of microturbines or build
another kind of small power generator nearby to fit its needs, instead
of stringing electrical cable across the countryside so it can draw energy from a nuclear power plant 1,000 miles away. This system elimi-

nates a lot of the seepage waste in distribution—not to mention the ungainly sight of wires across every horizon.

Fuel cells are ideally suited to this more decentralized energy world. They are quiet, safe, and environmentally benign and can run on whatever fuel source is most available at the site. Stationary fuel cells linked together—as in parallel computer processing—could provide enough power for small towns or neighborhoods. They could power remote facilities like that convenience store initially powered by a microturbine, or a cabin in the woods. In the future, you might have just one fuel cell power source in your car that connects to your house at night and powers your home's electrical system. It's not clear just what alternatives will become popular or commercially sensible in a wide-open energy future. What is clear is that decentralization will almost certainly continue and increase as we move our energy production from the central power station to the neighborhood and to the home. People are already thinking about tiny fuel cells to replace batteries in laptop computers and other appliances, so that they can work unplugged for days rather than hours.

The logic of decentralization will break out of the developed world, where inevitably it will first appear, and move to the developing world where arguably it is most needed. Fuel cells could be the way to bring clean, reliable energy to regions that would have to wait decades to amass the resources and effort to build huge centralized power systems and string power lines to all end users. These take massive projects that are extremely disruptive and tear up the environment. Today you would need to mow down paths through the rain forests to string up high voltage power cables in order to get enough electricity to run a business in inner Brazil or the Congo or Northern Thailand. The decentralized path seems better on all counts—from the practical to the environmental.

This kind of transformation in energy production won't happen overnight. It has started out slowly, though the advances in the late 1990s startled many industry insiders and made people accelerate their predictions of change. Wise government regulation can spur progress—like California's requirement that 10 percent of all new cars sold in the state in 2003 will have zero emissions. That requirement in a car-crazy state of more than 30 million people gave many of the auto companies a kick in the behind. But equally wise government deregulation can also spur progress—as California and some European countries did with deregulation of the electric utilities industry. Strict applications of some preconceived ideology are not what is needed. The Long Boom mind-set says use all the tools that are available; pull the levers that work.

The jury is out on which transitional strategy will prove most successful in the newly refurbished transportation and energy industries, but by 2050, the world will be run on hydrogen, or close enough to call the era the Hydrogen Age. Fuel cells will be the predominant energy technology, just settling in for a long reign. Or will they? By 2050, who knows what new technology will have emerged that is undetected on our radar screens of today? Which brings us to the next couple of chapters, the part of the book that really starts to stretch the mind.

Twenty-first Century Choices: The Making of a Long Boom

Part Seven: "Everyone Lets Go"

One of the greatest challenges for the world in the early part of the century was what to do about the environmental consequences of Chinese industrialization. The Chinese were trying to bring a billion people to a much higher standard of living at a very rapid pace. They were trying to accomplish in twenty years what had taken the United States a hundred years.

The problem for the world was that the Chinese were trying to reach that goal with old industrial technology and without paying for outside sources of energy. They were primarily using their only indigenous energy source, dirty coal, so the air quality over China—and beyond its borders—was rapidly deteriorating.

It is obvious from our mid-century perspective that to avoid utter disaster, China needed to take on the most advanced technology as rapidly as possible in every sector—industry, manufacturing, transportation, utilities. At the very least, China needed to import massive amounts of clean natural gas from central Asia and Russia.

But for years before and after the turn of the century, the Chinese did not see the situation that way, obstinately sticking to their original economic

plans until they were forced to dramatically change course. A series of disasters of ever greater proportion compelled China to transform its economic
development strategy from one based on low technology to high technology.

The first decade of the century brought continual news stories of industrial
and environmental breakdown. The Chinese public could tolerate factory accidents, massive chemical leaks, and toxic releases into the air—as long as
they seemed to affect mostly adults. But the evidence started mounting that
the unprecedented accumulation of pollution was starting to seriously affect
the children.

Children are extremely precious in Chinese culture, particularly since many
families were limited to only one child, so when thousands of children began
dying of respiratory diseases and strange cancers, the Chinese started to radically rethink their approach.

The issue came to a head in 2012. The Shanghai Winter was the final turning point.

The Sky Falls and the World Responds

By the end of the century's first decade, Shanghai was one of the most industrial cities in the world. Its industrial output far exceeded that of most countries—and almost all of it was driven by coal. More than 20 million people
lived and worked in its environs, and most of them heated their homes with
little coal braziers. Even apartment buildings several stories high had individual coal heaters in each unit.

The black pall of coal soot had hung over Shanghai for a decade, and residents had put up with it as the norm. But late in January 2012, a dense,
warm inversion of air moved over Shanghai. Over several days, the air got
grayer and grayer, and the light darker and darker. And the inversion kept
pushing the ceiling of soot lower and lower until, finally, people began to
die.

At first the casualties were the very old and very ill, who could not be protected from the air even shuttered inside their homes. Then it was people who
were less healthy, particularly those with respiratory illnesses like asthma.
And then it was small children, who couldn't find relief from the smoke and
were gasping to death right in their parents' arms.

A panic began, and a state of emergency was declared. Many of the most
vulnerable people were evacuated, and healthier people were ordered off all

the roads leading out of the city. All coal-generated power or heating sources were ordered immediately shut down.

The only alternative appeared to be a massive shift to electrical heaters and electrical power based on anything but coal. However, the electrical distribution system of Shanghai could not carry the proposed surge in electricity use. In addition, the electrical utilities would need months if not years to retool for natural gas or other cleaner energy.

The world community came to the rescue. People all over the world had been watching the daily drama with mounting horror, and those in the energy field knew there was probably only one answer to this problem: fuel cells.

Western companies like Siemens, DaimlerChrysler, and Asea Brown Boveri said they had inventories of hundreds of thousands of fuel cells that had been in production around the world. They said they could quickly retrofit fuel cells headed for vehicles to become stationary ones, and they could dramatically pump up overall production. Western governments then committed themselves to airlifting the fuel cells into Shanghai almost overnight, and within a matter of days, thousands of fuel cells had arrived in Shanghai from all over the world.

In every neighborhood and every major building, a powerful fuel cell was set up that used one of various fuel sources, from imported pure hydrogen canisters to regular gasoline. Electric heaters were sold all over Shanghai to heat homes.

Within a week, the coal pall began to dissipate. After two weeks, a heavy storm blew through and began to clear the air. Several more weeks of rainy weather brought out the sun in the end, and blue skies could be seen over Shanghai for the first time in years.

The sunlight brought a sense of relief but little joy. More than 200,000 had died in the catastrophe. Many more had suffered irreparable damage to their lungs. The horror would remain with an entire generation.

The Shanghai Winter led to an unequivocal commitment to transform the environment of China, to accelerate the rapid transition to new technology. It became very clear that the high-tech route was not only the only sustainable approach over the long term, but the only way to survive in the short run. China had double incentives and no other alternatives.

The Chinese people and the world community were now of one mind. A clear global environmental consensus was emerging.

THE GREAT ENVIRONMENTAL DEAL

THE AMERICANS AND EUROPEANS HAD BEEN offering TO HELP THE CHINESE UPGRADE ACROSS THE board, BUT THEY HAD RUN INTO PRACTICAL difficulties WHEN THEY TRIED TO follow THROUGH. SEVERAL PROJECTS HAD RATHER HAPHAZARDLY GOT off THE GROUND, BUT THEY HAD brought NO widespread CHANGE. Also, MANY WESTERN CONCERNS HAD LOST THEIR INVESTMENTS BECAUSE OF THE whims OF THE CHINESE GOVERNMENT.

AFTER THE SHANGHAI WINTER, THE CHINESE SHOOK UP THE world BY PUTTING A RADICAL PROPOSAL ON THE TABLE. THE PROPOSAL HAD BEEN floated before BUT HAD BEEN dismissed AS politically PREPOSTEROUS. THE CHINESE CHANGED ALL THAT BY THEIR COMMITMENT TO TAKING THE first STEP.

WHAT BECAME KNOWN AS THE GREAT ENVIRONMENTAL DEAL STARTED WITH THE CHINESE offer TO abandon ALL old polluting TECHNOLOGIES AND CHANGE AS quickly AS possible TO THE CLEANEST ONES AVAILABLE. THEY SAW IT AS BEING IN THEIR best IN-TERESTS TO LET GO OF THEIR NATIONALISTIC fears OF WESTERN INTERVENTION AND OF THEIR NEED FOR TIGHT CONTROL OF MATTERS PERTAINING TO ENERGY. THEY DECIDED TO TAKE THE WEST AT ITS word.

THE WESTERNERS SAID THEY WERE willing TO MAKE THE TECHNOLOGY TRANSFER AND HAVE THEIR COMPANIES SET UP THE INITIAL INFRASTRUCTURE, BUT THEY NEEDED THE freedom TO OPERATE THEIR businesses AND THE PROMISE OF A fair RETURN ON THEIR INVESTMENTS. THEY STRESSED THAT THE deal MUST BE ENTERED INTO WITH MUTUAL RE-SPECT AND TRUST.

CHINA ACCEPTED THE TERMS AND THE TECH RUSH BEGAN. WHOLE PLANTS THAT WERE ALREADY BEING BUILT FOR VEHICLES WITH INTERNAL COMBUSTION ENGINES SWITCHED IN MIDSTREAM TO BECOME FACTORIES PRODUCING TOP-OF-THE-LINE fuel cells. EVERYONE HAD ASKED THE obvious QUESTION: WHY follow THROUGH WITH building A FACTORY THAT WILL MAKE HIGH-POLLUTING CARS WHEN CHINA CAN immediately leapfrog TO THE CLEAN ALTERNATIVE? THIS SAME QUESTION AND ANSWER WERE APPLIED TO INDUSTRIES ACROSS THE board.

CHINA'S MOVE broke THE political logjam THAT HAD kept THE world FROM quickly switching TO NEW TECHNOLOGIES. ONCE THE CHINESE TOOK THE leap, OTHER developing COUNTRIES LIKE India OPENED THEMSELVES UP TO THE SAME DEAL. THEY ACCEPTED SOME LOSS OF CONTROL AND AUTONOMY BUT GAINED A HUGE boost ON THEIR developmental TRAJECTORY.

CHINA'S MOVE also forced THE developed NATIONS TO BECOME MORE AGGRESSIVE IN MAKING THE HIGH-TECH TRANSITION IN THEIR OWN ECONOMIES. THEY HAD HESITATED TO MAKE UNILATERAL SACRIFICES THAT WOULDN'T BE RECIPROCATED BY THE developing world. The United States had been particularly hamstrung by powerful domestic constituencies, like the coal industry.

But the new context of the 2010s prodded everyone to move as quickly as possible to the best technology. Now the developed world was racing with the developing world to a finish line that would benefit both.

The Ultimate Technological Fix

The really long-term solution to environmental degradation came with the adoption of nanotechnology several years after the most intense wheeling and dealing.

By around 2005, the science of nanoscale engineering was beginning to advance very rapidly. Both computing power and new kinds of physical tools were making it possible to operate on increasingly smaller scales at the level of molecules and individual atoms. A number of the breakthroughs came in Asia, especially in Taiwan and Singapore and, most of all, Japan.

Japan had recovered from its economic stupor after the turn of the century and had moved away from traditional manufacturing and into an economy based on smaller firms providing higher-value services, such as management, finance, design, and support services of all sorts, to business enterprises throughout Asia.

However, the Japanese had succeeded in the manufacturing era because they had a long tradition of craftsmanship in producing objects of high quality with terrific design, and they had huge numbers of talented engineers and a commitment to long-range scientific research. All of these assets came together to make Japan a nanotech power.

The Japanese started with some initial Western research, but they quickly became one of the most advanced competitors in nanotechnology. Many young people were drawn into the burgeoning nanotech field, and economic growth began accelerating again. The period from 2010 to 2020 made many recall the glory years of Japan in the 1980s.

Nanotechnology was one of the places where Japanese government-funded R&D was paying off handsomely. By 2010 the Japanese had managed to learn the U.S. venture capital model, so rather than government investments in private enterprises, there existed private venture funds that stimulated the creation of many new companies.

One key beneficiary was a company that came to be known as Nippon Nano. It acquired rights to commercialize software ideas coming out of the

GOVERNMENT-funded scientific RESEARCH, which had been enjoying huge increases in public money, and it became an integrated distributor of software
for the nanotech industry. Nanoscale engineering involved remarkably subtle
processes in both the design and the construction phases. Nanoscale devices
achieved staggering efficiency but were extremely difficult to fabricate.

Nippon Nano acted as a middle man licensing key nanotechnology software
to everyone. Its basic product was data files with intellectual property that
originated in other scientists' and engineers' work. It sold process licenses to
companies around the world, which then competed in using those designs to
produce new kinds of nanotech products and services.

This industry transformed every aspect of how we make things, from steel
to chips to automobiles to medical instruments. The opportunity for creating
material goods built on nanotechnology was almost unlimited, as was the ability to improve the efficiency and environmental impact of industrial processes.

Nanotechnology, more than anything, brought pollution levels down to the
minimal degree that we experience now in 2050. And Nippon Nano became
one of the most powerful firms of the twenty-first century—the Microsoft of
the nanotechnology era.

9

Technology
Emulates Nature

Advances in biological sciences are creating great new potential in agriculture and industry that bode well for the environment. The more humans emulate nature's sustainable practices, the better off we'll all be. However, some biotechnology breakthroughs, such as life extension and genetic engineering, will pose great issues that society must address. Ultimately, with nanotechnology, we will learn to make devices the way nature makes organisms—building them a few molecules at a time.

THE NEXT TECHNOLOGICAL WAVE that we will all ride is biotechnology, and this one will blow your mind. Biotechnology by 2020 will bring more change to the human species than we have experienced in the last *million* years. Through bioscience alone, we are going to change the nature of the human condition more fundamentally than in all our conscious attempts in all other fields in all previous eras combined. In just the medical field, bioscience will shift the health paradigm to such a degree that we'll look back on medical practices of today the way we now look back on those in medieval Europe. Today we say: Can you believe that doctors in those days used to think they could cure people by draining out bad blood? In the twenty-first century, people will look back and say: Can you believe that doctors in the twentieth century used to take knives and cut up people? That will seem equally bizarre.

Then look out for nanotechnology, another technology wave that will come rolling in soon after biotechnology. We will take what has been learned from many of the breakthroughs in bioscience and apply them to industry. Nanotechnology is flipping manufacturing completely upside down. Why do we want to dig materials out of the ground, melt them down, smash them up, throw a lot away, and then make products? We're going to be able to construct products atom by atom, very quickly, through billions of simultaneous actions, with no waste—like having an atomic Lego set that will ultimately make anything and everything. Nanotechnology and biotechnology, along with new energy technologies and future generations of our good old computer technology, are going to be the engines driving this Long Boom through the twenty-first century, and these technologies will cause repercussions long after what we define as the Long Boom.

THE BIOTECH BOUNTY

Here's a California story for you: In 1983, Kary Mullis was a research scientist in the fledgling biotechnology industry, working for Cetus Corp. in Emeryville, just across the bay from San Francisco. For a little break from the rigors of work, he took a trip to Mendocino, a beautiful town on the coast of northern California, about three hours drive outside the metro area. He took off for his trip in more ways than one: He dropped LSD, a powerful hallucinogenic, before he hit the road. Lucky for him—and all of us—he avoided any accident and had a breakthrough insight that would transform the biotechnology world. He kept seeing images of the genetic coils of DNA spin out of his mind. He watched as the strands stretched out and separated in a way that gave him an idea. Why couldn't humans stretch out the long coils of DNA, the fundamental genetic material that carries the programs organizing all life forms? Why couldn't we then just unzip the two strands of the famous double helix, the spiral ladder whose image has been studied by every schoolchild since Watson and Crick first described it? Then we could use RNA, DNA's cousin, to provide the four basic protein building blocks that could match up with each of the two orphaned strands to effectively duplicate the original DNA molecule. This whacked-out insight was refined into what became known as PCR (polymerase chain reaction), the common method of rapidly duplicating DNA. And PCR became the breakthrough that the biotechnology world needed. Before PCR, the extreme laboriousness and slowness of duplicating DNA were stymieing progress in this fundamental area of bioscience research. After PCR, DNA duplication became relatively easy, and experimentation exploded. In the meantime, Kary Mullis won the Nobel Prize for his—shall we say—unusual idea.

This PCR breakthrough, among others, ignited a boom in biotechnology in the 1980s that was in some ways very similar to what was happening in the personal computer world. There were many eerie parallels. A lot of the important activity in biotech happened in the San Francisco Bay area and around Boston, two hubs of the computer world. The small start-up biotech companies often spun out of research in the world-class universities located there. The University of California at Berkeley, Stanford University, and the University of San Francisco were all hotbeds. But so were some of the core universities in Boston like Harvard and MIT. Both these metropolitan areas had also developed strong venture capital communities primed to bet on risky projects. However, investors did not think long-term enough. Toward the end of the 1980s, the money spigot got turned off, and a lot of small biotech companies went belly up. Part of the reason was that the science of molecular biology was not as far along in its development as was computer science.

This brings up the distinct differences between biotechnology and computer technology. The main one has to do with time frame. Products in biotech take a long time to develop, mainly because they are used by humans and other life forms and can be dangerous. All biotech products need to go through a series of tests that ensure their safety. Governments have extensive apparatus to regulate drug trials and review the implications of widespread use. The biotech industry will always need to take safety precautions that the computer industry doesn't.

For that reason, the biotech industry has taken a different evolutionary path from the computer industry. The entrepreneurial stage is still very similar. But once a good idea becomes a viable product, the small start-ups are often bought out by the giant pharmaceutical companies. These companies have the resources to stay the course and the infrastructure to keep pushing these products through the regulatory hoops in Washington, D.C., and the capitals of other countries around the world. These are global companies, and many of the leading ones are based in Europe. They are good at the second stage of taking a nearly proven product and getting it to the public. They are not so good at sparking the next great idea. They're too big and bureaucratic, though that's changing somewhat. So the biotech system has evolved in a workable way that nurtures a symbiosis between highly creative small companies and the big companies with the infrastructure. After the big scare in the biotech bust of the late 1980s, the venture capitalists were lured back to fund a new round of companies. The 1990s brought a burgeoning biotech sector that remains almost completely off the radar screen of the public—partly because everyone is so mesmerized by companies tied to the Internet, which have extremely short product cycle times. These Internet companies rush to become publicly traded and hopefully household names, while the biotech industry keeps growing and developing products waiting for its time in the limelight, which will be soon.

The decade of the 2000s will prove to be the biotech decade. We're already seeing biotech products coming onto the market—though they are not headline grabbers yet. We're starting to get painkillers, like COX2, developed at the molecular level and very specifically targeted to certain kinds of pain. We have a new drug for Alzheimer's that helps protect the memory function of neural cells. Will it be long before we use similar techniques to *enhance* rather than just protect memory? And a whole new generation of cancer treatments is just coming to the market. There are about thirty cancer drugs—more than ever before—in the third and final phase of the clinical trials that the U.S. Food and Drug Administration typically requires before full approval. These drugs promise to extend lives and make cancer treatment much more bearable than chemotherapy or radiation, which have severe side effects and are brutal on the individual's system. The current chemotherapy involves killing not only cancer cells but also a lot of cells that are required to stay healthy. The new drugs are biological, based on naturally occurring proteins and genetic material. They are much less tough on the body's overall system, with few or very mild side effects. They won't necessarily cure cancer yet, but they will suppress the effects and make cancer much more endurable, extending the lives of patients much as the new protease inhibitor cocktails extend the lives of AIDS patients. These drugs are not just for one or two kinds of cancer. Already in the pipeline are drugs targeting cancers of the breast, prostate, lung, colon, liver, ovary, pancreas, kidney, and malignant melanoma, as well as inoperable brain cancer. Despite the ravages that cancer wreaks on so many families, these cancer drugs have not attracted much attention. They soon will. These are the biotech products that are emerging from the regulatory pipeline of trials. They are just the tip of the proverbial iceberg. The products that will really shake up health care are the ones that will emerge in the next decade. But first, the environmental dimension.

What does biotech have to do with the environment, the major topic of this section of the book? The answer is: A tremendous amount. What is biotechnology? It is human technology that emulates or leverages biological processes that nature has perfected through evolution over millions of years. Nature has evolved an amazingly complex and elegant system that is so far beyond what we humans have come up with that we may as well just start copying it as fast as we can. In terms of the environment, think of it this way: Our industrial system of the last few hundred years is a mechanical one based on thermodynamics. Almost everything we produce we heat up to extremely high temperatures or put under extreme pressure. We pound things and smash things and burn things and boil things—and we waste an enormous amount in the process. Nature works in a totally different way—on smooth, sleek biological processes. Nature produces things by growing them at reasonable temperatures and slowly changing the organic structure or the chemical composition. If there is any waste product in one growth process, it becomes an input in another growth process. So plants take in the carbon dioxide vital to photosynthesis and produce the "waste" of oxygen. Mammals use that oxygen, which is vital to *their* life process and get rid of carbon dioxide as a waste product. In the natural system, every part is fully integrated into the whole. One organism's waste, or output, is another organism's vital food, or input.

Increasingly, this is the way human-designed systems will work. Biology and biotechnology have much to teach us today. They are unlocking the secrets of how to produce things and waste less. Take oil refining. The way we now refine oil is to put the crude oil in huge vats and heat it to extreme temperatures until the various petrochemical products separate out: Gasoline rises to the top of the vat, heavier industrial oil sinks to the bottom, and various other products stratify in between. However, a lot of energy is used to heat the oil, the heating process creates emissions, and the production process creates polluting wastes. A biotech method of oil refining now being developed would use an organism to separate crude oil. Bacteria introduced into the vat of crude oil would work on the chemical composition in such a way as to spur the desired segmentation. This approach has not yet been realized and may never be workable on a large industrial scale. But similar biotech approaches involving hydrocarbons have been realized. For example, in the mid-1990s, a biotech product was developed for treating oil spills: A batch of bacteria applied to an oil slick break down the hydrocarbon molecules, which dissolve into the ocean. The organisms perform their job and then die. Again, this treatment does not work with huge spills where the breakdown can't be distributed widely. But it points toward the future use of benign bacteria and other biotech techniques to clean up our industrial messes and ultimately to supersede our industrial processes altogether.

Another example involves plastics, which are a mess to produce and difficult to dump. Our bodies produce complex polymers, which act much as plastics do. Nature grows these kinds of tough polymers all over the place. We're now far along on research to use biological processes to make plastics—in other words to grow plastics. We're close to being able to take ethylene, a core ingredient for one kind of plastic, and add bacteria to create plastic material—minus all the boiling and industrial waste. Someday soon we may even be able to grow plastic-like material from plants. These approaches may also allow us to make plastics that break down organically. A biodegradable plastic, or even one that is easily recyclable, would go a long way toward solving our landfill problems. Plastic in our dumps now could be around for thousands of years. It's a dumb way to package juice. Better to create a package that can dematerialize like a paper bag.

The original biotechnology, the granddaddy of them all, was agriculture. In the past, we have improved agriculture in three main waves: by developing pesticides, by fertilizing, and by breeding better plants. In all three of these areas, today's biotechnology is poised for big enhancements. Let's start with pesticides. In the past, we've scatter-gunned pesticides over whole fields in the hopes of protecting the plants we want to harvest. However, this approach is extremely wasteful because the pesticides travel far beyond the target plants through both the spraying process and the inevitable runoff. Also, the pesticides are often harmful to humans and other animals. One kind of biotech solution is to fine-tune the pesticide and the plant together, designing the pesticide on a molecular level to interact only with that specific plant and no others, and to be perfectly benign to other plants and human beings. Monsanto, a biotech company, has done this with certain kinds of soybeans that need very little pesticide of any kind. Or take the fertilizer side of the equation. In the past, chemicals, sometimes from petrochemical products, have been dumped on the soil to replenish the nitrogen and other nutrients. The result, again, is a lot of runoff into water systems and fertilization of the nearby weeds as well. One biotech innovation is to design plants that do their own nitrogen fixing or that grow fertilizers, that is, plants that fertilize themselves.

The real action in biotech involves the third area of agricultural improvement, breeding. People have been plugging away in this area almost from the dawn of agriculture itself. Breeding new kinds of plants, however, has been sort of hit or miss and has taken inordinate amounts of time. You took one kind of plant that, say, grows well in dry climates and tried to cross it with one that tastes sweeter. This method conjures up images of Gregor Mendel, the nineteenth-century Austrian monk who first figured out how male and female plants pass on their distinctive genetic material—but who spent his entire life trying to get different kinds of pea plants to cross-pollinate. It's a laborious process isolating plants with certain traits and then waiting through successive growing seasons to see results in future generations. Now, with biotechnology, we are dispensing with all this orchestration and cutting right to the chase. We manipulate the genetic code itself by figuring out which genes are responsible for what traits and how we can directly switch them on or off—or transplant them, though gene splicing, into another line of plants altogether.

This is where we enter the brave new world of genetic engineering. The possibilities are exhilarating. Once we've cracked the code and mastered the manipulation, which we're very close to doing, we can design plants to do whatever we want them to do. At the most fundamental level—through the genes—we could design superplants that, among other things, will take a lot of the load off the environment, like a plant that produces extremely high yields so smaller fields would support larger populations. We could design plants that will grow in regions of the world long off limits to agriculture, for example, a corn plant that will grow on the windswept steppes of dry central Asia. Plants designed to resist blights would do away with pesticides altogether; they might, for example, produce an odor that puts off predators. In other words, superplants could be designed that are extremely productive and also very low maintenance.

That's the exhilarating part of genetic engineering. There's also the terrifying part—at least for some people, particularly in Europe. Europeans seem to be more resistant to biotech advances in agriculture. They raise the specter of corporations creating highly productive superplants that spread out of control, crowding out natural vegetation and severely damaging the ecosystem. They warn that by disturbing the slow, natural selection process, we may create monsters that will rear their heads only generations down the line. We might strip plants of traits that will be needed years later. Europeans think the whole process is very unnatural. Something is not right. Americans, generally, don't seem to have nearly the same anxiety about genetic engineering in agriculture. To be sure, there is a strong organic foods movement in the United States that offers an alternative to mass-production agriculture. But the average American either is oblivious to these genetic developments or more comfortable with technological enhancements. The point is that through biotechnology we can gain ultimate control over the plant-breeding process. We can heighten the precision of our design choices and collapse the time it takes to reap the benefits. In many ways, we are just doing what we have always done—though not as haphazardly. We're quickly mutating plants in a laboratory rather than on special farms over years and years. Just as we gain the most control, people begin to have the most worries. And those fears have only been heightened with the parallel biotech developments in animal husbandry.

The same principles that work in agricultural genetic engineering work in animal husbandry. Instead of slowly trying to cross-breed exceptional animals over generations of trial and error, why not get right in there and tweak the genes? Until now, we've had to watch for the specific cows or lines of cows that, say, produce the most milk and then breed them. Biotechnology offers the chance to do all that and more through genetic pathways. We can deliberately create a cow that "naturally" produces much more milk than average cows or even than the cows today that get pumped up with hormones. Or our cow might be much healthier because various genetic diseases have been eliminated or physical attributes have been enhanced. Maybe our cow has shaggier fur to keep it warmer in the winter or a respiratory system more resistant to colds. This kind of cow would be doing its part to reduce wear and tear on the environment because one healthy supercow might produce the milk of three or four regular ones.

The logical next stage is cloning. We've already seen it happen and accelerate faster than almost anyone predicted. On February 23, 1997, Ian Wilmut of the Roslin Institute in Scotland announced the world's first successful cloning experiment in the form of a lamb named Dolly. The announcement was a shocker to the public and scientific experts alike. Many scientists believed that cloning mammals was impossible, merely a fanciful dream of science fiction, yet here was a researcher who actually pulled it off. The conventional wisdom then shifted to the idea that cloning was extremely difficult and would not be replicated in other animal breeds. Then on July 22, 1998, less than a year and a half later, a research team at the University of Hawaii produced twenty-two mice clones, seven of which were clones of clones from a single mouse. And then, less than six months after that, a research team at Kinki University in Nara, Japan, announced they had cloned eight cow calves from a single cow. Though four of the calves had died at or around birth, the cloning process had been remarkably easy. After that, the cloning announcements became more frequent and widespread, tending toward the routine. In fact, there were quite a few more cloned calves in Japan. Those behind the cow experiments said, in fact, that part of their motivation was to find ways to reproduce exact copies of superb producers of milk or meat. However, along with the talk about cloning comes a lot more anguished discussion. Cloning animals ratchets up the public anxiety even more than talk of creating superstrains of wheat. This time they're working on mammals, organisms that operate a lot more like people than soybeans do. If you can clone lambs, mice, and cattle, you can clone human beings, too. And so biotech moves out of the realm of plants and domesticated animals and starts to affect the human race, in a big way.

Human Bodywork

The medical field has done some amazing feats, particularly over the twentieth century. The health care system today is unimaginably better than any kind of treatment available in centuries past. We don't want to take anything away from the medical field's well-deserved glory, but frankly, what it's accomplished so far is rather crude. Seen from a future perspective, most of today's advanced medical practices are pretty traumatic. When a person has a failing heart, we tear open his or her chest, pull out the heart, put in the heart of a recently deceased human, and stick all the arteries and the skin tissues back together. From the perspective of the past, that operation is purely and simply amazing. But in the future, that same operation may seem bizarre: blood all over, and traumatized tissue, all the effort to fuse the patient back together and start the system again. The strangeness felt by those in the future will result from a paradigm shift in the medical field. Yes, another one of those paradigm shifts, this time in medicine. Now we treat a sick body from the outside. In the future, we will increasingly work from inside the body. For example, in 1998, scientists sponsored by the biotech firm Geron figured out how to cultivate human embryonic stem cells, the primordial cells in the human embryo from which an entire individual comes, and how to develop them into many, if not all, of the 210 different types of cells in the human body. It may be possible to create replacement tissues or organs from these stem cells. The development would start outside the body, but the tissue would be inserted into the patient so it could respond to local signals and integrate fully into the surrounding tissue. In this way, we may be able to eliminate the search for donors of organs that won't be rejected—and maybe even many kinds of surgery itself.

This breakthrough points the way to a whole array of gene therapy. The first step is understanding the human DNA sequence, a monumental task that is coming very close to completion. One big breakthrough came in late 1998 with the announcement that biologists had deciphered the full genetic programming of a worm. That may not seem earth-shattering, but up to that time, the genomes of only single-celled organisms like bacteria and yeast had been unraveled. This microscopic roundworm, barely one millimeter long, contained 97 million chemical units built up into almost 20,000 genes. If this DNA sequence were printed in an ordinary newspaper, it would fill nearly 3,000 pages. This roundworm was the first multicellular organism to have its genome laid out, and the genetic composition of humans, it turns out, has much in common with that of worms. The worm project employed 200 people working full time for ten years to identify all the genes. As they were working, they were also posting their results on the Internet so that scientists trying to identify human genes could compare notes. Once the function of a specific gene in the worm was known, the corresponding gene in humans could be identified, too. That process helped the human genome project, which is seeking to identify all human genes. It started as a government-funded project with the goal of completion in 2005. However, that effort got some competition from Celera, a Maryland company owned by the Perkin-Elmer Corporation, a maker of DNA-sequencing machines, which take advantage of powerful computer technology to rapidly sequence DNA. That technological breakthrough, along with the friendly competition, moved up the genome project completion date to the summer of 2000. Which means we can consider the human genome cracked. Now we need to figure out what to do with it.

There are about 4,000 hereditary human diseases, and many of them are truly horrible. There's a very good chance we can develop treatments at the gene level to solve killers like Huntington's disease or cystic fibrosis. We're at the point now of locating the genetic culprits in the human DNA sequence. Working with the genetic material of an adult tagged with the gene causing a specific disease is difficult and will take some years to fully figure out and perfect. However, doctors could relatively easily knock out any of those 4,000 disease-causing genes in future generations of kids. Rooting out hereditary diseases doesn't cause much controversy, but what do we do when we find the gene that controls height? Would parents want to control that gene, too? This is where we pass from using genetic information for disease prevention to using it to design human beings. And here we start to hit dicey ethical and moral turf.

What do we do when we figure out the gene that controls intelligence? At first, most people blanch at the thought of messing with that kind of fundamental attribute. However, on reflection, a reasonable argument could be made that it would be in the interests of the individual child and society in general if doctors boosted a low IQ to a normal one. The child would probably have a much happier, more productive life with no evident side effects. But then, what happens when a parent wants to pop a child's normal IQ of 100 to the genius level of 150? If the world is heading into the Knowledge Age, in which brainpower will be the most valued attribute, maybe we'd be better off with a lot more smart people. Then again, we might end up creating a two-tier society of the brain-enhanced class and the rest of us.

The genetic choices don't have to be just about intelligence. Some parents might want to soup up the physical attributes of their child. Some parents already put their children through intense regimens that produce world-class figure skaters or gymnasts. Tomorrow they might be able to design their kids to have the athletic ability of Michael Jordan. What are the societal implications of that choice? What are the rights of the children, who may not even like sports?

Do we modify humans in advance? The questions don't get much bigger than this one. And some argue that the risks don't get much bigger either because when messing around at that level, we can endanger the survival of the entire human race. That viewpoint goes something like this: Nature wants many options in order to evolve in whatever direction survival seems most likely. If one organism gets too stuck on one pathway and the larger environment changes, that organism will die out. Too bad for that organism, but the overall ecosystem will survive because other organisms were not caught on that doomed pathway, having headed in more fortuitous directions. Each single species, like *Homo sapiens,* should maintain as much genetic diversity as possible because the future is not predictable, and it isn't clear what attributes will prove to be useful later on. So if all seemingly useless or dangerous genes are knocked out of humans, we might become vulnerable to some unexpected environmental change. We don't really know now what genes we might need later. So the argument today is: Don't start messing with the genes. However, the counterargument is that we are extremely far from undermining genetic diversity. In the next 100 years, only a portion of humanity will be in a position to tweak their genes anyhow. And our increasing understanding of genetics will also allow us to react to impending environmental crises, such as a new disease epidemic. We're not like a helpless dinosaur. We're much more in control of our destiny.

"We are as gods and might as well get good at it." That was the opening line of the inaugural 1968 *Whole Earth Catalog,* the one that greeted the world with that picture of the earth floating in space. Stewart Brand came up with that line to set the tone for a catalog that wanted to get news of great new technologies and tools to as many people as possible. He actually built his line on a similar one from the 1968 book *A Runaway World?* by the British anthropologist Edmund Leach: "Men have become like gods. Isn't it about time that we understood our divinity? Science offers us total mastery over our environment and over our destiny, yet instead of rejoicing we feel deeply afraid. Why should this be? How might these fears be resolved?" Both Brand and Leach were trying to set an optimistic tone that ran against the prevailing pessimistic feeling of that time and the decades that came after. They were seeing all the scientific breakthroughs and new technologies coming on-line in the 1960s, and they wanted to get people to contemplate the heady possibilities rather than just stay stuck in dread. Their words resonate today as we face even more heady technologies and sobering choices. "We are as gods and might as well get good at it." We can't escape this responsibility. The fact is that we now have the tools that allow us to enter the realm that once seemed reserved for the gods. We are now well on our way to understanding the human genome. This is an intellectual endeavor that is expanding the horizons of human knowledge and that can't be stopped. Governments could not stop this exploration even if they tried. The medieval political and religious authorities may have temporarily stopped Galileo from studying the planets, but they barely tripped up the progress in our understanding of cosmology. No one can stop humans from figuring out what is true. So the fact is that we will soon have this understanding of genetics and the ability to control our genes. We should celebrate our good fortune but fully understand the very real dangers out there, too.

The environmental impact of all these developments in medical biotech works in a not-so-obvious way. It's easy to see a coming boom in the health care industries, helping fuel the overall Long Boom. It's not so easy to see direct benefits to the environment. But there is a development working in the background that most certainly will help in the care of the earth. It started out innocuously enough with an array of medical advances aimed at improving life. In the past, most of the attention in the medical field was on stopping bad effects that were already happening. Once a disease broke out, we went after it. Once something broke, we fixed it. Now there's increasing attention to improving the quality of life, especially for older people. Viagra drives home that point. Initially, it may have been developed for men suffering from impotence, but it has quickly been used to improve the sex life of many men and women. Viagra is prototypical of a whole array of new drugs. Viagra came out of advances in the science of molecular biology resulting in a harmless drug that affects a biological process. There are many more such drugs. Drugs are now available to slow or stop hair loss. One just coming out improves the elasticity of skin—in effect, returning much of its youthfulness. Soon we will see drugs aimed at improving poor night vision. Down the line we can expect to grow new tissue that will help shore up or restore deteriorating cartilage in aching joints—allowing people to move with ease indefinitely. People will maintain much more vigorous and healthy lives far longer, until they reach the end and die. That's development Number One, which feeds into development Number Two.

The human life span is getting far longer than most people think. We're talking additional decades, which on the surface seems preposterous but, with reflection, makes more sense. At the beginning of the twentieth century, the average life expectancy in the United States was roughly 47 years. Certainly many people made it past that age, but not too much longer. A person hitting age 70 was really rare. And many people died prematurely, bringing the average down. Today the average life span of an American is about 75 years. That's the average, meaning a lot of people live far longer. People in their 90s are pretty common, and the 100-year-old club is not at all an oddity. That means that in this century, in one rather prosperous country, the average life span was extended by about 30 years. And now we look back and cringe at the idea that most people back then only lived into their 40s. Well, here's the mindbender: We are now poised to extend the life span by more than 40 years. A very strong argument can be made that we're on the verge of extending the average life span to age 120. The overall average might not rise that high by 2020, but the trend will be clearly established. By the middle of the twenty-first century, that length of life will be the norm, and with the spread of prosperity, that will be the norm for much of the world.

Why 120? There seems to be a natural principle that affects cells of virtually every organism and limits the number of times cells can replicate. When cells can no longer replicate, the organism ages rapidly and soon dies. That principle is known as the Hayflick limit, named after Leonard Hayflick, who discovered the phenomenon. The Hayflick limit sets the maximum life span of the organism and so is different in each species. In a human being, the Hayflick limit sets the theoretical maximum human life span at 120 years. So extending life beyond 120 years proves much more difficult because we hit a fundamental biological barrier that we can't see how to surmount—at least not yet. However, extending life up to 120 years appears very doable. It's more a matter of creating the context for our cells to simply maximize their full growth potential. With our full array of biotech tools and our expanding knowledge of the life sciences, we will be able to ward off threats to our bodies, enabling the natural processes to proceed—aiding them when intervention is needed, and enhancing them in a pinch. The culmination of all the medical advances and gene therapy mentioned above will lead to the 120-year-old human being. And remember, these are not 120-year-olds who are comatose and on life support for the last couple decades. These are active, vital human beings who maintain much of the vigor of people 50 years old today.

Think about what 120-year-old life extension will do to people's sense of time. With this new longevity, today's 60-year-olds, about to retire, would be only halfway through their lives. A 40-year old would be considered a relative youngster, just emerging from the first third of life, the time of study and preparation, to make her most potent contribution in the next 40 years. Mary Catherine Bateson, an anthropologist, talks about how across history and all cultures, humans have been used to knowing no more than three generations, corresponding to the kids, the parents, and the grandparents—until now. We're already seeing more great-grandparents interacting with great-grandchildren—something that almost never happened as recently as 50 years ago. What happens when the 120-year life span allows five or six consecutive generations to live at the same time? At the very least, it will stretch people's sense of time. What we now think of as the distant future will become much more real because what happens then will affect not just the younger generations but you yourself. You might think differently about really long-term investments that will pay off only decades hence. That's fine—you'll still be around to reap the benefits. And your concern for the environment will only increase. Here's where medical biotech has a direct effect on improving the environment. If it will take a decades-long effort to reverse global warming, then let's do it. You'll have even more incentive because you will benefit from the positive long-term effects. The reverse holds true as well. People will be less apt to maintain an I-got-mine mentality and rape the planet of natural resources or leave a mess of pollution for the people coming later. Life extension is a development that will reinforce the more environmentally friendly mentality that the world needs. Life extension is completely in sync with the Long Boom.

Nanotech's Endgame

All stories need to start somewhere, and the nanotechnology story starts with Richard Feynman, the world-famous physicist, giving an after-dinner talk at his hometown campus, the California Institute of Technology, on December 29, 1959. There, he addressed a national society of experimental physicists in a speech called "There's Plenty of Room at the Bottom." Feynman started by chiding his contemporaries about their moaning that all the great fields of physics had been discovered and the pioneering trails already blazed. He went on to describe a new field where virtually nothing had been done but that held enormous potential: working with individual atoms, designing new kinds of microscopic tools to work at that level, and devising new ways of manufacturing in the vast spaces in the world of the very, very small. The more he talked, the more jaws dropped. Nobody had really thought about the possibility of working at that scale. It seemed impossible. But there was the great Richard Feynman saying that there was nothing in the laws of known physics that would prevent us from working down there. As he put it, "We are not doing it simply because we haven't gotten around to it." He further goaded them with "In the year 2000, when they look back at this age, they will wonder why it was not until the year 1960 that anybody began seriously to move in this direction." Feynman was ahead of his time in more ways—and more fields, for that matter—than one. He laid out this great challenge to the community of physicists, and not one of them rose to the occasion. The serious movement would only come later, once we crossed the threshold into the Long Boom.

Eric Drexler, from the moment you meet him, seems like an original thinker. Drexler certainly is in that class. As a graduate student at the Massachusetts Institute of Technology in the 1980s, Drexler was enough of a freethinker to buck the physics establishment and take up Feynman's challenge. The scientific community had balked at Feynman's idea, because most scientists believed that at the atomic level, matter was too uncontrollable, that the thermal motion of particles created an atomic turbulence that made it impossible to carefully order atoms—let alone manufacture products. Drexler's great insight was to point out that this was far from impossible because nature works at that level all the time. Nature has created all kinds of single-celled organisms having subcellular parts that operate as elegant biomechanical systems at the molecular level. For example, some bacteria have a simple but elegant rotator cuff embedded in the cell wall that allows a tail-like part to turn and propel the cell forward in liquid. This rotor is exquisitely designed and perfectly fits the function. It's made up of a handful of molecules, which are themselves composed of atoms. Drexler just pushed the obvious parallel: If nature can get a handle on atoms and fuse them together to make tiny but elegant tools, why can't human beings? He laid out his ideas in a 1981 paper in the *Proceedings of the National Academy of Sciences,* and later in 1986 in his groundbreaking book *Engines of Creation*, which kicked off the serious study of nanotechnology. You can see how, right from the start, nanotechnology was inextricably tied to biotechnology. It can almost be seen as an extension of biotechnology and, going back to first principles, biology itself. Through molecular biology, we study how nature works at that level. Through biotechnology, we try our hand at emulating and improving upon those practices in the organic living world. And with nanotechnology, we take those design principles and strike out on our own to build things in the physical, nonliving world.

Given that dependency, nanotechnology has been on a developmental track in stutter step with biotechnology. There's a built-in lag time of roughly two decades. The 1980s was the decade of cracking the fundamental design principles. Drexler's book in the middle of the decade spurred more serious thinking in other quarters. The 1990s were more about coming up with the initial tools and starting to play around on the atomic level. Of course, computers played a big role in enabling these new tools and allowing people to work at an extremely small scale. Take the atomic force microscope, a device that has an extremely fine point only a few atoms wide. When an electric charge is sent through the tip, the charge nudges an atom or two at a time. Human hand movements on a computer mouse can be scaled down to the level that pushes an atom one way or the other. The atomic force microscope is not just a manipulator. The charge nudging the atoms can also pick up an electronic image of the atoms, which is blown up through computer simulations and computer graphics to give the operator a "picture" of the atom—something that the lens on a regular optical microscope could not see.

The first technical breakthrough came in 1989, when Don Eigler and Gerhard Schweitzer of the IBM Research Division at the Almaden Research Center in San Jose, California, used the tip of a scanning-tunneling microscope to line up thirty-five individual xenon atoms, one at a time, to spell—what else?—IBM. This picture of the atomic-scale IBM logo blew away the staid world of particle physics and got a lot of people working on simple experiments. By the end of the 1990s, many initiatives were coming to fruition, and many of the heavyweight technology corporations—like Lucent, NEC and Sun—were devoting serious resources to nanotech research. The Foresight Institute, a nonprofit organization headed by Drexler that spreads the word on nanotechnology, and the Institute for Molecular Manufacturing were holding annual nanotechnology conferences keynoted by Nobel Prize winners. The 1998 conference in Silicon Valley drew 300 people from eighteen countries and had five simple nanoscale devices showcased. One team from the Netherlands had developed a nanotube transistor that might someday work as a molecular-level wire. A team from Japan announced a new class of carbon nanostructures called *bucky horns,* which along with the already-developed buckyballs and buckytubes, are the crude early building blocks of nanotechnology.

The 2000s will be the decade during which a more rigorous manufacturing process will be crafted. A Texas start-up company called Zyvex has already begun serious work on designing a molecular assembler that will be able to manipulate individual atoms or very small particles. Right now we can only nudge the atoms around with an atomic force microscope and the like. But this machine will be able to pick atoms up and assemble them with others. However, the company fully expects that the development process will take until the middle or the end of the 2000s. The following decade will see an explosion of commercial assembler applications. They still will be crude and only a flicker of what is to come.

Among the first products in the 2000s might be chip sensors not larger than a single cell that can be injected into a person's bloodstream to take readings of some biological function. You can imagine the development of a cheap single-celled machine designed to identify and perhaps kill a virus or other pathogen and then turn itself off to be flushed out of the person's system. Another early product might be simple superstrong materials designed from the atom up, and at such a density and with such reinforcing substructures that they could bear excruciating loads. The problem we face when working at the level of atoms is that it takes a lot of atoms to make a product that we can even see. For example, the head of a pin can hold about 400,000,000,000,000,000 atoms. That's 400,000 trillion atoms. What makes future visions of nanotechnology plausible is the possibility of parallel processing like that in biological growth, where billions of simultaneous processes occur. Parallel processing in nanotechnology would involve billions of the nanoassemblers simultaneously doing their part to construct a tiny portion of the material. If enough of them are working, the material will soon add up.

The really serious, widespread commercial products in nanotechnology will probably not come until the 2020s, about a twenty-year lag time from the boom in biotech products after the turn of the century. Here the products can range from the mundane but dirt-cheap to the bizarre. The superstrong material used the decade before for something the size of a ball bearing might be cheaply produced in such quantities in this decade that we could build reusable rocket ships or whole buildings that have the strength to rise 100s of stories or be built deep into the ground. Or, moving in the other direction, our command of working at the atomic level would allow us to keep shrinking our electronic circuitry to build ever-more-powerful computers. The current generation of silicon-based computers faces a natural barrier by about the year 2010 because the photographic lithography technique used now will not work at the submicron level that we're projected to reach. In other words, Moore's law is built on the logic that every eighteen months engineers will be able to design a chip with twice as many transistors in the same size space. But by about 2010, we will have shrunk the size of the chip so much that our old techniques will not operate effectively. That's when we might port over to the new techniques of nanotechnology and enter the realm of nanocomputing.

Nanotechnology's real repercussions will be felt after 2020 and increasingly throughout the twenty-first century. The Long Boom era will crack the code of basic nanotechnology and begin to orient people to the future technological possibilities, but it will not reap the benefits of this watershed technology. That's not to say that effects won't be felt. Just knowing that nanotechnology is coming and understanding the fully realizable potentials will deeply inform the public debate about our destiny in the latter Long Boom years. This is particularly true when it comes to our deliberations about the environment because nanotechnology will have an enormous impact there. Theoretically, there is no more efficient way of producing things than through nanotechnology. There is no waste, every atom is present and accounted for, and only the atoms that are truly needed are built up. Given that hyperefficiency, theoretically only the absolute minimum of energy is needed to perform the task.

Nanotechnology also shifts our perspective on natural resources. Building needs to begin with the original atoms of some element, but after that, those most basic materials can be mixed into more complex molecules and materials. Some mining of the earth will remain because if you want to build something with the properties of tungsten, you do need some tungsten atoms to start with. But those tungsten atoms would be as efficiently used as possible, and they could be rearranged and easily reused via nanotechnology. However, many products and things that we use could be made up of much more common elements—the ones that are virtually limitless. We could take common elements like carbon and, through nanotechnology, easily create lumps of synthetic diamonds, for example, which nature creates by putting carbon molecules under enormous pressure deep in the earth. Today we also can create synthetic diamonds through intense pressure, but we use lots of time and expensive equipment to do it. Nanotechnology could do it with little energy and no equipment—making the whole process dirt-cheap. We could have inexpensive, abundant material with the strength of today's diamonds.

And that's just the start. Once you have figured out how to manufacture billions of these microscopic assemblers working tirelessly like tiny Energizer bunnies, you can steer them toward a remarkable range of environmental tasks. Sometime in the twenty-first century, we may find it cost-effective to use nanotech to produce cheap solar cells so tough that they can be used to repave our road system. That way we can create a large enough area of solar cells to collect a substantial portion of our energy needs without using any more land that's not already being used. In fact, we might collect so much excess solar energy that we could use it to break down the tons of excess carbon dioxide put into the air in generations past. Nanotech holds out this kind of prospect of going back and cleaning up many of the industrial messes of the twentieth century. Or we might find that what we thought of as "wastes" in the twentieth century will actually be the raw materials for building products with nanomachines in the twenty-first. Instead of mining deep in the earth for our raw materials, we will simply mine our landfills—cleaning them up in the process.

All of this may sound an awful lot like science fiction. Nanotechnology actually started as the distant dream of far-out science fiction that future generations 1,000 years from now would figure out how to build everything by the atom. Science fiction often works that way. The dreamers lay out the implications of technologies that are seemingly impossible. And then the scientists and engineers, often avid consumers of science fiction, plug away and find the actual technologies. We've seen this dynamic play out again and again. Drexler's genius was that he was the one to ground those distant dreams of nanotechnology in reality. His book *Engines of Creation* took what the science fiction writers said would take 1,000 years and made a convincing case that it could be accomplished in less than 50. That book transformed many readers' view of the future. It predicted a world which, through nanotechnology, will allow people to retain their material goods and live affluent lives. Nanotechnology will provide the pathway to a future in which a rapidly growing economy is completely in balance with nature.

Getting the global economy perfectly in balance with the natural environment will not happen by 2020. Our job is to start to rechannel the global economy in that direction. We begin by stopping any increases in planetary pollution, and then we nudge the amounts down. We use all the new and cleaner technologies at our disposal and bank on those just coming down the line. With this kind of continuing effort, by the end of the twenty-first century the planet will be able to support in relative splendor a projected human population of 10 billion. It's feasible that everyone on the planet could live what we now consider a middle-class life. And that kind of global lifestyle would not lead to environmental catastrophe. On the contrary, the air, water, and land should be in much better shape than they are now. This is not a dream of science fiction. This is a plausible future that should bolster our resolve and give us peace of mind today.

10

PREPARE for Wild Science

The progress of scientific knowledge has by no means come to an end. We can expect major breakthroughs in physics and biology because some of our theories don't yet make sense of certain known facts. These scientific advances, if and when they come, may remake our conception of the universe and result in some major technological surprises.

HAVE WE LEFT OUT ANY AMAZING technologies and scientific discoveries that will occur in this Long Boom? Plenty, though we don't know what they are. This is where we enter the world of wild science, where almost anything can unexpectedly happen and change the context of everything else. In fact, we can almost count on some big scientific discovery within our time frame that will send reverberations throughout the world—perhaps turning it upside down. The signs are everywhere that we are in the midst of many paradigm shifts in many fields, and science is not immune. However, many conventional scientists today say that most of the basic science explaining the world has been cracked and all that's left is to fill in the holes. We've heard that refrain before.

At the end of the nineteenth century, the song of the end of science was commonly heard. In those heady times of industrialization, scientists, and the public who idolized them, believed that all the major discoveries had been made and they had nature and the cosmos pretty much figured out. Actually, they didn't have a clue what they were missing—whether tiny things under the surface or distant things far out in the stars. For example, nineteenth-century astronomers were pretty proud of their telescopes, which let them more clearly examine pinpricks of starlight in the sky. But with the development of more powerful telescopes in the 1920s, astronomers realized those pinpricks weren't stars at all, but entire galaxies. That one discovery, that the universe has billions of galaxies rather than just billions of stars, blew open the doors of astronomy. Or consider the discovery of the electron. Before 1897, no one had any idea that every single particle of matter was composed of a proton, a neutron, and an electron spinning madly around the other two. Yet the electron helped define the entire twentieth century. It led to some of our greatest achievements, such as the creation of computers, and it drove us into some of our darkest moments, with the dropping of the atomic bomb.

Not that there weren't clues lying around at the end of the nineteenth century that pointed to the need for different theories. Periods before a scientific paradigm shift are often marked by evidence that can't be explained by current theories or that can be explained only through extreme contortions of those theories. The classic example of scientific contortion is the Western obsession with the Ptolemaic system of astronomy. Ptolemy, the second-century A.D. astronomer and mathematician from Alexandria, had posited that the earth was the fixed point in the universe, around which all other celestial bodies moved, and he devised a complex system to try to explain the irregular courses that those bodies took. To Westerners, that theory was gospel until the Copernicus paradigm shift of the sixteenth century, which built a completely new model that was elegant, internally consistent—and true. (For the record, the Indians of the subcontinent never traveled down the earth-centric path. This was a Western folly.) Another example is the photoelectric effect, which happens when an electric current passes through a dark body and produces light. We couldn't explain it—until Einstein's series of papers in 1905 that laid out his special theory of relativity, arguing that energy and mass are equivalent, and that under certain conditions, one becomes the other, the key constant being the speed of light: ($E = MC^2$). Less than a decade later, after mastering a new form of mathematics called Rie-mannian geometry, Einstein elaborated on those ideas in his more comprehensive general theory of relativity in 1912. That theory re-framed all of physics and our understanding of much of the universe.

The point is that there is a delicate interplay between experimenta-tion and theory. An experiment uncovers new data that don't fit the old theories, and then new theories must be devised to explain them. Those theories then stimulate new experiments, which test the the-ory and provide new data that force additional theoretical refine-ment. The third element in the equation is tools, defined in the broadest sense. Sometimes they are physical tools, but often they are tools of the mind, like new mathematical languages. Einstein needed the more complex math of Riemannian theory to work out and artic-ulate general relativity. This scientific method keeps driving the evo-lution of our understanding of the world.

Today, in some ways, we have a scientific situation similar to the one a century ago. For example, we can't account for a big chunk of the mass that, according to current theories, should exist in the uni-verse—we're talking *90 percent* of the mass, which we call dark mat-ter, partly because we can't find it. Something seems screwy here. Or according to our big bang theory of creation, the universe is expand-ing out from that initial explosion in one of two ways: Either it has been expanding at a steady rate after that first shove into the empti-ness of space, or it is expanding but decelerating because of the grav-itational pull of all the bodies in the universe. However, we now have new telescopic tools that can measure parts of the spectrum previously unexamined: x rays and infrared and ultraviolet radia-tion. New evidence collected from observations taken in these parts of the spectrum in 1998 showed that the universe is actually *acceler-ating* its expansion. We have no way to account for that phenome-non, but it's a sign that the current paradigm for understanding the universe may be due for an overhaul. Some scientists even think our understanding of physics is analogous to the understanding just be-fore Galileo opened it up in the early seventeenth century. We don't truly understand the fundamental rules, we don't know where to di-rect the most attention, and we're not even sure what questions we should be asking.

THE BURGEONING BRAIN TRUST

Unlike seventeenth-century Europe, we have developed an awesome infrastructure to handle any and all new ideas. Think about it. Think about the sheer brainpower we have amassed over the years. There's a common, though unverifiable, assertion that 70 percent of all the scientists who have ever lived are living and working today. We do know that tens of millions of scientists are working around the world today. These are people who have completed at least twenty-one years of formal schooling: twelve years through secondary school, another four years for undergraduate work, at least five years for a Ph.D., and perhaps a postdoctorate degree after that. These people are in all fields imaginable, dedicating all their intellectual focus to expanding the scope of human knowledge in some relatively narrow area: black holes, insect species in the rain forest, the molten core of the earth, how the mind works, bones buried a million years ago, creatures living seven miles under the ocean, the cause of the common cold—the list is endless. And these people are completely unknown to the general public. They're just doing their jobs, expanding their intellectual horizons, adding their little piece to the sum total of what is known.

What's more, there are millions more scientists and engineers now working on advanced degrees. In fact, there are getting to be so many that some people consider it a problem. Because much of a university's prestige comes from high-end research and the number of illustrious alumni in their fields, many institutions have expanded their programs for advanced degrees to bolster their reputations and attract better students and more funding. This expansion, however, has produced far too many candidates for the number of current vacancies in university teaching and research positions. So, many of these people are heading into the private sector and bringing their expertise to companies working in fields like biotech.

The number of people with just undergraduate degrees also continues to increase at a brisk pace. These college-educated people are very receptive to scientific advancements. They know the basic language of science and can appreciate from a lay perspective the importance of the announced breakthroughs. They also make up a very powerful political constituency that can influence the direction of wise public policy and funding in response to science's needs. This group of college-educated people is getting huge. In just the United States, roughly 40 percent of the population has gone to college—about 100 million people. Europe adds another 100 million, Japan about 40 million, and Russia another 20 million. Plus there are many parts of Asia that value education highly and have many people with university degrees as well. A conservative estimate of the numbers globally is about 350 million. Other ages, right up to the twentieth century, had only a handful of people with university degrees or equivalent training. At the most, there were hundreds of thousands in the nineteenth century. We have hundreds of millions.

It gets better. All these tens of millions of scientific minds, along with the increasing number of the college-educated, are getting wired together through the Internet. They now have a global medium through which they can communicate instantaneously with any other individual, or any tailored subgroup, or the entire community virtually for free. Scientific research used to take years to work itself into the scientific journals, which were printed on paper and mailed to the network of scientists in the club. And then challenges to the research would take months, if not years, to surface through those same journals. Now the research is often published on the Internet or sent by e-mail. The prestigious paper journals are still around, but many of them are changing to electronic form as well. As a result, the time needed to spread the word on new discoveries has been cut to almost nothing, and it's now disseminated as well to all the ardent amateurs outside the scientific clubs. These are the folks who often think out of the box or raise the obvious point that everyone else overlooked. And hidden somewhere is some young genius who will add a fresh insight and delight the world.

The Internet is also capturing a magnificent collection of data generated in all fields. Since the 1970s, we've seen an exponential increase in the amount of data we have amassed, partly because we keep increasing the capacity to store it. In the 1990s, we have linked millions of computers and will ultimately link millions of databases. So all these brains are sitting at a machine that can instantaneously connect them to any colleague and any piece of information. For

those who don't yet have access to the Internet, there's the ubiquitous global medium of television that can get news out to the masses.
The journalists watch the Internet and then move the stories out to
everyone.

On top of all that, the economy has developed a system that is extremely good at seeking out new ideas and rewarding those who
come up with them. Those huge numbers of graduates with advanced
degrees are in luck. They may not get a tenure-track university job,
but they do have a strong incentive to join industry, a think tank, or
a research organization, or to start their own business. The economy,
as it is wont to do, has taken advantage of the situation surrounding
the universities. Some companies have enticed Ph.D.s to work in set-
tings where they can still devote a quarter of their time to their own
pure research. Other researchers—including top professors themselves—create their own start-up companies to pursue their original
research and hopefully to sell their ideas for big bucks.

The rewards system for innovation has pumped up the pace of scientific discovery and has collapsed the time it takes for good ideas to
move toward practical applications in the marketplace. In the San
Francisco Bay area, this system has become a fine-tuned machine.
Students now come to Stanford and other universities in the region
with the explicit plan to do research with an eye toward forming
their own company. The venture capital community has a web of
scouts out looking for great ideas with big potential, and they quickly
connect the right idea to large amounts of capital and bring financial
and managerial expertise to help guide that idea to a successful product. Then they hope to bring the company to the public stock ex-
changes, where they will raise additional capital from public
investors—and cash out on their own investments. The potential capital to be mobilized is gargantuan. There are trillions of dollars out
there in the global marketplace just waiting to rush toward a great
idea.

Here's the situation: Human beings have collected a wide array of
knowledge in our 10,000 years of recorded history. That's our baseline, our foundation, the starting point for today. We've got all that
knowledge well documented and easily retrievable through a global
computer system. We've also spent generations and invested im-

mense resources building up the intellectual capacity and the advanced education of a large portion of people, numbering now in the hundreds of millions. They have expertise in every field imaginable and they now have been turned loose to figure out and improve the world. We've connected all these smart people together so that they can instantaneously share every new thing they learn and then take immediate feedback so they can refine their ideas. We've saved trillions of dollars worth of liquid capital that can move just as fast through that global network as can ideas. We have designed a highly adaptable, remarkably efficient, problem-solving apparatus. We have built a web of extremely motivated, extremely competent, often brilliant brains that love solving problems. In short, we have primed a finely tuned knowledge machine that can take on the challenges of the twenty-first century as well as exploit the windfalls that come our way. We are ready for anything. Some one of those roving brains out there in the world is going to make some mind-blowing discovery. What will it be?

To Infinity and Beyond

How about warp drive? Right now all theories of physics hold that nothing can travel faster than the speed of light. That is an absolute limit, which is a bummer, because that means humans would be hard-pressed to travel to the stars. Barnard's star is a fascinating star, the second closest to the sun, less than six light-years away. To get there, we would need to travel for six years at the speed of light, which we also have no idea how to do. If we traveled about fifty times faster than the fastest-ever manmade object, which was the interplanetary probe *Voyager* at 37,000 miles per hour, traveling to Barnard's star would take 2,000 years. And Barnard's star is our next-door neighbor. The really interesting stuff is hundreds or millions of light-years away. That's why the concept of warp drive, the method of propulsion on the *Star Trek* television series, has been so tantalizing. Warp drive allows the Trekkies to travel faster than the speed of light through warping space by a method that is never explained on the show. Most serious physicists have dismissed it as claptrap. But Miguel Alcubierre, a respected Welsh physicist, recently published a well-received paper arguing that warp drive might actually be possible within the limits of Einstein's general relativity. Theoretically, a sufficiently large gravitational force could warp the fabric of space in such a way that a spaceship could cross through that wrinkle in space at a relative velocity that would not break the speed of light. When it emerged on the other side of the wrinkle, and the warped space went back to normal, the spaceship would have traveled much farther than another spaceship moving through normal space at the same speed. That's the theory, which no one has been able to fault. People have raised obvious questions, like how you could harness the energy needed to warp space in such a way. But you never know. NASA thought warp speed sufficiently credible to include it in its Breakthrough Propulsion Physics workshop in 1997. NASA is trying to do some long-range planning on its mission deep into the twenty-first century, and although warp speed is a long shot, if possible, it could change everything. Without it, we're stuck in our boring little solar system. With it, who knows?

Or maybe we'll devise an antigravity device. We really don't know much about gravity despite studying it since Isaac Newton got bonked by an apple. We don't understand why it exists, where it comes from, or how it works. We know that all other forms of energy exist at a particle level, and a particle of gravity, called the *gravitron,* has been theorized, but we've never found one. Other theories of gravity have been similarly weak. There have been some generally accepted conclusions about the laws of gravity, such as that it is a constant force that can't be manipulated by anything. Then in 1993, the Russian émigré scientist Eugene Podkletnov claimed he had inadvertently negated gravity. He was testing a superconducting ceramic disk by rotating it above powerful magnets when he noticed that small objects above the disk appeared to lose weight. It seemed that the superconducting disk was shielding the small objects from the force of gravity—at least a little bit. The objects seemed to have their weight reduced by about 2 percent, but even that was astounding. If that process could be refined and the shielding focused, we might be able to levitate anything into the air. We could, among other things, transform transportation on earth. When Podkletnov tried to publish his peer-reviewed article in a respected physics journal in 1996, the

mainstream press got it first, the skeptics had a field day, and he became a laughingstock. But when the laughter died down, other scientists began taking the idea seriously, and the possibility still remains.
We seem to be able to manipulate all other forces, like electricity and
magnetic fields. We learned to manipulate light long before we really
understood it. We just have never found a way to manipulate gravity—but we might.

Or maybe wild science will open the doors to zero-point energy, a
potentially limitless source of energy that could be found everywhere. We know there is such a thing as zero-point energy, which is
the energy that exists between the particles inside an atom. We actually can see direct evidence of this energy when we slow down atomic
particles at the temperature of absolute zero and still observe motion.
At that temperature, no motion can come from heat-related energy,
so the energy has to come from somewhere, and we call that somewhere zero-point energy. The question is: How much energy is there
in that state? If the amount is too small, it might not even be worth
pursuing. But if it's large, we might be able to someday solve all our
energy problems. The other question is how we get at that energy and
unlock it. Maybe it's too bound up in the basic structure of the atom
and we will never be able to get it out. On the other hand, some
think zero-point energy is actually at work in the vacuum of space,
periodically being transformed into hydrogen atoms as part of the
spontaneous ongoing development of the universe.

Maybe zero-point energy is too far-out. Then there's always cold fusion, the ability to create energy through nuclear reactions at low
temperatures. We now create atomic power through nuclear fission,
which breaks down the atomic nuclei and creates both power and
waste. We're spending billions trying to master nuclear fusion, which
creates power by fusing atomic nuclei under extreme temperatures.
On March 23, 1989, Stanley Pons and Martin Fleischmann announced the discovery of cold fusion in one of the most widely covered science stories of the decade. But these two relatively unknown
scientists immediately came under withering criticism from the scientific establishment for incompetence and fraud. Their experiment
was deemed a hoax, and the whole notion of cold fusion has become
discredited. Or has it? Since 1989, laboratories in eight countries have

spent millions of dollars on cold fusion research, and a significant body of evidence has built up, though little has been published. And now some highly qualified and respected scientists are starting to talk openly about the possibility that someday cold fusion just might be for real. And if it's for real, then we might have a cheap, safe, limitless energy source that makes even hydrogen power seem old-fashioned.

And while we're at it, what about contacting aliens? Now *that* would be wild. Contacting intelligent life somewhere out in our galaxy would probably be about as big a wild card as you could ever throw into the mix of human history. Who knows what would happen then? Yet it just could happen. The theory used to be that planets were rare within galaxies and that life on those planets would be even rarer. But we're coming across new evidence that planets are much more common. Our most powerful telescopes are picking up faint signs of planets around many nearby stars. And we're also coming across evidence here in our solar system that extraterrestrial life might not be as rare as we thought. We know Mars once had water and might still have some under the surface. In 1997, we discovered a meteorite on earth that seemed to have originated on Mars and showed signs of fossils from an ancient life form. This could not be proven, but it sparked interest in getting to Mars and finding out more. So now we're sending out small unmanned probes to Mars to seek signs of water and, if we're lucky, maybe even bacteria still alive. Farther out in the solar system, the *Galileo* spacecraft in 1997 sped within 125 miles of Europa, one of Jupiter's moons, and took close-up photos that indicate warm water might lurk just under the icy surface, providing a possible habitat for some kind of life form. This is certainly a long shot that nevertheless will eventually be examined. But if our solar system has possibly seen life arise in several places, might not other solar systems have seen life arise as well? This is the basic logic of Drake's equation, which calculates the number of stars in the universe that might have planets capable of supporting life as we know it. Given the trillions of stars in the universe, the probability that other life exists is extremely high. At least, that's what Frank Drake argued back in the 1960s, long before we even realized the abundance of planets. Today the odds are even higher.

Since the early 1960s, we have systematically searched for radio transmissions from alien civilizations. The search for extraterrestrial intelligence, or SETI, is a maddeningly slow and difficult process. At the main radio telescope in Arecibo, Puerto Rico, scientists working on Project Phoenix have directed their search to only 1,000 of our galaxy's 400 billion stars, mostly the closest ones, within about 200 light-years. They scan 2 billion channels of a relatively quiet part of the electromagnetic spectrum on the off chance that the supercomputers doing the analysis will come across something out of the ordinary that might have been artificially created by other intelligent beings. It's like searching for the proverbial needle in a haystack, and it's gone on for nearly four decades with no results. But now new tools and strategies may allow SETI to expand the search to 100,000 other stars. The project has gotten more resources through private funding, much of it from the moguls of the technology world, like Paul Allen of Microsoft and Gordon Moore of Intel, who are partial to long-shot but big-payoff projects.

We can laugh at some of the wild conjectures about what wild science will bring us, but we would be foolish to think that there won't be huge scientific discoveries that will bring profound consequences in the near future. Anyone told 100 years ago that in 50 years moving pictures would be sent through the air or machines would be able to see through the body and photograph the bones would have considered such stories insane. Now everyone takes television and X rays for granted. The same thing will most certainly happen to us. The next great breakthroughs will initially boggle us. They will then profoundly affect us. And eventually, we'll take them for granted, too.

TWENTY-FIRST CENTURY CHOICES:
THE MAKING of A LONG BOOM

PART EIGHT: "EXPANDING INTO SPACE"

WELCOME back for THE final episode of "TWENTY-FIRST CENTURY CHOICES: THE MAKING of A LONG BOOM." I'M SALMA AboulaHoud, ANd I'll bE TALkiNG AbOUT ONE of THE biqqest choicEs THAT THE qlobAl community took iN THOSE first dECAdES of THE CENTURY—THE decisioN TO MOVE bACk iNTO SpACE.

WE NOW REALIzE THAT THE TWENTY-first cENTURY WAS THE bEqiNNiNG of THE REAL SpACE AqE. SpACE is SUCH A pERVASivE pREOCCUpATION for MOST pEOplE NOW, iN

2050, but in the late twentieth century, space exploration had lost public support.

There had always been opposition to spending the relatively huge sums on cutting-edge space technology when that same money could be spent helping so many human beings on earth. That sentiment existed in the 1960s but was overridden by the perceived importance and excitement of the space race between the United States and the USSR.

Space exploration at that time was mostly a product of the Cold War. Rocket technology was developed partly to build up arsenals of intercontinental missiles, and "Star Wars" satellites were developed to defend against them. The race to build a space station was the USSR's attempt to thump their chests. The race to the moon served the same purpose for the Americans.

When the Cold War died down, enthusiasm dropped. The explosion of the U.S. space shuttle *Challenger* undercut confidence. The Russian space station *Mir* became a comic debacle. People were fed up with it all.

The twentieth century ended up as a false start into space. We now have the advantage of taking the long view of space exploration. We also tend to have a different appreciation of time itself.

We see the year 2000 as a watershed in human history, not the least reason being that it marks the beginning of humans' truly engaging space.

When people look back 1,000 years from now, so many of our current fascinations will be blown away like chaff in the wind. People will see only a few significant developments, and one will surely be that humans permanently shifted their gaze from the ground to the galaxies.

The year 2000 will be the demarcation line between Before Space and After Space. People will be able to make that statement from the vantage point of watching 1,000 years of space exploration and seeing how fundamentally it shifted humans' conception of themselves.

Step One: The Space Station

The shift between eras started with the building of the International Space Station, which was considered a boondoggle at the time. Many wondered whether the minimal gains in scientific experimentation were worth the $60-billion cost. They rightly pointed out that much of the science could be gleaned with available tools that were much cheaper. However, the space station was significant not for the science but for the symbolism. People of that

TIME LEARNED MUCH, THOUGH NOT ABOUT SCIENCE. WHAT THEY LEARNED ABOUT WAS GLOBAL COOPERATION.

THE INTERNATIONAL SPACE STATION WAS THE FIRST COMBINED GLOBAL EFFORT BEHIND A MAJOR SPACE PROJECT. IT BROUGHT TOGETHER A DOZEN NATIONS, INCLUDING THE ONCE WARRING RUSSIA AND UNITED STATES. IT DREW IN SPACE NEOPHYTES LIKE JAPAN AND ITALY AND BRAZIL AND SHOWED HOW SMALLER COUNTRIES HAD MUCH TO CONTRIBUTE.

BUILDING THE STATION TOOK MORE THAN 150 ROCKET AND SHUTTLE LAUNCHINGS TO LIFT MATERIALS AND WORKERS. IT TOOK AN UNPRECEDENTED NUMBER OF SPACE WALKS TO DO THE CONSTRUCTION—MORE THAN ALL PREVIOUS SPACE WALKS COMBINED.

AND ONCE OPERATIONAL IN 2005, THE STATION ALLOWED MANY ASTRONAUTS TO GET USED TO LONG-TERM EXPOSURE TO SPACE, THE NEW NORM IF HUMANS WERE TO SERIOUSLY EXPLORE THE SOLAR SYSTEM.

WHILE HUMANS WERE GETTING THEIR SPACE LEGS IN THE FIRST DECADE OF THE CENTURY, UNMANNED PROBES WERE THE ADVANCE TEAMS PREPARING FOR EVENTUAL HUMAN ARRIVAL.

CHEAP, SMALL, POWERFUL COMPUTERS OVERTURNED THE OLD METHODS OF EXPLORATION, AS THEY HAD IN MANY OTHER FIELDS. INSTEAD OF HUGE, CUSTOMIZED SPACE VEHICLES, THIS DECADE SAW THE PROLIFERATION OF MANY SMALL PROBES USING OFF-THE-SHELF TECHNOLOGY.

THEY WERE ABLE TO CHECK OUT ALL THE PLANETS, AND MANY PASSING COMETS AND ASTEROIDS, WITHOUT RISKING HUMAN LIFE OR SPENDING MUCH MONEY. THE NEW FINDINGS PIQUED INTEREST AMONG SCIENTISTS AND THE PUBLIC IN SEEKING MORE DEFINITIVE ANSWERS BY SENDING ASTRONAUTS TO FOLLOW UP.

STEP TWO: THE MOON BASE

A MOON BASE WAS THE NEXT LOGICAL STEP. THE 1969 LUNAR LANDING STOLE THE DRAMA FROM THE RETURN TRIP TO THE MOON ALMOST FORTY YEARS LATER, BUT THE SERIES OF MISSIONS BEGINNING IN 2008 HAD MORE PRACTICAL VALUE AND MORE LONG-TERM CONSEQUENCES.

THE FIRST LUNAR BASE, COMPLETED IN 2013, FACED THE EARTH. THE BASE, NICKNAMED DRY DOCK, STARTED MODESTLY ENOUGH AS THE SUCCESSOR TO MANY SPACE STATION EXPERIMENTS, BUT IT SOON GREW INTO THE SITE FOR THE EARLY MINING OF MINERALS AND MATERIALS THAT COULD BE USED FOR MAKING FUELS AND SUPPLIES FOR LONG-TERM SPACE VOYAGES. THAT BASE LATER GREW INTO THE INTERPLANETARY LAUNCHING PAD USED BY OUR ERA'S GENERATION OF ROCKETS.

THE SECOND LUNAR BASE, NICKNAMED Black Eye, WAS COMPLETED IN 2015 ON THE FAR SIDE OF THE MOON AND BEGAN AS A BASE FOR COORDINATING EFFORTS TO EXTRACT WATER FROM ICE CRYSTALS IN CRATERS AT THE POLES. THIS WATER WAS NEEDED FOR THE FUEL FACTORIES AND THE LONG-TERM CAMPS ON THE NEAR SIDE.

BUT SOON Black Eye CAME TO HOUSE THE LIGHT AND RADIO TELESCOPES THAT WOULD PROBE THE UNIVERSE WITHOUT INTERFERENCE FROM EARTH'S RADIATION OR THE SUN'S HARSH LIGHT. THE MOON, WITH NO ATMOSPHERE AND VIRTUALLY NO GROUND MOTION, PROVIDED THE PERFECT BASE FOR TELESCOPES. MANY STARTLING DISCOVERIES CAME FROM THAT ONE SITE OVER THE NEXT THREE DECADES.

THE MOON BASES ALSO FIRED UP THE GLOBAL PUBLIC'S INTEREST IN FINALLY BEING ALLOWED TO GO VISIT THEM. SPACE TOURISM BOOMED, STARTING WITH THE BASIC ORBITAL PACKAGE IN 2009. PEOPLE COULD PAY $100,000 FOR THREE DAYS OF ORBITING EARTH ON THE SUCCESSORS TO THE SPACE SHUTTLES. DESPITE THE STEEP PRICE, AND TALES OF SPACE SICKNESS, THE WAITING LISTS QUICKLY EXTENDED TO A DECADE.

THE SUNNY-SIDE Dry Dock MOON BASE WAS AN EVEN MORE EXOTIC AND EXPENSIVE JOURNEY. A LUCKY FEW WERE ALLOWED TO GO THERE, AND THEY BECAME CELEBRITIES ON THEIR RETURN HOME.

STEP THREE: MISSION TO MARS

THE RISING INTEREST IN SPACE CAME TO A HEAD IN THE MISSION TO MARS, PLANNED OVER THE SECOND DECADE OF THE CENTURY AND CULMINATING IN 2020.

THE GLOBAL COMMUNITY HAD LEARNED MUCH ABOUT THE CHALLENGE OF COOPERATION IN BUILDING THE SPACE STATION AND THE MOON BASES, AND IT WAS READY TO INCREASE THE CHALLENGE WITH A TWO-AND-A-HALF-YEAR MISSION BY SIX ASTRONAUTS FOR A 500-DAY STAY.

THE MOUNTING EVIDENCE THAT MARS ALMOST CERTAINLY ONCE HELD LIFE—AND POSSIBLY STILL DID—ATTRACTED THE SUPPORT OF THE SCIENTIFIC COMMUNITY, BUT THE GLOBAL PUBLIC WAS ALSO ATTRACTED TO THE CHALLENGE AND, FRANKLY, THRILLED BY THE RISKS.

AS WITH THE MOON MISSION IN THE 1960s, THE GLOBAL OBSESSION WITH MARS HEIGHTENED DAY BY DAY. UNLIKE IN THE 1960s, ALL COUNTRIES OF THE WORLD FELT A PART OF THE EFFORT.

WE ALL KNOW THE DETAILS OF THAT HISTORIC VOYAGE, WITH THE FAMOUS FIRST STEPS BY SHEILA FISHER AS SHE BOUNDED OFF THE *Harmony* LANDING CRAFT IN JULY 2020. IT WAS ALMOST FIFTY YEARS AFTER NEIL ARMSTRONG HAD BOUNDED OFF THE *Eagle* ONTO THE MOON.

Almost the entire population of 8 billion people watched the historic television images beamed from 35 million miles away. They saw humans walking around a desert planet with an inhospitable atmosphere of carbon dioxide. The *Harmony* had landed near the bed of what had been a wide, flowing river, though now all that remained was red sand and rocks.

It was hard not to reflect on the fact that Mars may once have looked much more like Earth. Or that someday, with the destruction of the ecosystem, the Earth might look much like Mars.

And the audience saw the astounding image of Earth seen from Mars—not much bigger than Mars seen from Earth. It was a very small blue orb in a very black sky. Not much bigger than a star.

That image drove home the point to people at that time that they lived on a fragile little planet that could destroy itself and become like Mars, that all organisms crammed on Earth were intricately interdependent and needed to find a way to live together on that tiny little place.

The images from Mars drove home another point: The people on Earth were truly one global society, one race—the human race. The divisions people imposed on themselves looked ludicrous from afar, and a planet of warring nations, the state of affairs that had defined the previous century, made no sense anymore. Far better to channel the aspirations of the world's people into collectively pushing outward to the stars.

Those images, and the entire Mars mission, made a deep impression on the global community at that time. As we know, they kept pushing outward, as we still keep pushing. With this Space Age, the real Space Age, there's no end in sight.

PART FOUR

Birth of a Global Civilization

I F WE CAN SOLVE the key political and environmental problems laid out in the previous two sections and continue the global Long Boom, then certain consequences will follow. The growing global economy will swell the numbers of the new global middle class, well-off people who share certain values that transcend borders. This new middle class promises to be a force pushing for widespread changes, including greater democratic control of all aspects of the economy and society. And the burgeoning economy will bring affluence and rising standards of education, which almost always translate into a rise in the status of women.

Section IV looks beyond the technology and the economy to their wide-ranging effects on the many other aspects of our lives. Over the course of the twenty-first century, we will probably see such fundamental changes in our technology, science, government, and arts that we will begin to talk about a new kind of civilization, a global civilization. This civilization will coexist with the world's other great civilizations, which will continue to thrive.

These long-term social and cultural developments are not inevitable: We must not squander our historic opportunity and fail to achieve the full potential of the Long Boom. So this section also lays out ten guiding principles that will help bring about the Long Boom vision and will help anyone thrive in this emerging era. A more positive future is totally dependent on what we do today. We need to choose to create a better world. So we end the book with a challenge—and a choice.

11

The New
Global Middle Class

A key measure of success of the Long Boom is how many people are enjoying the benefits of a middle-class lifestyle. The growth of the new global middle class will be both a beneficial consequence of the Long Boom and a driver of continued economic expansion. These people will share many attributes and attitudes because they are increasingly exposed to a common global media and culture. They will be highly influential in the century to come.

URING THE FIRST HALF of our Long Boom era, the world has watched the emergence of a new global middle class. This somewhat hidden but inexorable trend is one of the key drivers bringing on a more positive future. On the simplest level, you can understand the phenomenon as an explosion in the numbers of middle-class people around the world. After World War II, the making of the middle class mostly took place in North America, Europe, and Japan—regions with about 800 million people by the 1980s. Though there were poor people in those societies, the majority belonged to the world's middle class, which also included a smattering of elites and affluent people in other parts of the world. It took the Long Boom era to start to spread the wealth. In the 1980s and 1990s, the developing world began to grow economically to the point where a significant middle class emerged. By the early 1990s, the middle-class numbers in the developing world approached roughly 400 million and were expected to double in a decade, particularly in Asia, which maintained the consistently highest growth rates. The Asian middle class alone—excluding the Japanese who had already made it—was expected to grow to 700 million people by the year 2010 and to have an estimated spending power of $9 trillion. The Asian crisis in the late 1990s forced some middle-class newcomers back into relative poverty, but many others hung on.

By 2000, midway through the Long Boom, roughly 1 billion people could be regarded as belonging to the global middle class. That's about one out of every six people in the entire world, and those numbers are poised to grow in the second half of the Long Boom. More than 3 billion people are actively participating in the global economy and positioning themselves to try to catch the next growth wave. About half the people in the Asian tigers of South Korea, Taiwan, Hong Kong, and Singapore had worked their way into the middle class by the 1990s. Nearly 20 percent of the emerging tigers of Thailand, Malaysia, and Indonesia had reached that point before slipping in the Asian crisis in 1998, though many will scramble back. About 10 percent of China's 1.2 billion people own their own homes. That's over 100 million people who are making the first steps to middle-class lives. And then there are tens of millions more middle-class prospects in Latin America—Mexico, Brazil, and Argentina—and pockets around the world. An estimated 30 percent of Russians have the middle-class mind-set, though not the wealth to go with it at this time.

The precise numbers of the global middle class are maddeningly difficult to come by. Middle class in the United States means something very different from the same category in India or Botswana. Some think of middle class in terms of income, some in terms of purchasing power, some in terms of education or even values. From a Long Boom perspective, being middle class is as much a state of mind as a material condition. The first characteristic has to do with becoming free from basic material wants. Members of the global middle class have reached the point where they don't worry about food or shelter and are on their way to accumulating consumer products to make their lives easier. From a global perspective, we're talking about achieving the basics: a television, a refrigerator, a washing machine, and the like. People need to accumulate enough material goods and achieve enough economic security to liberate the mind. Which brings up characteristic number two. Members of the global middle class place an extremely high value on education both for themselves and for their children. This has always been true of middle-class people, across nations and eras. They understand that education will allow them to remain in the class and will allow their children to do even better. Education becomes central to their lives, and a large proportion of their resources and time is devoted to it. Which then leads to characteristic number three.

Middle-class people always eventually want an increasing amount of personal freedom and control over their own lives. This *always* happens. A person gets his or her basic material needs met, gets a decent education, and eventually he or she will want freedom. This desire might first surface in social issues like wanting the freedom to choose their own mate. Then it might appear as wanting the economic freedom to choose their own line of work. But eventually it means wanting the freedom to speak one's mind and have some say in how the community is run or who will lead the nation. In every case in which a country has experienced strong economic growth and a burgeoning middle class, the pressure for democratic political reform has eventually followed. It might not happen right away. The emerging class might defer such reform in order to sustain the growth longer and avoid violent conflict. But at some point, the middle class is unable to repress those desires and will force the change.

Moderation is another one of those middle-class characteristics that bode well for our future. Middle-class people are relatively moderate in their political views. They have too much at stake to risk being mesmerized by radical plans to overturn the status quo. The dispossessed, who have nothing to lose, and the very rich, who will always survive, are more susceptible to the seductions of radicalism. Middle-class youth might toy with revolution, but once they buy a house and build a stake in the society, they rapidly lose interest. Some people wring their hands over this moderate bourgeois trait, but it's

completely in sync with the Long Boom mode of operation. As long
as the general trends are heading in the right direction and the world
is evolving toward a more positive future, having a large, stable middle class is fantastic. They are a political force acting as political ballast that keeps the ship from tipping too far to the left or to the right.

One final relevant characteristic: Middle class people have the freedom to think about the future. They are freed from the wants that
keep others focused on survival in the present. In all other eras, only
the handful of people who made up a society's elite had the luxury to
think that expansively. Today, we have a sixth of the world's population in a position to think beyond the day-to-day. For example, middle-class people care deeply about the environment and make
protecting the environment a political issue that must be dealt with
now. In general, middle-class people can afford to engage their minds
on higher-level problems, the ones that depend on a vision that's
more long-term.

The Truly Global Media

What about the global dimension of the global middle class? So far
we've talked only about the growth of the middle class in various regions of the world. You might think the label reflects the idea that
the rise of the middle class is simply a global phenomenon, happening simultaneously but separately in many different places. Although
that's true, the label carries more meaning. The global middle class
actually is taking on the characteristics of one integrated class
throughout the whole world. The members of the class share so many
characteristics and values that increasingly what specific nation they
come from is much less important. Their identity is more and more
membership in this class rather than citizenship in a particular nation. They are communicating with each other and sharing common
media. They are becoming truly global people, and this is really new.

Increasing globalization is inevitable as technology links more and
more of the world together. You may as well begin tracking it and adjust your plans to its inexorable spread. This genie isn't going back in
the bottle. The world has arrived at the point where the interconnections across the planet have reached a critical mass, and their number

and volume can only increase. And on the backs of that technological infrastructure, the globalization will spread.

Take the media. At the very beginning of our Long Boom era, Ted Turner came up with the concept of a global television news station, CNN. The name—Cable News Network—reflects how dependent the new media were on the new infrastructure of that time: cable. After CNN became wildly successful in the 1980s, global competitors popped up—notably Rupert Murdoch's Sky Television. Again, check out the name, which reflects a dependency on the new infrastructure of the 1990s: satellites. With the spread of satellites and receiving dishes around the planet, the truly global medium of television saturated the world. The typical person around the world could choose from twelve channels, according to a Roper survey in the mid-1990s. North Americans have the largest selection, averaging twenty-seven channels. Western Europeans received an average of fourteen, Latin Americans and central Europeans have twelve, Middle Easterners have eleven, and Asians, nine. It's not that all these channels beam programs into the void. People throughout the world, even in developing regions, spend large amounts of time each day watching TV. Middle Easterners watch the most television of any major region, an average of 3.6 hours per day. North Americans, including Mexicans, are second, with 2.9 hours.

Though all regions have local shows produced in local languages, much of the programming comes from two main sources, the United States and Britain. Hollywood sitcoms, television series, feature movies, and old reruns are often the standard fare in many of these countries. The only difference is the language in which they are dubbed. MTV, the music video channel, which also began in the early 1980s, now reaches about 290 million viewers in 83 countries. CNN alone now reaches 200 countries. It has become the ubiquitous common news source for the roving ranks of the global middle class. No matter what hotel room you end up in, there's your CNN.

Cultural critics in many countries regularly express concern about the impact of U.S. media on their societies. But we're not heading into a future of one homogeneous global culture that will suffocate the multiplicity of magnificent cultures found around the world. People always worry that the advance of a global culture will mean that everyone will munch nothing but McDonald's hamburgers and just stare at a tube showing reruns of *The Simpsons*. That simply will not be the case. We will see the emergence of a subtle, complex, variegated global culture that will overlay the world's existing cultures without snuffing them out. All the signs since the early 1980s indicate that local cultures are blossoming right alongside the spread of globalization. The people of Provence are just as fiercely devoted to their 800-year traditions of cuisine and song and dress and myths and dialect as they ever were—perhaps more so. They can still appreciate those old ways while flipping through a magazine with Benetton advertising.

The layering of a global culture over local cultures will resemble something like what has developed in the United States. There is clearly an American culture that almost everyone absorbs, understands, and mostly appreciates, but each region of the country still retains a very distinct culture that residents identify with. And then there are finer and finer cultural distinctions and identities that are even more rooted in specific localities. So an individual can be a part of American culture, and New England culture, and Boston culture, and even the culture of the working-class South Side. Any visitor can list huge differences between the people of Grand Forks, North Dakota, and Mobile, Alabama. But people from both places laugh at the same *Seinfeld* jokes. Something similar is going to happen in the world at large. A global culture will emerge, and virtually everyone will be fluent in it—yet paradoxically, the tiniest cultures will also flourish.

The World Wide Web is the new global medium that is perfectly suited to this paradoxical development. In many ways, the Web is enabling both global cross-fertilization and the enrichment of local communities. At the global level, the Web allows extraordinary access to the broadest range of information in a depth that only recently would have been inconceivable. You can think of the Web as the medium of that rising global middle class. A member living in a country with poor local media can tap into the same *New York Times* delivered to every magnate in Manhattan. All members of the global middle class can get their hands on the same data and raw material at the same time. The result is a common base of understanding and shared experiences that was impossible as recently as the early 1990s. One of the first big shared experiences that proved the point was the spring 1997 chess match between world champion Garry Kasparov and Deep Blue, IBM's supercomputer. The official website reporting the six-game series registered 74 million "hits" from 106 countries over nine days, which translated into 4 million individual visitors. That event was a watershed for the nascent media and just a taste of what is to come.

However, the Web also allows local communities to stay stitched together across wide expanses of physical space. A member of that global middle class roaming far across the world on business can instantaneously tap into information from home, like the hometown newspaper or local high school sports scores. And the Web is a boon not just to physical communities, but also to communities of interest. A person living in isolated rural Montana and fascinated by flamenco music would be extremely lucky to find others nearby with the same passion. The local radio stations are unlikely to devote any of their precious time on scarce airwaves to music with such a limited draw. And how many magazines are published about the subject? But the Web will now allow that person to become part of a lively group of fellow enthusiasts from all parts of the world—including Spain itself. And people can publish their thoughts on the art without waiting for some interest from a print publisher. And soon that person will be able to pick up an infinite variety of music channels streaming across the Net. Far from dying out, flamenco will flourish with the new globalization.

The Plane People

Take any international flight. After you sit back and enjoy the film, undoubtedly something from Hollywood, take a look around you and study the people, the plane people. The youths—no matter what nationality or what ethnicity—all dress the same. In mid-1999, the visor of a hat turns to the back of the head. In 2000, it may well turn to the side. No matter what language they speak, the music in their Walkmans will be similar, falling within a range of current global hits. There will be very few exceptions. Despite growing up in disparate localities, each kid in that plane will have somehow learned the code. The adults, likewise, will have a dress and conduct code that generally applies across nationalities. You can study the subtle variations among people as they sip their French wine and read their English-language magazines.

These plane people are the new global middle class. Besides consuming the burgeoning global media and culture, they're traveling. The numbers are truly astounding. In 1980, about 287 million people took international trips as tourists. By the late 1990s, that number had more than doubled to 595 million international tourists a year. The World Tourism Organization predicts that by 2020, that number will nearly have tripled to 1.6 billion international tourists a year—out of an estimated population of 7.8 billion. That will be 20 percent of the people in the world making a foreign trip. In that same twenty years, spending on travel is expected to grow fivefold from a base of $4.2 trillion in the year 2000. (That spending includes travel, room, and board plus discretionary expenses. And that is *trillion*, not billion. The travel industry accounts for 10 percent of the world's annual economic output.) These numbers point to a planet on the move. Today the global airline industry flies about 6 billion trips a year. Even Americans, traditionally stay-at-homes compared to Europeans, have 45 million passports in circulation.

The plane people, the new global middle class, are becoming one. They are getting much of their news and information from common global media. They are getting a big dose of their entertainment from the global culture industry. They are buying similar products and wearing similar clothes. And on top of it all, they are criss-crossing the planet, visiting previously foreign countries at a mind-boggling rate. As they sit in those planes, they are chatting to a person who is the mirror image of themselves. Then they bump into them, or others just like them, in the hotel, or the museum, or the street café. They like these plane people. They seem to have just as much in common with them as they do with their compatriots back home. And the middle-class people they deal with and meet in the host country—they're not bad either. They're like the plane people—only on the ground. This is a world that is globalizing at a fevered pace. From the Long Boom perspective, this is a beautiful development in the interests of long-term geopolitical stability and peace. The more the global middle class grows, and the more familiar they become with their cohorts across national borders, the more the prospects for peace improve.

Date: Friday, December 23, 2010
Begin File: 12:20:15 P.M., American Pacific Standard Time
End File: 1:11:43 P.M., American Pacific Standard Time

I'm in the hills of northern California. I'm writing to you folks even though I'm with most of you. I'm taking a noontime walk by myself into the woods while you hang out or prepare tonight's holiday feast. I needed to get away from the cabins and the kids and do my annual letter. Can't skip a year at this point. This year I'm writing with my new Talkman. For the technophobes among you, it looks like those old Walkmans that we used to have for listening to music tapes long ago. Was that the 1980s? Man, we're getting old. Anyhow, now they actually capture your voice and immediately transcribe all the words onto a computer disk, cleaning up the language as you go. It actually does an excellent job in transcription, making me sound much more melodious than I actually sound to the naked ear. I can then ship it over the Net before I make it back to the cabins, and you can flip it on your book tablet this evening or even print it out just like old times.

I'm writing you this letter because I love you guys. I love this community. I love Mol and Amy. There is a lot of love around here, a lot of warmth, good feeling. A lot of sense of accomplishment. We did much in the last ten years. We worked our tails off. But it feels good, because we made it through. We made it through our various crises, all that craziness and hard times, all those ups and downs. And now we are gathered once again for the holidays at the cabins that we've dubbed the Summit. What a difference this place has made for all of us. We still don't gather quite as often as I'd like and enjoy the peace of this place nearly enough. I still would like to notch back a level of intensity in my life. But there's such a difference between the pace of our lives today and the insanity of ten years ago. How did we pull that off? I've got my candidates for the answer.

For one thing, we became full-fledged knowledge workers. Ten years ago, we barely understood what that term meant, and we certainly didn't understand how those workers would be compensated. But we soon figured out that good ideas, indeed, held great value, and that as long as we kept learning and evolving and coming up with good ideas, we would be compensated quite well. We began to be paid for the products of our fertile brains rather than paid for sitting at a desk for sixty hours a week. Compensation was not tied to time. What a concept! One really great idea could provide income for quite a while—creating more free time for other pursuits.

The promise of the technology also finally began to deliver. This Talkman is a big help. I can do my knowledge work when and where it's convenient, before Mol is up in the morning, or when Amy is out on a date for the night. I can do it right now walking down the pathway, taking a stroll in the hills surrounding our Summit, looking at the beautiful views of the Pacific Ocean through the trees. Partly because of the technology, we were able to force a lot more flexibility into our organizations and create a lot more variations in how we could work. That allowed us to stay deeply involved in our personal lives and the lives of our children while carving out periods of intense concentration and creativity focused on work.

The technology, the adaptable organizations, and the higher levels of compensation gave us all more ability to choose. More than any other generation, we were able to make more individual choices about how we wanted to tailor our lives. Some kept throwing themselves into moneymaking, and they made gobs. Some dedicated themselves to changing the world—and they found great fulfillment. Others, like us, did some of both but channeled quite a bit of energy into personal passions. Not that making those decisions came easy. You know my struggles over boundaries. As the ability to work everywhere expanded, everybody needed to establish boundaries between work and home—but in the end, we laid down the line exactly where we wanted it. No boss told us what to do. No homogeneous model existed. We were free to design our own model. It was the ultimate triumph of diversity. I chose to create my life by focusing more time on my family—Mol and Amy. I'm feeling good about my choice.

I'm fifty now, and all of us in this network are at the point where we are near the top of our respective fields and are in a position to exert our maximum influence. I feel accomplished in a way that I never thought I would feel ten years ago. A theme of this letter is accomplishment—not total accomplishment, but I feel pretty good. I feel proud because I was part of a country that mostly lived up to its opportunity. As a people, we rose to the occasion, and I was a part of that. And we are in a very different world right now, partly because Americans made many wise, magnanimous decisions. But more than that, I think that as a group, we did our part to help make the world a better place. Who would have thought that we could help realize the high-minded ideals for the world that we talked about in our radical youth? Who would have thought that this group of idealists could really make an impact?

Not that the world is free from all problems. The environment in the past decade has been slowly getting worse, reminding us that we've got to solve this problem once and for all. At least we're living in a world where we have hope that the environmental problems can be solved. It looks as if the world could actually begin lowering overall pollution levels soon, but we're not there yet. That's our big challenge for the next decade. It still terrifies people that we won't turn the corner from expanding to decreasing pollution. Like an ocean liner plowing straight ahead, it's hard to turn this baby. And we've got the big Caspian Sea Crisis going on. Who knows what's gonna happen there? And some regions of the world, like Africa, still haven't participated fully in the boom. We have ignored a lot of people around the world. We need to help them out. Our work is not yet over. We really need to keep pushing. But, you guys, let's reconnect for a few days.

12

THE EMERGENCE
of WOMEN

*The widening opportunities for women have been a central part of
the story of the expanding economy of developed nations throughout the twentieth century. We can expect the same to happen in a
global context in the coming decades. Not only will women benefit
from the Long Boom, but the Long Boom will benefit from unleashing the talents and energies of half the potential workers in the
world.*

O N THE BACK OF THE INEVITABLE rise of the new global middle
class comes another inevitable development: a rise in the status of women all around the world. The empowering of women on a
trajectory toward full equality with men is inevitable. In many ways,
it's simply a function of the spread of that global middle class. The
historical record pretty clearly backs up this symbiotic relationship
between the rise of the middle class and the rise of women. The rise
of women has a direct correlation to the development of the two pil-
lars of the middle-class lifestyle: increased affluence and education.
The best test case is in Western societies that experienced the growth
of a large middle class in the first place and for the most sustained period of time. This kind of broad social change does not happen im-

mediately but only through waves of changes that build on each other and play out over a long time. You can roughly describe the rise of American women, and the women's movement that accompanied it, as coming in three waves.

The first wave occurred from about 1880 to 1920, the era of the great rise of industrial society. In the United States, those forty years marked the transformation from an agrarian nation of dispersed farmers to an industrial nation of densely populated cities. That period also saw the birth of the modern American middle class. It was in this relatively new environment of the nascent middle class that certain thresholds of affluence and minimal education were attained, including by women and girls. That minimal taste of freedom brought a big push for the most basic political rights—including the right to vote. That era was filled with the struggle of the suffragists for basic voting rights, pretty much Square One in the journey toward equal political rights and equal protection under the law. In 1920, women won the right to vote through an amendment to the U.S. Constitution, closing that wave of changes and moving onto the next one.

The next period in the rise of women could roughly be classified as between 1920 and 1960, which coincided with the rise of the mass consumer society and the further broadening and deepening of the middle class. Part of that rise in the status of women can be attributed to the proliferation of cheap home appliances. This was the first era in which most U.S. homes became electrified and partially automated. The period started with people still talking about the home electric motor, one big motor that could be hooked up to various appliances, one at a time. So you'd use to it power your sewing machine for a while, then lug it into the kitchen to power a fan, and then maybe connect it to a new machine called a vacuum cleaner. The paradigm quickly shifted as the electric motors shrank in size, increased in power, and dropped dramatically in price. They got so small and cheap that individual electric motors could be installed in each of the individual appliances. Meanwhile, the electric power grid had fingered its way through cities and neighborhoods and into almost every single room in every house. The appliances could be plugged into the uniform electric socket found everywhere. (Does this sound familiar? We're in the midst of the same proliferation of cheap computer chips and the extension of the soon-to-be ubiquitous telecommunications grid today. It will have a similarly widespread, yet different, social effect.)

This technological development of cheap home appliances did not so much liberate middle-class women from housework—they had already been liberated by domestic servants. In fact, after agricultural workers, domestic servants were the second largest class of workers in the United States around 1900. The appliances "liberated" these domestic servants from their work *and* their livelihood and forced a migration of working-class women into other jobs, including factory work, which was more like the work men did. The onset of World War II accelerated that process for women of all classes, who were needed to help keep the economy going while the men went to war. When the men came back from World War II to rejoin the economy and take their old jobs, women were not as receptive to going back to the home, though most did. However, this displacement could be seen as the beginning of a slow buildup of discontent among women. This period of 1920 to 1960 saw a slow accumulation of advances for women but no widespread breakthrough in their status. For example, the opportunities for higher education for women started expanding in the 1930s and showed substantial growth, though the numbers of women entering college did not reach critical mass until the 1960s. On the other hand, the opportunities at the workplace did not keep pace in the 1930s, 1940s, and 1950s, and college-educated women were tracked into certain kinds of work, such as elementary-school teaching, and were prevented from getting other jobs with wide responsibilities. This circumstance helped contribute to the pressure cooker effect of built-up resentment among women seeking widespread change. That would explode in the next era, starting in the 1960s.

The third wave of changes, in the period from 1960 to 2000, was driven by the Baby Boomers, the cohort that started to move through the system of higher education and the workplace like a boar down the throat of a python. Born in the postwar boom, most of this huge number of young people were living in unprecedented affluence. Not only was the middle class still expanding, but a substantial upper middle class evolved. And some of the key beneficiaries of this next stage in the evolution of the middle class were women. This was the first generation in which women were accorded roughly the same access to higher education. Almost as many Baby Boom women went to college in the 1960s as men did. By 1988, the actual numbers evened up, and then more women than men were enrolled in institutions of higher education. This statistic was no fluke because the tilt toward women has been growing year by year. By 1996, there were 8.4 million women and only 6.7 million men enrolled in college, according to the U.S. Department of Education. By 2007, the department projects, the gender gap will be even larger, with 9.2 million women enrolled and only 6.9 million men. What's more, women outnumber men in every category of higher education: in public, private, and religious institutions, in four-year and two-year programs. The skew is even larger among those pursuing part-time studies, and among older people, and African-Americans. The same gender trend is now playing out in lower education, too. In 1992, the publication of a controversial study by the American Association of University Women, "How Schools Shortchange Girls," fueled the perception that young girls face widespread inequalities in the elementary and secondary schools. The study declared that girls faced biases from preschool to high school, through texts and tests geared to boys and through teacher neglect. At the end of the decade, however, by almost all measures, girls actually beat out boys in school. They got better grades, had higher reading and writing scores, had higher class ranks and more school honors, and were more likely to take advanced-placement tests.

This equality for women in education set in motion a chain reaction that has reverberated through other parts of the economy and society. Those highly educated Boomer women enter the workforce and prove that they can do just as good a job as—if not better than—their male colleagues. Over time, their own self-perception changes, as well as the views of the men they work with. As they advance through their careers, they take on more managerial responsibility and leadership roles and begin to change the organization itself and the environment for women who are entering the organization under them. Sure, they hit glass ceilings that surreptitiously protect concentrated centers of power held by men, but these days, they bump into that ceiling far less frequently, and with time, those ceilings will go, too. The rising education of women plays out in many spheres, from the macro, like the economy, to the micro, like the home. These women usually marry partners who are their equals, and their relationships evolve as much more equal and balanced than those of the past.

That more equitable couple then raises the next generation of children, who are more likely to see this equality as the way of the world. Whether girls or boys, they are more likely to grow up in an environment where women are the equals of men. The parents reinforce this equality each day, and the community they are raised in appears to hold those same values. So a young girl born today, at the end of this third stage in the inexorable rise of American women, will see much less of the stereotypical prejudice that women are not equal to men. To be sure, she won't confront a perfectly equitable environment, and she might be thrown off by media images of women, or latent cultural stereotyping, or discrimination. But she is far more likely than women in the past to believe she is equal, that she will mostly live her life as an equal with men. Compared to her Boomer mother, who struggled to get a higher education, or compared to her grandmother, who had few options but the home, or compared to her great-grandmother, who could run a household but not vote, that girl will be free to pursue her dreams.

Roughly this same three-stage process took place in Europe and is occurring to various degrees all over the world, though mostly with a time lag. Every time the economy becomes sophisticated enough and potent enough to grow a substantial middle class, prospects for women begin to rise. So we see a lot of places that have entered the first phase, in which women have been accorded basic political rights like the right to vote. This right may also depend on purely political factors apart from a country's economic development—like international pressure to conform to standard human rights.

As to the second phase, much of the world seems stuck there. Certain countries have developed large middle classes, and many of the women in these countries have experienced more affluent lives and even higher education, but they remain locked out of the core economy and involvement in the larger society. They are trapped in that pressure cooker stage of increasing frustration and resentment, and they are at the point of busting out and entering the next stage, which will move them toward real, full equality. However, the rise of women is not an automatic outcome of economic growth. Cultural factors play a huge part in thwarting or facilitating the rise. These cultural forces can be so strong that they overwhelm the quite powerful economic forces themselves. No country is a clearer example than Japan. By all measures, Japan is as economically developed as the United States and Europe and has as big a middle class, if not a bigger one. Yet Japanese women are locked out of almost any important role in the economy beyond raising the next generation, which, granted, is extremely important. Japanese women of recent generations have been highly educated, but they have been stymied in their career development and have not been able to contribute to the Japanese economy at large. This situation is doubly bad. It has led to built-up resentments that have women about to explode. It has also led to a lethargic economy that is about to implode. The Japanese economy has many problems, but one of the most fundamental is that the Japanese utilize only half their talent pool.

THE FEMALE FUTURE

Let's take a head count of everybody on the planet. Let's see a show of hands of everyone who is female. Good. Now let's see the hands of everyone who is male. OK. Looks as if we have a pretty even split. Now, how many of you women really feel as if you have a fair shake in the world and just as good a deal as men? Almost certainly most women in the world would feel like second-class citizens. This male-female divide is one of the most, if not the most, fundamental on the planet. Everybody confronts it almost every day. Few live without daily interactions with the opposite sex, and everybody sees the rifts between the sexes, how they don't communicate and don't get along, how one side, usually the males, exploits the other. If the Long Boom contemplates mending the rifts between the Western and Asian civilizations, between the Left and the Right on the political spectrum, then it's worth reflecting a bit on this rift of all rifts, the one between women and men. If we're thinking about building a better future for

the world, then that future better work well for the female half of the
population. So we can sit here and make the moral appeal that treating women equally is the right and decent thing to do. That's a fine
argument, but it just hasn't worked despite its periodic appeals
through the ages. Another effective argument for treating women
equally might be made on economic grounds. It's not just for the best
interests of women, but for those of men as well. We'll all be better
off in the end.

Women are different from men. As they say in the software business, that's a feature, not a bug. For a long time, those pushing for
equal rights for women stressed the ways in which women are the
same as men, so that they would be accorded equal treatment. Whatever the tactical merits of that approach, it's not accurate. Because
two things are equal does not mean that they are identical. They can
be equally valid or valuable, but different. So women and men are
not the same, and the source of their value to each other is in their
differences. That value comes through in individual relationships and
the economy as a whole. The typical woman sees the world somewhat differently from the typical man, perceives different information as more important, takes away different feelings from the same
situation, thinks through a problem differently, and expresses herself
differently. Women have far more in common with men than not,
but they still may have a slightly different mind-set and a slightly different set of values.

Our basic rule of twos holds that you always want at least two
healthy alternatives in any situation, two vigorous forces playing off
each other. You can't get more fundamental than the two forces of
men and women, the yin and yang that from the beginning of time
have acted as the metaphor for all interdependent but distinct forces.
Ideally, to make a healthier whole, you want both those forces actively
engaged in your society and your economy. The rule of twos has never
been more important than in the new knowledge economy emerging
today, which values infinite variations in new ideas and great diversity as a source of those ideas. Any company or organization or industry or nation wants to create the context that will allow diverse minds
to rub up against each other and spark the next great idea. You definitely want women in the mix. Without them, you've lopped off half

the potential ideas right from the outset. With them, you have an intermixing of the masculine and the feminine that could create some interesting new synthesis. By extension, the drive for diversity carries beyond drawing women into the mix. Women are the forerunners of other groups that have been left out of the flow of the mainstream economy. Their efforts for inclusion predate the efforts of other minority groups. But the same arguments apply all around. You can argue for their inclusion from the basis of fairness toward the individual. Or you can argue for the good of the system, the economy as a whole. They both point in the same direction. Diversity is good.

When societies do not allow women to freely participate in the economy, they are entering the global economy with only half their potential hard workers, half their potential knowledge workers, half their potential child prodigies. This is an obvious point, but it bears repeating, given the way women are treated in much of the world. In the United States, for example, women are starting small businesses at twice the rate of men. They already own an estimated 8 million firms, employing about 18.5 million people, and generating more than $3 trillion in sales and revenues. Part of the secret of the Long Boom will be tapping into those resources offered by women and allowing their potential to come out. This increasing participation of women in the global economy will be part of the long-term energizers of the Long Boom into the next century.

We are not suggesting that the process of equal inclusion of women will be easy. Women in many countries are still trapped in subordination to men through systemic discrimination and violence. They face entire legal systems that severely tilt the playing field against them and toward men. For example, women in many countries—by law—cannot have a controlling share of the family income, even though numerous studies show that when women control household income, they allocate more resources to the nutrition, health, and education of children—all vital to a country's economic development. Women face similar systematic discrimination in access to education. Although gender gaps in education are closing worldwide, the number of girls enrolled in school still falls well below the number of boys, especially in secondary schools and above. In some extreme countries, like Afghanistan, girls are not even educated. Since the

Muslim fundamentalist Taliban took power in 1996, all girls have been shut out of school, all women have been denied the right to a job or any position of visible authority. A few have been stoned to death for appearing in public without the proper attire—even if they simply don't have the thin mesh covering the front of their eyes. The case of Afghanistan's war against women is extreme, though the use of violence to enforce systems of discrimination is not. Some of the violence is state-sanctioned, but much of it is carried out in a social context by men, who often know the women being punished and use violence to keep them in their subordinate place. The state often looks the other way or does little to stop the violence and rectify the situation. A World Bank analysis of violence against women in thirty-five industrialized and developing countries found that about one-third of all women have suffered abuse at the hands of an intimate partner. Other analyses of rape statistics in these countries show that as many as one in five women will be a victim of rape in her lifetime. Yet in many countries, particularly in Latin America, a rapist is exonerated if he offers to marry the victim and she accepts.

The rise of women will be difficult to achieve without directly challenging the legal and quasi-legal systems denying women fundamental civil, social, political, and economic rights. Some of this challenge—especially of the most egregious violations—has to come from direct pressure by the global community. However, many of these systems are cultural in origin and are very complicated to challenge or change. The rise of women in the West, as described above, came within a culture that for centuries held a fundamental value of human equality in the abstract, even though this equality was withheld from women and nonwhites. This egalitarian ideal could be cited by those seeking change.

Non-western cultures need to work out the evolution in the status of women in their own way, perhaps in a better way than the West has handled it. The strong family unit is of high value to Asians and Latin Americans, for example. This value gives them a social cohesion and even an economic asset that they don't want to lose. However, the general lot of women in those societies can be improved and their roles enhanced. The cultures involved will have to choose how to achieve these goals. Values have a way of evolving to fit practical realities, particularly economic realities. That's not to say that values are arbitrary, but they are social constructs that change when the environment changes. In the old economic reality of Saudi Arabia, awash with oil money, women were not allowed to drive cars, so they needed to be chauffeured everywhere, and hundreds of thousands of drivers were imported from other countries to fit this peculiar need. However, with the collapse of oil prices in the late 1990s, the austere new reality is bringing pressure to send the chauffeurs home. Will Saudi women start driving soon?

The world is heading not just toward more global economic growth, but also toward more democracy. Political democracy, in a broad sense, is becoming the price of admission for deeper engagement in the global economy and the greater global community. Whose voices are going to be heard? Increasingly, those voices are going to be women's. As political systems move toward more democratic structures, half the population voting will be women. A peasant woman's first vote in her life might not be distinguished from the vote of her husband, but later, she may vote differently. And an educated middle-class woman first given suffrage may cast an independent vote right from the start. The polling data in Western countries clearly show gender differences in votes on numerous issues. As the Long Boom proceeds, an increasing number of political, economic and social institutions will become more democratic and women will increasingly participate. More and more, women's voices will be heard and their influence felt. Their values will shape all of us.

Date: 2020.12.17
GPS Position: 12.3 kilometers SSW of Capetown
Start: 14:12:48 P.M., Greenwich Mean Time
Finish: 15:03:02 P.M., Greenwich Mean Time
Selected Languages: American English, Mandarin, French

I'm standing on the thin point of the peninsula south of Capetown, where two great oceans meet. The Atlantic Ocean comes down on one side and slams up against the coast off my right foot. The Indian Ocean comes down on the other side and slams into the base of a rock cliff just off my left foot. The two oceans are mingling out in front of me, and I can't tell where one ends and the other starts. Think of the Atlantic Ocean as Western civilization, as Europe, North America, and Latin America, coming down through that giant ocean that has defined so much of their common history and reinforced their civilization. And think of the Indian Ocean as Asian civilization, as all the great Asian peoples who have been linked by those waters and the subsidiary seas that have carried all the communication and trade for centuries. Here, off this point, Western civilization and Asian civilization meet and are completely blended, completely interconnected. And that's what we've done in this world, that's what we've pulled off in the last forty years. We've merged two sides of the world, we've interwoven a dense web of connection that knows no boundaries. It's metaphorically in front of me here in Capetown.

Capetown reminds me of San Francisco, and all of southern Africa reminds me of California. The natural environment is very much the same. There are the beautiful beaches and great surfing. There are the mountains that can get pretty darn cold. The dry hills are perfect for wine making. The rich farmlands produce high yields of crops. The deserts bake you in the middle of the day. It's California all over, except upside down. Here I am writing my year-end letter in the middle of summertime. The sun is warm, I'm in shorts, and a cool breeze is coming off those oceans. This isn't the Africa that most people think about. They still think of Africa as sweltering jungles, and broken-down infrastructure, and people demoralized by war. Despite quite a bit of progress, the image sticks, and it's not completely out of sync with reality. Which is partly why I am here.

I came to Africa because of *empathy*. Over the years, I've found that through empathy, everything can eventually get solved. It was the secret to smoothing out my personal relationships because, when you really feel what that other person is feeling and really understand what that person is going through, progress can always be made. Through empathy, the channels for feeling and understanding open up. It's the starting point for figuring out solutions together. Empathy had been largely absent when it came to thinking about Africa. The global community had essentially ignored the region through the second half of the twentieth century. We let too many atrocities happen. We didn't provide nearly enough help for Africans to solve their problems. At least in the last ten years, we've started. Amy moved here two years ago to do her part. And now Mol and I have moved over for an extended spell.

The same merging that I was reflecting on between the West and the East has been taking place over the last forty years in other areas—certainly here between blacks and whites. In 1980, South Africa was a war zone, with blacks fighting apartheid. The whole of southern Africa was seething with black revolutionary movements fighting white control. Today blacks and whites are building on a couple decades of working together, and those fundamental racial divisions are truly melting down. We haven't totally healed that breach between black and white yet. It runs deep in the minds of many people. But that's changing more and more, thanks to a generational change in mind-set. The same goes for the breach between Western civilization and Islamic civilization. In 1980, Iran held U.S. hostages, and Israel was fighting Palestinians who had taken over southern Lebanon. But today those warring, hate-filled relations have been left behind. The last ten years have seen a real rapprochement, partly because both sides have started to empathize. Men and women marked another severe divide in 1980. Men ran almost everything, and women were locked out of power. Now the difference between the treatment of the sexes is negligible, and power is remarkably evenly distributed.

What made people empathize more? They saw everything. Everybody saw everybody. The whole world got so interconnected technologically that every region literally became like a person's backyard. The big breakthrough came with the whopping bandwidth that made video connections common. With screens the size of picture windows, people could look out their windows and see a Mongolian neighborhood as easily as the house across the street. Video cameras were pointed everywhere, and millions of people created videos. Regular phone and e-mail contacts across the world also came with a visual component. That stimulated even more physical travel, which contributed to greater understanding. So many people witnessed problem areas firsthand that they started thinking that the problems needed to be solved once and for all. We were all bumping into each other much more frequently, and one way or the other, we've all got to thrive. It was like that old movie Network from our youth in the 1970s. The guy who anchored the T.V. news stood up and got his entire audience to open their windows and yell, "I won't take it anymore." This time it was a very different network that solved the problem—the interconnected network rather than the monolithic broadcast one.

It's interesting how empathy became a practical strategy that worked within the networked economy of increasing returns that has underpinned the Long Boom. In the old world, empathy was a weakness because it diverted energy to others that people felt should be used for individual advancement. But as scarcity gave way to plenty, people realized that empathy was a strength because it bound the individual to the community and brought even greater returns to everyone in the end. Fear begets more fear; love begets more love—which kind of world would you rather live in? I know what I choose.

So here I am on this rocky point, looking out over the Atlantic and Indian Oceans, writing another year-end letter. The amazing thing this year is that I'm talking into a device that not only transcribes my words, but also simultaneously translates them into other languages. It then links up to satellites and routes the various versions over the Net to our extended family, which, over the last ten years, has spread all over the world. As a courtesy, I put the letter into Chinese and French so all family members can read it in their native language. You can hear my letter as I talk, or you can pick it up and read it. In this case, I'm not using video. You have to imagine this scene as I describe it. I'm still a writer at heart.

I'm balancing on these rocks and thinking about how we finally balanced the economy and the environment. The situation at the turn of the century was way out of balance, and the world in 2010 was still cockeyed. But now in 2020, we're finally getting it right. We aren't totally there yet, but we have finally stemmed the growth of pollution and waste. We are now decreasing those levels and are even starting to clean up. Over the course of the century, we can expect to get back to a balanced planet. It's as if we're walking on one of those horizontal bars, and it's steady and we're sure-footed, and we're walking very skillfully down it. We had been leaning in one direction and were about to tumble off, but we got our balance, and now we are walking the line.

I'm breathing in this fresh ocean air and thinking how alive I feel. You guys, we all have ducked the death dart. For generations, men were dying in their mid-fifties. Many of our fathers didn't make it much beyond. Mine didn't. Yet most of the men among us are turning sixty this year. And we are a healthy bunch. I've been told I could easily live to be a hundred, and it's not just limping life—it's a very alive and mobile life that once was associated with life at age forty. I could live into the middle of the century. I never would have imagined I'd live until 2050. But we are thinking longer-term now. If I do live that long, I just hope Mol will be with me. I can't imagine life without Mol.

It's about time we turn over the world to Amy's generation. She's now twenty-five and shows all the exuberance and energy that we had when we first seriously entered the world. She's much better prepared than we were. She's spent the last twenty years learning about the new systems our generation set up. She and her cohorts have got this connected global environment down. They're just coming out of their formative years and taking their rightful position in the global community. We're all going to be better off because these kids are going to run things right. They're going to build things far beyond our expectations. They'll outachieve their parents' generation in much the same way as we outachieved our parents.

Just as I say that, I can hear the deep, slow beat of music resonating from someplace down the cliff, probably on the beach. Those who are listening to the verbal version of my letter can hear the sound in the background. We're all very familiar with the music coming out of Africa. It's not even considered African music anymore, but global music, the sound of the new world. Africans have really tapped into something vital with that sound. Music is a perfect model for something that communicates across cultures and ignores all the other barriers that humans put up between themselves. Music is a form of communication that is translingual, transcultural, transcivilizational. A common music is the perfect expression of this nascent global civilization. We still don't all speak the same language. We can simultaneously translate, but it's still rough—translation never approaching the precision of poetry. So translated passages never really move you. But music does connect across cultures, and Africans have found the way to connect with everyone. Africa has become the real center of a new global sound, a global language that is rich and subtle. It's a means to pull us all together through musical harmony. That's it. The secret key to the new world was not empathy or balance, but harmony. We've created a harmonious world.

13

The Guiding Principles

With so much change taking place around us, everyone faces the question: What can I do now to build a better future? We offer ten core principles that have worked in almost all situations over the last couple decades of the Long Boom. We suggest that they inform all our choices in the years ahead. They will sustain the Long Boom and help everyone thrive.

I F THIS LONG BOOM comes about, if the global economy churns at historically high growth rates for a couple decades, then one thing is certain—change will be the norm. You can debate about whether change is good or bad, but if we have a Long Boom, we're going to be confronted with a lot of change. Torrid economic growth always brings with it a lot of social, cultural, and political repercussions. It's the hallmark of boom times. Think about the booming 1960s in the Western countries. With affluence and prosperity, people start thinking expansively and begin challenging old ways of doing things. The talk of reform and even revolution often fills the air. So if change is increasingly going to be the norm, then what can a person do about it? Certain approaches would be better than others. For example, a dynamic approach would work better than a static approach. But the guidance doesn't stop there.

As unpredictable as the future might seem, we think there are certain key principles that can be relied on to thrive better in the years ahead. Ten of them seem to us worth highlighting. These are fluid principles meant to direct, to influence, to nudge people in the right direction. And they are malleable, subject to revision over time. Yet these principles are not arbitrary or simply good values that we prefer out of a batch of choices. They are principles we believe work better in the new reality that's emerging around us year by year. Those countries, or companies, or individuals who follow them tend to thrive in the new environment. Those who disregard them tend to flounder. However, the more people do follow them, the more likely we are to see the conditions promoting and reinforcing the success of the Long Boom. These principles are not easy to follow. Some of them directly contradict principles that worked extremely well in the past. That said, all these principles are doable. All we have to do is set out to follow them with resolve.

Go Global

Going global is the first principle, which affects all the others. This is the major event that's defining our era, the watershed for the world. Before this Long Boom era, everything was organized on a subglobal level, within nations or cities or localities. What passed for global engagements at that time were really international. They were interactions between and among nation-states. During this Long Boom era, everything started truly going global. The technology, such as satellite-based telecommunications systems, went global. The boundaries of nations became less relevant. The economy, first through leading industries but increasingly through all fields, started becoming global. Already all the major players are global corporations. They used to be called multinationals when they were simply operating in more than one country. Now their market is the entire world. Our business relationships and even our personal relationships are going global. Our media and mass cultural experiences are going global. Our values are becoming global. You name it. Every realm of human interaction is spreading out to fill that global space. After this Long Boom era, we will be truly global, and future generations will look back on the fundamental change that took place today: The world went global, and it happened in the historical blink of an eye.

Today we need to think through *everything* and figure out how it fits into that new global context. We need to question every preconception and every policy to see whether it makes sense in this new light. Every nation must go through this soul-searching. As just one of the pieces, how does it fit into this much greater whole? Each country is now really analogous to one of the 50 states of the United States—it is one of the 200 or so states in this new global whole. A country's decisions now often affect more than its own population. For example, a country needs to think through its national telecommunications policy from a global perspective. Each country is now one node in the global system. What do you do about breaking up a monopolistic company that is dominant in its home market but is simply a small fry in the entire global economy? If your borders are truly open and foreign competitors can come in, then that old trust-busting policy needs a rethinking. This goes for subnational entities, too. The state of Connecticut has always thought of itself as competing with other states in the northeastern region or even the entire United States. Henceforth, the state should really think of itself as competing with the province of Yorkshire in England or the region around Osaka in Japan. Cities should try to be the best not in the state, or the nation, but in the world. They need to promote worldwide that they have, say, the best craftspeople for glass blowing. They need to convince others that they are definitely worth checking out in that global market. Every unit needs to figure out how it best fits into the global picture.

The global logic will just keep shooting through every aspect of human organization. Industries need to figure out how they can thrive in a global environment and then take steps to ensure that they do. It will be harder to survive if you're a national mobile phone industry that's on a technical standard out of sync with the rest of the world. That may be happening in the United States, which is moving down a path in conflict with the truly global standard for mobile communications (GSM) that Europe established early on.

A company's potential global market through electronic commerce is huge. IBM aired a wonderful television commercial in 1998 showing a couple from Ohio visiting a quaint shop in Italy. The couple proudly told the owner how they sold their products through three stores in their home state. The Italian woman nodded approvingly and then said that she sold in one of those stores, too. Her guests' look of surprise prompted her to explain that her e-commerce traffic was not only with Ohio, but with Capetown, and London, and the list went on. This global chant has become widespread in the business press, but for large segments of businesspeople, particularly in small local businesses, the message has not sunk in, and the full implications are being ignored. E-commerce really does change everything. It allows a little business struggling to sell enough in a local market to thrive in a huge global one. It allows a niche business choked off from growth by a lack of local talent to tap into human resources from anywhere. It takes one of the fundamental conditions defining any business opportunity—the size of the market—and blows it up to gigantic proportions. Not only has the message not sunk in to most businesses, but it's also barely pierced the consciousness of nonprofit organizations. How do schools rethink education to make this global value the prime one? Organizations geared to social change need to think through their desired changes in a larger light. And, of course, individuals need to reorient their gaze to this global perspective, too.

Open Up

The principle of opening up is as fundamental as going global but even more black-and-white. Just remember: "Open, good. Closed, bad." In almost any situation—government policies, business strategies, technological innovations, or individual philosophies of life— the more open option is better, and the more closed option is worse. Individuals should infuse everything they do with openness and stretch their minds. In this more open, expansive mode, good things will follow. Being open to new experiences and new people expands personal and professional networks, whereas a closed approach cuts people off from all the things that make it easier to perceive where the world is heading and where they fit in.

For businesses, the open strategy clearly is the long-term winner. There might be short-term gain in closing your company off from all others, shielding a proprietary formula or methodology and going it alone. But that short-term gain will be at the expense of long-term success. Apple Computer made that fatal mistake by choosing the closed route in rabidly protecting its proprietary operating system. Microsoft at that same juncture chose the open route and created an operating system that worked on virtually any computer. The open strategy works over time because whatever you hold close to your chest today will be obsolete tomorrow, plus the new formulas and methods for success will be created in the interaction with others in your field or out in the marketplace. You want to keep the channels open to potential employees or colleagues or partners in future ventures. You want to keep your options open to be able to change direction if the market or industry that you're currently comfortably situated in collapses overnight.

The open strategy is just as reliable for countries but much more difficult to pull off. Most peoples of the world today instinctively support a more closed strategy for their nations. This is even true of the developed countries, which have benefited so unambiguously from greater openness. For example, a large segment of the U.S. public still supports protectionist policies that clearly would undermine the boom they now enjoy. Not only Americans but people all over the world still harbor a lot of fears about the wild world outside their national borders and the different people that inhabit that world. They are very reluctant to open up. That impulse is irrational, counter to the evidence, destructive to global economic growth, and anathema to the Long Boom. Clearly, on every level, countries need to open up and integrate into the larger world. Today borders need to be opened as much as possible to the free flow of products, many of which are parts of products being aggregated elsewhere. A rational, efficient global economy demands that kind of circulation. It's like greasing the parts of the engine of the car. If one part doesn't move, the performance of the other parts is undermined.

Borders also need to be opened to the free flow of capital. That's the second pillar on which the global economy will run. A highly productive global economy will need capital to move to where it can be most efficiently used. This position is harder to swallow for countries that saw the ravages of the swings of capital in Asia in 1997 and 1998. Safeguards need to be installed that will mitigate the damage of huge, quick swings, but the concept of the free flow of capital is absolutely essential to a full-functioning global economy. Trading products has always been a hallmark of the international economy, but moving capital freely around the world has been much less prevalent.

Which brings up the third pillar, people. Borders need to be increasingly opened to the free flow of people, of labor, of talent. This is probably even more difficult to swallow than allowing money to move in and out. Most nations today want to control the flow of people because they fear an influx of unwanted people or an outflow of top talent. As difficult as it is to come to terms with, the global economy will need that free flow to function properly. Most of the labor at all levels can stay put and let the technology and capital come to it, but much of the real value of the cross-fertilization of ideas and the transfer of knowledge comes from direct human contact. The bodies have to move around. Borders will increasingly need to open up in the years ahead.

At the highest level of world systems, the open mantra also applies. International institutions, like the newly formed World Trade Organization, need to rigorously promote and expand open trade. Institutions like the International Monetary Fund need to encourage the open flow of finance. Think of it as a circulatory system moving the lifeblood of the global economy—capital—to all the parts of the body. You don't want the blood vessels around the heart to be wide open and supple while the vessels in the arms and legs are clogged up with cholesterol. Same goes for the new global economy. You can't have a wide-open, lightning-fast, highly calibrated electronic financial system in the most developed countries and then have national banking systems in the developing world completely ossified. The quicker we get the circulation flowing and the heart pumping, the better off we all will be.

There's one other area where world systems need to actively promote much more openness. We need more open speech, otherwise known as free speech. If we're heading into the Knowledge Age, we need open information systems and open debate. Even more than the free flow of capital, the global knowledge economy will need the free flow of ideas. We're going to need access to accurate information everywhere in the world. We're going to need wide open forums to carry on rigorous debates in all fields. And we're going to need an open system that can get the distilled truth out to all peoples. Only then will the twenty-first century's knowledge economy really hum.

The choices the world faces between open and closed routes into the future are very clear and very stark. Choosing the closed route will move us into a vicious circle that spirals downward and inward. We start with relatively closed societies and a fragmented world. With more insular attitudes and policies, the individual nations will turn inward, and the world will break down into isolated blocs. This situation will strengthen traditionalists and ensure more rigidity of thought. The economy will stagnate, and the level of poverty and general frustration will increase. The result will be conflicts and increasing intolerance, which will lead us to even more closed societies and a more fragmented world.

On the other hand, if the world chooses the more open route, this leads to a more virtuous circle of growth and expansion. Open societies turn outward and strive to integrate into the world. Openness to change and exposure to new ideas lead to innovation and progress, which grows the economy, brings rising affluence for more people, and decreases poverty. This leads to growing tolerance and appreciation of diversity. If you and your family are doing well, you are more apt to be generous and to help out others. This then brings us to a more open society and a more integrated world. No one understood this better than George Soros, the financier who made a fortune in global currency trading, and who then invested much of his wealth in a nonprofit organization called the Open Society, which finances and supports initiatives around the world that help to open up societies. The idea is that a small project that opens up a closed system will lead to an opening that can expand by itself. For example, Soros went to Hungary before the breakup of the Soviet bloc and funded one simple project of bringing in copying machines. Until then, there were no generally accessible copiers, and the state controlled all the means of printing. Suddenly, with Soros's copiers, people had the means to create instant newspapers and circulate controversial ideas. That dy-

namic created more and more openness. Eventually, no one, not even
the authorities could stop it. Which brings us to the next point.

LET GO

Let go of the control of the past era. We can't control the present the
way we could the past. And the future is going to be even more beyond any individual's or any organization's control. No one is in control—and that's OK. Walter Wriston, the former chairman of
Citibank, was recently asked about this phenomenon: "Who is in
charge if nobody is in control?" Wriston answered, "Everybody." It's
not that the world is completely out of control. Everybody is in control to a certain extent, doing her or his part to make the whole system sing. It's just that no one individual or organization can control
situations the way they could be controlled in the past. That kind of
centralized control is gone. No one knows that better than Mikhail
Gorbachev, who had to take a huge leap of faith and let go of the
control apparatus of the centralized communist economy and state.
To a large extent, his hand was forced by historical forces beyond his
control. Still, he took a courageous stand against the large control
constituency of which he was the head. We're still watching the wild
reverberations today.

But former communists aren't the only ones who need to learn the
new habit of extending the fingers and pulling back the hands. Many
people in the West are just as frightened of letting go and moving
into seemingly uncontrollable, or radically decontrolled, situations.
The British could not let go of their need to control their currency
and their own national economic policy, and so they failed to join
the pioneers on the Continent launching the Euro. The French and
Germans and others accepting the Euro showed far more strength in
letting go of the known course of staying with their national currencies, and leaping into the unknown. All the evidence indicates their
gamble was a good one. The overly conservative British lost out, and
they now know it.

Letting go does not mean succumbing to chaos. The out-of-control
situation we advocate does not equate with anarchy. Letting go is
about trusting people. The Long Boom in general comes out of a Jef-

fersonian tradition of believing in the fundamental worth and capability of ordinary people. We're shifting from methods that controlled people to ones that coordinate them. Think of the analogy of a traffic grid. The so-called authorities set up the parameters (cars must stay on the roads). Then a few rules (drive on the right, or left, side of the road). Then they install traffic lights to settle the potential clashes of interests (when it's red, stop; when it's green, you can go). And finally, the system is opened up and individuals take over. The traffic gets coordinated, not controlled, and everyone trusts others to be competent and do the right thing. That level of trust is quite high when you think about it. Every day you drive down roads where you completely trust that the person driving toward you will stay on the right side of the line. You are trusting some complete stranger who is driving a machine weighing thousands of pounds at speeds often more than sixty miles per hour. You do this every day, hundreds of times a week, and you don't even think about it. That's the kind of trust we're developing on many different levels of the global society. Managers who run companies or organizations will increasingly have to let go of their need to control those under them. Networked organizations are marked by radically distributed decisionmaking and autonomous workers. The more you try to control knowledge workers, the more you undermine their value, which comes from their independence, their creativity, and their free thinking. When you box them up, they don't work.

The impetus to let go comes not just from some democratic impulse, but from the sheer demands of the mounting complexity of our society. Sufficiently complex systems can't be controlled. We have reached that level of complexity, and we are going to far surpass it in the coming years. Once again, we can turn to our wise old teacher, nature. Nature has perfected out of control systems. Biological systems are great models for what human-designed systems could come to be. Kevin Kelly, the former executive editor of *Wired*, laid this out beautifully in his groundbreaking book *Out of Control: How Human Systems Are Emulating the Biological*. At the microlevel, individual organisms are extremely complex but not strictly controlled by their brains. For example, many organs of the body do not need the brain to function. Like distributed computer systems, the body has much distributed intelligence through its DNA programming. Most functions in a body are carried out in reaction to a local stimulus, autonomous from the central nervous system. The brain is more like the coordinator, the higher-level system that carries out some rarefied higher functions but mostly helps integrate all the subsystems. At the macrolevel, the biological models are even more applicable. An ecosystem is an extremely complex system made up of billions of individual actors, and there is no direct method of coordinating it. There is nothing approaching a master coordinator like a brain. Everything is self-directed and moves in response to the actions of the other parts of the environment. The only guidelines are certain laws of physics that can't be evaded (gravity will always pull water downhill and the like). Yet, in that out-of-control environment, all the parts find ways to elegantly interlink and are woven into a fabric of interdependence. When one part changes, all the other parts in the vicinity adapt. Granted, nature took millions of years of trial and error to arrive at that masterpiece of an ecosystem, but what a beautiful system to behold and to study. You can sit in a meadow or a wetland or some wilderness foothills and learn a lot about the way human societies could evolve.

Don't lose heart that we humans are incapable of such beauty and complexity. We've built some extremely complex systems, such as the global marketplace, that already work on these letting-go principles, and we've built some powerful tools to help us master these principles. We now have computers capable of tracking billions of functions at a time, and we have intellectual and mathematical models, like complexity theory, to carry the insights of nature into our realm. Complexity theory was born in the attempt to track the complex gyrations of the mushroom clouds of atomic explosions, where billions of independent variables all come together. But since the 1980s, complexity theory has evolved to try to apply to human systems like market behavior and global economics. Much of the early work was done in more offbeat places like the Santa Fe Institute, but now the theory has gone mainstream—and it looks as if its influence will only grow. We have a lot of work ahead to understand how to emulate nature and build human systems of hypercomplexity, but rest assured that there are lots of brains out there picking away at their portion of the problem. In the meantime, start loosening up and heading toward a future of more letting go.

Grow More

Taken in a literal sense, growing more is a fundamental hallmark of the Long Boom. Economic growth is good. We need much more of it. Living in the context of increasing prosperity has beneficial repercussions in many directions beyond strict economics. Everyone is better off living in the midst of plenty. To some people, this point is obvious—an economic axiom that doesn't deserve highlighting. But to many others, economic growth is seen as highly suspect if not outright dangerous. This is particularly true of many environmentalists, who see a zero-sum game of more economic growth automatically translating into more damage to the environment. With the increasing environmental anxiety about global warming, this no-growth or slow-growth attitude could become more ascendant. So the "Grow more" principle needs elaboration here. First, taken as a whole, the world is a pretty poor place. Probably half the people in the world live in conditions that a visitor from the nineteenth century would find perfectly familiar. For example, of the 4.4 billion people living in developing countries, nearly three-fifths lack access to safe sewers, a third lack access to clean water, a quarter do not have adequate housing, and a fifth have no access to modern health services of any kind. The prosperity that spread through the twentieth century reached about thirty advanced industrialized countries but stopped far short of reaching most people outside that club. For example, the richest fifth of the world's population consumes 86 percent of all goods and services, and the poorest fifth consumes just 1.3 percent. The richest fifth eats 45 percent of all meat and fish, uses 58 percent of all energy, has 74 percent of all telephone lines, and owns 87 percent of all vehicles. Any basic sense of fairness would argue that we can't kill the growth juggernaut now. We need to expand it so that its benefits reach ever more people.

The Long Boom is not about normal levels of growth. That's the second point. We're talking about pumping up the growth rates of the global economy to levels that are much more ambitious than historical norms. We think the new conditions of the New Economy warrant more heady targets. In the four full calendar years from 1996 through 1999, the U.S. economy grew at a 4 percent annual pace. This is growth in a very mature economy with an extremely high base of more than $7 trillion in gross domestic product. During certain quarters, the growth rate surged to more than 5 percent and sometimes nearly 8 percent. The U.S. economy is the prototype of the new global knowledge economy, and much can be learned from it about global expectations for the future. It is very plausible that the entire global economy could grow at a steady annual 4 percent rate— it hit that level just before the 1997 Asian crash. It's conceivable that rates eventually could push to more like 5 percent and possibly even 6 percent. These kinds of growth rates would reflect big strides taken by developing countries working off smaller bases with plenty of development to fill out. In Asia in the 1980s and 1990s, countries frequently hit growth rates of 7, 8, 9, and even 10 percent. More parts of the world could enjoy that kind of growth, countering the relatively slower rates of more mature economies, and pushing the overall global rate up. The third point is that the growth strategy promoted by the Long Boom will be built on new technologies and techniques that would create much less stress on the environment. We're talking about low-impact growth, a new but attainable goal—and an indispensable one at that.

The principle of "Grow More" has a more natural organic interpretation as well. This principle is one of several that are rooted in biological metaphors and that take inspiration from the study of nature. In the natural world, growth is an integral part of the life process. All living things grow. They go from some embryonic form and develop through various stages of maturity. When they get damaged by outside forces, they enter a healing process that is simply a variation of the growth process. All healthy organisms grow. We see this in plants and animals, and we watch it in the human realm most obviously with children, but the principle also works at other stages of life. Personal growth at every age should be seen as a positive development. Growing emotionally, mentally, and physically makes people come alive and feel energized. And our human artifacts, the businesses, organizations, and systems we devise, also need to be engaged in a constant process of growth, not so much because they need to grow for strictly economic reasons, but because growth is a healthy process in and of itself. When an organization, like an organism, stops growing, it begins to die. For organizations or individuals, the equation is pretty simple: Grow or die.

Always Adapt

Units within a growing system must constantly adapt to survive. The logic is simple: Growth over time will change the environment to such an extent that old behavior eventually won't work. Those units that adapt with new behavior more appropriate to the emerging environment will thrive. Those that don't adapt will flounder. This is another one of those biological principles rooted in an observation of nature or, more specifically in this case, evolution. We go right back to our original metaphor of the totally interdependent ecosystem. All the autonomous moving parts of plants and animals ensure that the overall system will be continuously in flux, with no predetermined end state. That means that all the pieces, the individual species, are in play, and only the ones that stay aware of what's around them and react incrementally to ongoing changes will stay in the game—stay alive. Those that disregard the changing environment will certainly be phased out in the long run. Take the simple example of two species of wildlife in Colorado. Mountain lions could not adapt to the encroachment of human development on their territory. They needed large areas to hunt for game, and they were so fierce that humans could not coexist with them. Mountain lions could not adapt to the new environment, and so their numbers are dwindling to dangerously low levels. However, deer were able to adapt to more developed environments. As herbivores, they posed no direct threat to humans, who actually liked having them around. So now deer have proliferated so much that they are actually becoming a pesty problem in suburban developments. You could almost say they adapted too well. Now, as humans shift tactics and allow limited hunting to cut their numbers, they may have to adapt again.

This game of evolution is a difficult game to play. You never can know all the players. There are far too many of them, and they change all the time anyway. The parameters and even the rules are constantly changing as well. So the possible situational outcomes are myriad, and keeping track of all the variables is very difficult. And the stakes of evolution are high. You make the wrong decisions, and your species dies. The only tactic in that situation is to keep adapting—keep that dance going as long the music plays. Of course, species don't actually think through their options or consciously adapt at all—with one exception, latter-day human beings. We're the first species that can consciously choose to adapt and make pretty good calculations about the best way to proceed. That's good, because we may have to react to a changing planetary environment and somehow fix it. But that's also good because our human systems have evolved to such complex states that the same strategies that work in evolution now work in the human-made world. In the changing global economy, in our complex modern society, constant adaptation is the only tactic that makes sense. In a slight variation of the point from the "Grow more" principle, adapt or die.

Keep Learning

The mechanism for adapting in today's world is, pure and simple, learning. And never has learning been more important than it is now. Of course, education has always been an advantage. Of course, people were more likely to get ahead if they were more educated. But the reality is that an education was not a necessity for reaching the middle class in the Industrial Age. A person could drop out of high school and go to work in the steel mills, auto factories, coal mines, or rubber plants and earn a solid middle-income wage. With that level of economic success, the worker could afford to buy a house in the suburbs and send his or her children to college. Indeed, that was the greatness of the U.S. economy in the post–World War II era. Few similar opportunities will exist in the Information Age. Without an adequate education, one that includes becoming computer-enabled and globally aware, people will have great difficulty thriving in the new century.

Attaining a higher educational level is necessary in the New Economy, but not sufficient. The New Economy moves at a pace never seen before. The rate of innovation and change has become pumped up to what is called Internet speed. Today's expertise can be rendered irrelevant in a couple of years. The challenge to everyone in the New Economy is not to master a specialty, but to continually learn. Lifelong learning will be the key to success in the future. Individuals will be able to use networked learning processes to continually assimilate new knowledge. They can use learning as a way to reorient themselves if they get trapped in a line of work or an industry that's dying for reasons far beyond their control. They can use learning to continually make themselves more valuable in a knowledge economy.

The scary way to frame the situation is that learning is everyone's only chance. The world is changing so much that an individual has no choice but to learn and to learn fast. The world will not slow down for anyone. The more positive way to frame the situation is that learning is the vehicle for all the opportunities that will open up in this new era. If you're feeling stuck or yearning for more, then learning is the way to get unstuck and improve your prospects. Learning isn't just hitting the books. It encompasses intellectual and emotional growth in all directions. It's about experiential learning that expands capabilities and skills in all kinds of ways. It's about acquiring knowledge in unconventional areas and following your own passions. Mental capabilities are the new source of wealth, so we have to get smart and learn a lot.

Nowhere in the world has that been more clear than Singapore, which is the perfect example of a learning society. Its only resource is people and the capacity to organize them. When Singapore became independent from Great Britain in 1959, few would have believed that a tiny city-state with no resources, very little useful infrastructure, and limited capabilities would be one of the richest places on earth by the turn of the century—yet it is. Singapore's success came because it learned ferociously. Singapore insisted on education and rewarded educational achievement. It became a highly meritocratic society with almost no corruption. It invested heavily in the continuous adaptation of its organizations, so that they could move from lower-value tasks to higher-value tasks as quickly as possible. And it provided the opportunities for the continuous learning of people who had to adapt along with the economy. Its greatest challenge now is becoming more democratic, finding an appropriate democratic mode in what has been largely an autocratic society. It now will have to learn democracy, and it will.

Value Innovation

In companies or organizations, learning finds expression as constant experimentation and reliance on innovation. That's why the New Economy is so identified with entrepreneurship. The entrepreneur exemplifies the search to find new ways to do things better, to expand the frontiers of applying knowledge. Entrepreneurial traits are increasingly needed at every level of an organization and the economy. All the people in every department of a large corporation or institution need to keep learning about the changes in their markets to keep coming up with new ways to improve their area of responsibility. They need to expect the unexpected and to welcome innovations that come from all quarters. If they don't, they and their organizations will be unlikely to succeed in the New Economy.

In the old Industrial Age economy, you could hear many clichés: "Keep it simple, stupid"; "If it ain't broke, don't fix it." These phrases fit the processes of industrial production and actually worked well in those contexts. But if production is learning in the Information Age, then valuing the results of learning is clearly productive—as well as rewarding and fun. The corollary to "Keep learning" is to value one of learning's key outcomes: innovation. Innovation takes a certain kind of creative brain, and some are more endowed than others. But everyone can *value* innovation. This is particularly important today because we're in a historical moment when we need to make large structural changes in our economy and society. We need to support those who are doing the innovation because it benefits us all. This is trickier than it sounds, because for many people what's valued most is tradition. That mind-set has people habitually looking backward. We should continue, of course, to appreciate and learn from history and traditions, but we must also constantly look ahead. To value innovation is to welcome and embrace the future, to be open to what constitutes advancement, to befriend progress. Innovation is what got us to the historic opportunity of the Long Boom. Valuing innovation is one of the guiding principles that will enable us to fulfill its promise.

Innovation is now the central wealth creation mechanism of the knowledge economy. In some measure, it always was, but it is now much more. The innovations of agriculture and metalworking throughout the industrial economy were all applications of knowledge. What is different now is how many different areas of society are being transformed by knowledge, and how rapidly that knowledge itself is advancing. It's the scope and scale, the pace and spread of knowledge that make this truly a knowledge economy—very different from an industrial one. An important implication of this wealth creation process is that because the rewards for innovation in this New Economy are very high, an enormous number of people are motivated to innovate. The entrepreneurial venture capital system is a very powerful motivator for new product and service development, and the competitive pressures of the world economy are an enormous incentive for large companies to continuously innovate. So businesspeople today must accept the reality that if they fail to innovate, they will fall behind.

In a more positive sense, we need to innovate in order to create a better world. The kind of output that we could expect from an industrial economy is not likely to sufficiently raise the incomes of large sectors of society and narrow the income gaps over the long run. It just cannot grow fast enough. Also, if the industrial economy became the ubiquitous form of economic activity throughout the world, it would be highly destructive to the environment. We need innovation to create high-value economic growth, growth that creates jobs, increases productivity, and continues to raise incomes. And we need knowledge-intensive growth, rather than physically intensive growth, because we need to reduce the environmental impact of generating that income. We need a high degree of innovation to solve a number of fundamental problems. Fortunately, the motivations for innovation are now so high that it is very likely we will solve them.

GET CONNECTED

"Get connected" is also a fundamental principle for the new networked economy. This new knowledge economy would be going nowhere without the connections that have been made between computers. When personal computers were stand-alone devices in the 1980s, all their real potential lay ahead. When these computers started getting connected within offices and companies in the early 1990s, their potential started being realized. The public advent of the Internet around 1994 kicked the whole shebang into high gear. The Internet connected all the diverse subsystems and created extremely dense interconnections. The "Get connected" logic works for the system because more people added to the network increase the value to all the members already on. The logic works for the individual because being connected to the Internet becomes more valuable each day. Anybody can now find something on the Net that interests or benefits her or him in some way. But simply being connected to the network is itself worth it because it means being a part of the flow of ideas and transactions taking place in the world community each day.

Networking is the central metaphor of the New Economy and is fundamentally about connecting people—with or without the technology. It is about drawing from diverse pools of skilled people. One of the central activities for any worker in this environment is building a personal network to help solve problems, accomplish tasks, and find other opportunities. One of the key tasks of any company or organization is to establish networks outside that can help accomplish goals once achieved in-house. Making that new connection is the first step in the process of networking. And deepening these connections is what makes networks solid and lasting. Connect with people and thrive.

BE INCLUSIVE

The flip side of going out and getting connected is being inclusive and drawing other people into the network. Being inclusive can be seen as being altruistic—looking out for the other guy—and also as serving a person's self-interest by expanding that person's network. The direct payback might not be immediately apparent. Over time the newly included person will contribute something of value. The wider and more diverse your network, the more valuable it will be to you in the long run.

Being inclusive goes back to our theme of the increasing value of both diversity and integration in the New Economy. The world is becoming an increasingly complex place, so it's no use working only with people who are a carbon copy of you. You want people in your network who will challenge your thinking and sharpen your mind. You want them to come from a wide range of backgrounds and learning experiences, and also to have contacts and familiarity with different cultures and regions of the world. That way you'll have a better chance of figuring out the optimal solutions. As everything goes global, you want guides who can help you interpret the world out there.

This "Be inclusive" principle applies even more to larger communities, all the way up to nations and civilization blocs. The first phase of the Long Boom, in the 1980s and 1990s, was the rough-and-tumble experimental phase, marked by rugged individualism. Margaret Thatcher and Ronald Reagan focused on dismantling the old centralized, bureaucratic industrial economy and creating a more dynamic, entrepreneurial economy. They were successful on both counts, and they helped put forces in motion that we're still reaping the benefits of today. However, they did not pay much attention to the collateral damage. Many workers and their families were lost in the transition, and large segments of the population were shut out of the benefits that came with the changes. There is no point in debating now whether more could have been done at the time to help all sectors of society move ahead. That's the past. The point for the present is that many people still need to be drawn into this New Economy and into the middle class. Despite the impressive growth in the United States, many pockets of the population are still struggling to find their niche. And in countries in earlier stages of this transition to the New Economy, the casualties are running high. In some parts of the world, like Southeast Asia, whole nations are reeling from global forces partly beyond their control.

This is a time to be inclusive. The early adopters, the stronger and more advantaged segments of society, have been given the time to focus their attention on their own transitions and on getting the basic framework of the new system in place. Now they need to think deeply about ways to help bring the rest of society along. Govern-

ments at the national and more local levels need to help less fortunate people learn how to succeed in this new environment. They
need to aggressively reach out and draw these marginalized people
into thriving networks. The politics of the second half of the Long
Boom will be the politics of inclusion. The formula is already working
for political parties that saw this early. In Europe, the political debate
and overt political control are dominated by parties of the people,
those coming from the Left, which explicitly talk about this agenda
of inclusion. In the United States, the Democrats are closer to pushing and benefiting from this same message, though some Republicans
are talking about "compassionate conservatism." Those domestic
agendas need a parallel track in international affairs. The politics of
inclusion for a truly global community means that the more developed countries need to aggressively help less developed countries
struggling to make the turn into the twenty-first century. Many of
these countries, particularly in Asia, are trying to modernize and certainly have the will, but the transition is a tricky one, and even those
with the most assets need an occasional nudge. The Western nations
need to demonstrate global leadership that offers the needed assis-
tance and opens the global networks wide. They can do it for others
or they can do it for themselves, but only when more regions of the
world have made the transition will the global networked economy
truly sing.

You can't open up your network and include diverse people and expect that they will behave and think the same as you. You need to
tolerate the differences that they bring into the network, not out of
politeness but because that's where their value lies. The principle of
tolerating differences is one that underscores some of the other principles. If you go global, then you inevitably will come in contact with
very different people and cultures and opinions. If you can't be tolerant of those differences, then get out of the global game and stay
home. The same goes for opening up and all that entails. The truly
open-minded person needs to tolerate seemingly bizarre ideas because it's never certain where truth lies. What once was wacky can
suddenly turn into the norm. In his own time, the painter Vincent
Van Gogh was considered an insane person, but today crowds all over

the world line up to see his paintings. And the principle of letting go also implies that we need to embrace the principle of tolerance. If we are going to let go of the controls, then we must be ready for unexpected consequences. A manager who allows workers the freedom to do their best must also be prepared for the worst. Those workers might come up with something far different from what the manager expected or they might flat-out fail. The good manager doesn't want the end results preordained or predictable. The corollary to "Let go" is "Let live." Stay with that tolerant attitude.

Stay Confident

The Long Boom concept is optimistic about the future, so an appropriate last principle is "Stay optimistic." Maintaining an optimistic attitude can be a successful strategy for dealing with change. It allows you to focus on a positive course while filtering out more negative alternatives and disturbing evidence that might undermine your resolve. But "Stay optimistic" is a little too feeble or lightweight for one of the core guiding principles, particularly the final one. Optimism implies picking up on only the positive elements, making the best of a situation. But we are not merely optimistic about the future; we are confident about the future. We are confident of the ability of the global community to deal with the challenges that lie ahead. We are confident that our children will inherit a world that is better than the one we have now. This book is about spreading that confidence by laying out many of the world's assets and resources, by showing all the ways we can pick up on the growing potential of the present, and by drawing the through line from here to a better there.

"Stay confident" is the animating principle that will sustain all the other principles and make this Long Boom fully happen. Right now the world is in a highly anxious state. Many people are anxious for good reason: They live in countries that are flat on their economic backs. Others are anxious because the global economy is doing a transitional pirouette and they're not at all sure where it will land. Others can't deal with these new technologies, or can't afford them, or don't understand them—yet they're being told that's the way of the future, the only way to go. Toss in the approach of the new millennium and people's anxiety gets even greater. And when people get uptight they can do strange and dangerous things: They can jump to conclusions and get paranoid about others. They can make rash decisions that are overly self-protective and even hostile. They can get in a supremely selfish mood. This is a time to "Stay confident." Maintaining confidence can cut through the anxiety. There's something very profound and soothing about Franklin Delano Roosevelt's famous line during the Great Depression: "The only thing we have to fear is fear itself." Fear is often way out of proportion to the actual danger on which the fear is based. People frequently feel much more anxious and fearful contemplating something bad than they feel actually experiencing it. Fear also has the potential to get out of control and lead people to take actions that really do make everything worse. So FDR said to get a handle on the fear. In other words, "Stay confident."

Staying confident is not just a mental fabrication to lull the mind into calming down. The confidence comes from a deep realization that the global community *can* rise to the challenges. We are fully capable of dealing with the transition into the twenty-first century. We know how to handle many of the most pressing problems and we have the tools and the knowledge and the brainpower to figure out whatever problems come up next. The confidence also comes from the understanding that the global community is not some abstraction, but all of us. We're all in this together—which takes us back to the first principle. We're all now an integral part of a global community. Not only that, but we're open and ready for anything—the second principle. Also, everybody's got a bit of control in how the world will proceed—the third principle. We'll grow together and evolve in a healthy way. We're fully capable of adapting to the challenges of the future. We're going to stay balanced and connected, feeling good about each other. No one is going to be left behind. Everyone is going to accept everyone else's differences. In diversity there is strength. And we know we can do this—as long as we stay calm and confident and face down our fears.

Date: 12/02/2050
Start: 10:09:22 A.M.
Finish: 10:15:59 A.M.
Selected Languages: American English, Arabic, Cantonese, Zulu.
Idea Tool memory enhancement on.

I am in a cabin at the end of my life. Although I've lived a long, robust life, I'm told that at age ninety I don't have too much longer to live. So I've come back to the place of my birth. I've come full circle, all the way back to where the story began in 1960. I'm not literally at the place where I was born, but at a cabin near the border of Canada in the heartland of the United States. The cabin is perched on a beautiful wild river—still wild after all these years. My father was one of those guys who never bought new lumber and straightened all his old bent nails, but he built this incredible little cabin, a magnificent place on the bluffs. This is the place where we grew up in the summer as kids. I first crawled here; I took my first steps here. It's very hilly, so I'd roll down the hills into the brush. I spent many meaningful moments here with my father, mother, siblings, and friends. And all of you who have been here know that the cabin is one of the emotional touchstones in my life. It's the plot of earth to which I feel most connected.

It's late in the year and really cold in this part of the country. The frost is already coming in the mornings, and the trees long ago lost all their leaves. I really miss Mol right now. I always thought that she would outlive me, and I never thought I'd have to carry on after her. Luckily, though, I have Amy. Mol lives on in Amy. Amy is thriving like her mother and still only halfway through her life. She has raised another generation, and not only that, but her daughter is now raising another generation. Amy is now a grandmother, and I'm a great-grandfather. I have a really special connection with my great-grandchild—named after me. The layering of generations was really quite unexpected. We didn't think about it with the early medical breakthroughs back around 2000, and certainly not in the 1980s. But four or five generations now live simultaneously on the same plot of ground in a way that we have never experienced before. You all are in similar situations. Almost all of you have kids and grandkids and great-grandkids, too. Most of you will outlive me and may even see a fifth or sixth generation. I'll probably be the first of you to pass away. But there's at least one last year-end letter to write.

I'm an old guy and hung onto my old Talkman well into the 2030s. I loved that thing. But now I have switched to recording this as I think. The thought patterns are basically picked up by some biotech, nanotech tool that I couldn't begin to explain to you. My grandchildren and great-grandchildren turned me on to this new "idea tool." I was always somewhat of a technophile, so I decided to try it out. I think through what at one time I would have written, and the implant basically records it. I've just learned how to think more focused thoughts and more clearly in one part of my brain. It's not the same way we used to think in 2020. But I've learned how to focus my mind in a certain space with a certain intensity. I can write a narrative through thought patterns in the same way I might speak them out—only much quicker. You're still reading words. They have been able to translate the thoughts into text but haven't been able to upload it whole-sale into other people's brains. They haven't been able to make that complete interconnection yet. But that is a promise of the late twenty-first century. In the end, they are actually trying to communicate fully, mind to mind. But that's beyond me.

When I think back on my life, it's really astonishing how much the world has changed. It's equally astonishing how little we understood about what really was happening around us until just after the turn of the century. None of us really had a clue back in the 1980s and 1990s. We Boomers should have recognized the early signs of what was to come, but we completely missed them. We really were trapped in our time. But now, in the year 2050, it's crystal clear. The entire world has made a massive leap forward. By anyone's standards, the world we live in now, in the middle of the twenty-first century, is a much better place to be. You can make the comparison using almost any measurement—general prosperity, improving environment, stable population, technological wonders, scientific breakthroughs, rising standards of living, or lowering levels of poverty, or of violence, or of whatever problem you choose. You pick the category and we're much better off today.

Who would have thought that by the year 2050 we would be able to pull the vast majority of the world's population into a decent middle-class lifestyle? The average person now lives at a material level once reserved for just elite Western nations. Virtually everyone is beyond the absolutely miserable conditions that more than half the world's population lived in just fifty years ago. Reaching that material threshold took a huge amount of growth in the global economy, and no one ever thought we could do it without completely destroying the environment. We were convinced that the coming century would bring a meltdown in the polar ice caps, rising sea levels, bizarre weather, rampant disease—all of which turned out not to be true. And almost all the basic fears we grew up with—that a faceless enemy will wage total war, that intercontinental nuclear missiles would come screaming over the horizon, that life as we knew it would be eradicated in a flash—all that is gone. When those threats receded, other ones took their place: terrorism, biological warfare, the crazy rogue nation that would still launch nukes. All these things never really materialized, or if they did, we severely contained them or nipped them in the bud. And now we are looking back on 100 years without a major world war. Not since World War II have the world's most powerful peoples waged all-out war against each other. We've had our skirmishes and close calls, but we've now hit a plateau where world war is essentially a thing of the past. Who would have thought it?

When I think back to my childhood growing up here, one of the most powerful feelings I have is one of connection. I felt so connected to my family and this cabin and the land itself. When I left home as a young adult, I severed those connections and entered a world that appeared very fragmented and far-flung. Far from connected, everything seemed contentious. The rest of my life was spent trying to get connected again. I learned the hard way, over decades of trial and error, and anxious moments, and setbacks and confusion, and wrong turns, and all the other traumas that went into my life. I've learned that at every stage of my life, the thing that got me moving in the right direction and opened up opportunities was to get connected. The more connection, the better. The deeper the connection, the better. Connection worked on all levels. On one level, it described the spark that flew between two human beings in the most intimate moments, between Mol and me. It also described the bonds between me and Amy and me and my best friends, you guys. Connection is what we always craved more of between us. It's what kept us gathering at the Summit and other spots of the world, year after year. It kept me writing to you for a full seven decades.

Connection worked for the world, too. You could say it saved the world. We had no idea what would come out of those early connections in the old days of the Internet, which entered our lives almost sixty years ago. The

Internet was the conduit to this deeper connection between peoples, cultures, civilizations. But it was really just the initial means for everybody to connect on far more meaningful levels. Over time, our technology just blended into the background. We started seeing each other across these vast expanses and started really communicating, and sharing experiences, and building understanding. We had no idea where that interconnection would lead. We still don't. And it was through that connection that wars and violence and all the things that haunted us for so long started to lessen. Connection was one of the secrets of the future of the planet, and also of my life. That's what my lifetime has been about: seeking that feeling of interconnectedness, trying to stay connected right until the day I die—and just maybe after that, too.

14

The Choice

The Long Boom isn't inevitable. We have to make it happen. The great opportunity of our era must be seized by the generation responsible for the world today. We have the potential to create a much better world in the twenty-first century for our children and the generations to come. Doing so depends on the imperative of economic growth today. Failing to achieve high growth now will result in a dark future. We face a choice.

THERE'S A FAMOUS IMAGE of President John F. Kennedy that is relevant here: the newsreel clip of him delivering his speech that challenged the nation to send astronauts to the moon. After laying out an ambitious social and economic agenda for improving the United States, Kennedy said, "We will go to the moon, and do the other things, not because it is easy, but because it is hard." The politics of Kennedy's time was one of challenge, one of sacrifice and hard work. The fact that landing men on the moon within a decade was going to be extremely difficult actually energized and motivated that GI generation. They liked the idea that they were being called to sacrifice. The 1960s were a time of great challenges. Kennedy's generation met those challenges in not only going to the moon but also in tackling such issues as civil rights and expanding investment in education. Our times are filled with equally daunting challenges. They are not the same challenges, but they are equally important and historic in nature.

Kennedy issued his challenge almost exactly halfway through the previous era, the forty-year period from 1940 to 1980 that incorporated the post–World War II boom. They were at a critical juncture then, halfway through their boom, as we are now, halfway through ours. We've seen where we've come from since the early 1980s, and we have a good notion of where we can go. We now have to rise to the challenge and do it—if not for ourselves, then for our kids. What kind of a world do we want to hand over to our children? We'd want to give them a world that meets the three criteria laid out at the beginning of the book: We'd want a world growing ever more prosperous so that affluence spreads to sectors of society and regions of the world where such development was previously considered preposterous. We'd want to hand over an ecologically sustainable economy so our children can hold solid hopes of living full lives without environmental trade-offs. And we would want to leave a more peaceful world with decreasing levels of violence. That world would be so technologically interconnected and so economically interdependent that world war and even large-scale regional war would be ludicrous. We have it in our power to hand over that kind of world to our children, in our lifetime. We just need to start now and make the right choices.

The new generation born after 1980 we call the Long Boom Generation. This is the generation born and raised in the two decades just before the new century, studying and coming of age in the two decades after it. These kids will grow up completely in sync with the many new computer technologies that will seem foreign to their elders. They will internalize right from the beginning how these technologies work and how they can exploit them best. This deep understanding of networked computer technologies and their possibilities comes from enmeshing their lives with these machines almost from the moment they started to think.

The Long Boom Generation will come of age implicitly understanding all of the Long Boom's other new technologies—those beyond digital computing. They will grow up comfortable with biotechnology, deeply appreciating the benefits but also calmly assessing the risks. This will contrast with the older generation's acute anxiety and occasional hysteria over how to deal with biotech. This younger generation will be predisposed to buy a fuel cell car and use alternative energy. They'll have no attachment to the dirty old internal combustion engine. And this generation will also be the ones fascinated by the new field of nanotechnology—the real virgin technological turf left for them to pioneer. This generation will accept as a given that economic growth must be in balance with nature. From their very first days they have been surrounded by messages that they shouldn't litter, that air and water pollution is criminal, that natural habitats need to be preserved. They now feel these values and will carry them on. And this generation will see themselves as global citizens. With media saturation from sources all over the world, with local cultures feeding into the global culture, with more travel abroad and more exposure to foreign visitors, these kids will refine xenophobic stereotypes out of existence. A member of this generation will think of himself or herself as a kid in the world—a global kid.

This generation will come out of the Long Boom just hitting their prime performance years. The oldest of the generation today are in their late teens. By 2020, that leading-edge cohort will be entering their forties and the bulk of them will be in their thirties and late twenties. They will then be ready to take over a big portion of the work in the world and begin looking far out into the twenty-first century, their century. Given the expected advances in biotechnology and medical technology, their average life span could easily be at least 100 years, if not 120 years. These members of the Long Boom Generation will see not just the beginning of the coming century, but the end of it too. Their playing field will be the whole of the twenty-first century, a marvelous century, filled with great advances and surprises—and more than a few challenges.

The Long Boom Generation will be able to pick up from our efforts and work on higher-level problems that are out of our reach right now. Our kids could take on the full century's ambition of regenerating the natural ecosystem of the planet. They may aggressively root out all poverty—finally healing the divide between the richer North and the poorer South. Or they might truly mend the rift between the civilizations of the West and Islam. Or perhaps this generation will find its destiny in evolving new philosophies or a new form of spirituality that transcends the vicissitudes of various religions. Or maybe this generation will create new art forms or means of human expression. This will be the generation that wrestles with the curve balls pitched by wild science. Maybe this generation will be the ones to finally contact—or even create—other intelligent beings. This Long Boom Generation could take off in any of these directions and exploit many of the possibilities of the twenty-first century. These kids could enjoy the civilizational payoff of the Long Boom. But then, it all depends on what we do today.

THE IMPERATIVE OF GROWTH AND THE TRAGIC ALTERNATIVE

Every generation has its major challenge, and our challenge essentially is to bring about the Long Boom. You can quibble about the name or many of the specifics we laid out, but the opportunity of our era is to sustain a vast global economic expansion that goes a long way to solving many fundamental problems that have plagued the world for generation after generation. We believe that sustaining a high-growth strategy for the global economy is the only option. It is imperative that the world maintain economic growth rates of between 4 and 6 percent for at least the next twenty years. The only credible alternative is to bore full speed ahead.

High economic growth solves the core issues facing the world today. First of all, it helps solve the problem of the gap between the haves and the have-nots by pulling many more people into the haves category. It makes societies rich enough to pick up even those at the bottom. In the United States, the main mechanism is through job creation. In Europe, the mechanism still is mostly through social welfare, which if it is going to continue to work in the future must be based on a thriving economy. Either way, these societies need the increasing wealth to try to solve the problem of large numbers of marginalized or poor people. And without more global wealth, rectifying the extreme inequities between the developed and developing worlds will not happen.

Second, economic growth helps solve the environmental issue of the rapid destruction of the biosphere. Normally it would do exactly the opposite: Extreme growth would put extreme stress on the environment. Indeed, using our current industrial technologies, more growth does exactly that. But that's the point. Our current capital stock, the sum total of all our technologies, simply isn't good enough. It pollutes way too much and is far too inefficient. We need to replace the bulk of it—and fast. It's the only way to turn the corner on an environmental catastrophe within the next fifty years. So we need to rapidly migrate to much more environmentally benign technologies. Luckily, in almost every economic area of consequence—from transportation to manufacturing to energy production—there are whole new generations of technology coming that are much cleaner and greener. Only a high-growth strategy will turn over that capital stock rapidly enough. This is a monumental project that will take decades to fully complete—even at the rapid pace. At a slower pace, we may never pull it off.

Third, high growth throughout the world reduces major sources of conflict. As long as almost all countries—and all social classes within countries—see their prospects rising, one of the major sources of violence is undercut. People are much more likely to fight over scarce resources than when confronted with plenty. They are more likely to turn to violence—whether it's major war or petty crime—when they fear for their material survival. An expanding pie gives people legitimate opportunities to improve their lives. Why turn to the more desperate measures of crime or war? That's not to say that all the sources of conflict will disappear. People will still fight for other rational and irrational reasons, from pride and honor to greed and sheer miscalculation. However, in general, high growth will bring a greater alignment of interests because almost everyone has more to lose by a collapse of the international system and the growth juggernaut. The interdependencies created by integration get undercut by violence of any kind. In short, growth is the right thing to do all around. It is the best way to achieve social justice, environmental quality, and a reduction in violence.

If high rates of economic growth are imperative, then the only way to sustain that growth for the long haul is to be inclusive. This is absolutely crucial. Opportunities to obtain wealth, and the benefits of economic growth, must be shared broadly or the growth

won't go on. There's no way around it. If we don't provide access to
the new economic game for everyone, we'll either kill the growth
quickly, by causing a political backlash, or we'll kill it slowly, by
lessening demand. The backlash will come—indeed is already stew-
ing—among those who feel left behind or outright excluded from
the good times. Don't underestimate how powerful those passions
can be or how easily they could be tapped by skillful politicians.
And these lessons apply to the whole world. The developed countries in the West can't expect their economies to grow much more
unless much of the developing world gets back to expanding its
middle class. Any high-growth strategy has to be an aggressively inclusive one.

There is a very real tragic alternative to the Long Boom. Creating a
high-growth global economy is not a done deal. It is important to get
the policies and the institutions right. A low-growth or even no-
growth alternative could emerge—with disastrous results. It would
lock in the current social structure with almost no hope of improving
prospects for the many. The relative ratio of haves to have-nots would
remain virtually fixed. The momentum needed to move quickly to
new generations of green technologies would never materialize.
There'd be no capacity to act boldly to make that environmental fix.
And without expanding opportunities and prosperity, much focus
would be redirected to fighting over what's left. Conflict would almost certainly increase. In this scenario, fear and deprivation lead to
increasing protectionism and trade wars, and declining international
commerce. This brings the possibility of deflation, lower standards of
living, depression, and possibly even war—this time with biological
weapons. This is a very bad scenario. The outcome is tragic not only
because it's bad, but because we could have done much better. We
have the technology to solve many of our problems. We have the
tools, knowledge, and brainpower to figure out what we don't know
now. The outcome is tragic also because the victims who will bear the
negative consequences of our failures will be the generations that
come behind us.

We authors all have children. Schwartz has a son Ben, age nine;
Leyden has a daughter Emma, age seven; and Hyatt has two sons,
Zachary, age twelve, and Jared, age sixteen. They all are the recipients

of the dedication of this book. These children—our kids and their cohort around the planet—have so much potential, and they're growing up in a world with so much potential, that it would be an absolute tragedy to let them down. We offer this Long Boom book as a contribution to avoid such a tragedy and help unlock all the potential surrounding us. The Long Boom is not a prediction—this can't be stressed enough. The future is not predictable but it can be influenced by human actions. People working together can shape the future through their concerted efforts. That's why we put this challenge to you as a choice.

Your Choice

Think of this Long Boom book as a first-draft vision, a rough outline for a course that the world could follow. We believe that right now the world has no comprehensive vision of how to evolve in a way that will benefit everyone. In the post–Cold War era, people seem to have little idea where the world should head or how to make it better. We want to help solve that problem by offering this Long Boom vision, this set of ideas, to get people started thinking positively about our future and our destiny. By all means improve this draft. We hope you will do so.

Achieving this Long Boom all comes down to making the right choices. The responsibility for choice falls at many levels. The whole global community must make collective choices moving toward greater openness and interconnectedness. Individual nations must choose to opt into the evolving global system. No one can force them. This is not about control, but about opportunities and choices. Choices must also be made by social groups and communities, and by industries and companies. But ultimately, the choice rests with individuals. Ultimately, each individual will have to choose either to move forward toward a more positive future or remain with the status quo. But before you make that final decision, you might reflect on that hypothetical person looking back on our era from the year 2050 because in the end, that person could well be you. Anybody under the age of about fifty stands a decent chance of living to see the year 2050. Basically any Baby Boomer could live that long, including you.

What will you say to your great-grandchild in that year 2050? With life extension, connecting with great-grandchildren who are themselves adults will be increasingly common. What will you say to yours? Will you say that you faced up to the challenge of an anxious world in transition around the turn of the century? Will you say that you helped build a more positive global community in the ensuing decades? Will you say that you made sacrifices for future generations? Will you look your great-grandchild in the eye and say, "I did all I could for you"?

Afterword

MEMO TO THE
PRESIDENT-ELECT

THE YEAR 2000 PRESIDENTIAL CAMPAIGN is just beginning in the United States as this book gets published. Suppose the president-elect of the United States wanted to achieve the Long Boom vision. We would suggest a few steps that would get him or her started, as reflected in this e-mail.

http://www.president.gov
To: The President-Elect
RE: Achieving the Long Boom
Date: January 15, 2001

Congratulations on your election victory. Embracing the New Economy and countering the fears of globalization were key elements in your campaign's success. So was your confidence in approaching the future with optimism. You gave people hope.

These were great first steps in achieving the Long Boom vision of a better world. The next step is to get the public to understand that strong U.S. leadership in the world today is essential, and that without it there is no chance this vision will be fully realized. The United States must pragmatically and symbolically step up to accept the responsibilities, obligations, and opportunities of being the world's only superpower. This means not only paying up on our dues at the United Nations and recommitting if not boosting our contributions to the International Monetary Fund, but also helping Russia financially through its painful transition to democracy and free markets, and continuing to engage China as it embraces the New Economy. Our nation's security is much greater with a strong democratic Russia as opposed to a weak communist or totalitarian one. Similarly with China, we cannot withdraw from the arduous process of building an ever better relationship even though the path is filled with bumps along the way. The alternative—a cold war, or worse, with China—is far more dangerous to our national interests.

The United States should also lead efforts to integrate global regulatory frameworks in the financial, legal, and environmental arenas. Together with the IMF and other developed nations, we must assist developing countries in the critically important task of building solid political institutions that will ensure legal and financial stability. Our support for democracies and democratization around the world must be unyielding.

The United States and its allies must clearly articulate standards of international conduct for all nations, and be prepared to confront those who fail to adhere to these standards. To address the new threats that lie ahead, you should direct the military to adopt a new strategy. It is no longer necessary to be prepared to engage in two simultaneous major wars. There is not even one competitive superpower today, and that will not change until at least 2015. Revising our military strategy would enable us to save substantial amounts of money—to be better invested as discussed below—at the same time as we improve our ability to deal with the localized conflicts and terrorist threats that present today's challenges.

I know that your pollsters tell you that people have little interest in foreign affairs and even less in being the world's policeman. But you must use the unique platform of the White House to constantly explain the direct relationship between successfully playing our global leadership role and achieving a Long Boom vision that is in the interests of every American citizen—indeed of people everywhere.

The United States must lead the world in understanding the importance of high-growth economic policies. The Long Boom vision is based on sustainable global growth rates of between 4 and 6 percent, which would more than double the world's wealth in the next twenty years. Old-style Keynesian policies no longer fit the New Economy. We can have high growth and increasing wages in a world of low unemployment and no inflation. And we can do this because technological advances have significantly increased productivity, which makes the economic growth sustainable and noninflationary. You need to appoint a successor to Alan Greenspan who understands this completely, and who will not unnecessarily raise interest rates in response to economic growth, but will do so only if and when inflation is a real problem.

Your new Secretary of the Treasury must have diplomatic as well as managerial and financial skills, to take the case for high-growth economic policies around the world. But we need to lead the way. The United States is the world's supereconomy. We can afford to tolerate short-term trade deficits in order to help struggling developing countries increase their standards of living and thereby become larger consumers of our goods and services in the future.

Not everyone thrives in this new global economy. Domestic opposition to many of the important and necessary policies, like open trade, comes from those afraid of being lost in the cracks in this New Economy. The fear is real, as is the danger. Some people lose jobs and have great difficulty reestablishing themselves. We must adopt specific policies designed to help those people. We must improve and modernize the safety net. The approach should be to protect the person, not the job. If a job is unproductive, it is costly to thousands of unnamed others to prop that job up artificially. Doing so raises prices to all consumers and limits their choices of products and services. Instead we must help the person whose job is lost by providing tax credits, out-placement support, extension of health care coverage for the unemployed, and easy access to government-funded training programs that train people for tomorrow's jobs, not yesterday's.

It is difficult to help those lost in the kind of transition we are now going through from an industrial economy to a knowledge economy. It is easier to prepare the next generation to not ever be in a position of being left behind. We do this through a bold commitment to improving our educational system. The key to success in the Long Boom era is to create a learning society. You must help Americans understand that education is not something that stops when a person reaches his or her twenties. It is a lifelong process. You should support specific policies that at a minimum: require states to establish educational standards for K–12 schools; promote charter schools in the public school system, thereby creating competition between the public and private school systems and more choices of schools for parents and students; invite private-sector initiatives to devise better ways to deliver education; fund the wiring of all schools and provide universal, free Internet access for students; provide seed funding to develop distance learning for adults; fund the development of on-line libraries, which would make access to knowledge universal, convenient, and free; and initiate new global learning grants in conjunction with other nations that give young people the opportunity to pursue higher education at the same time that they get exposed to countries other than their own. These policies should be viewed not as expenses, but as investments.

Voters responded to your call to protect and enhance our environment. Accelerating the turnover of old facilities and equipment to new advanced technologies is enormously beneficial to the environment. Tax incentives as well as setting higher standards should continue to be used to provide encouragement to companies to do so. The federal government should be a leader, not a laggard, in adopting and adhering to higher standards.

Finally, you must adopt a policy that once again has the federal government making large investments in scientific research. We are at this moment of great historical opportunity in part because of sound government policies long ago. None was more important to getting us where we are today than the huge resources invested by the federal government in support of pure scientific research. The Long Boom vision is predicated on the pace of technological change accelerating. You can ensure this happens by restoring the role of the federal government as the chief supporter of science. One way both to spur rapid science and technology development and to excite the public would be to commit to a global effort to send a person to Mars by 2020. Another is to fund research in new, promising technologies, like nanotechnology that holds out the promise of allowing rapid economic growth completely in balance with nature.

Your opportunity as the first President of the new century is enormous. Your legacy can be as the person who led the way to the Long Boom vision of a better world. These steps are the first to take in building that legacy. Call on all Americans to help. Continue to be optimistic. Fulfill the hope your campaign created. Provide the bold, visionary leadership that we and the world need.

The Story of
the Idea

T HE STORY OF THE IDEA of the Long Boom began in the summer
of 1996 in the midst of general pessimism in the United States.
Most Americans at that time believed that their country was in decline, that the world was spinning dangerously out of control, and
that children were destined to live worse lives than their parents.
They felt insecure about their jobs and the long-term prospects of the
U.S. economy, despite many encouraging signs that were starting to
emerge. They seemed stuck in a negative mentality that had been
pervasive since the 1970s and could not be shaken even with such
breakthroughs as the end of the Cold War.

Against that gloomy backdrop, a project began at *Wired* magazine
in San Francisco to create a positive scenario of the future. It would
need to be able to convince a tough-minded audience that this vision
of the world could be realized in the near future. Peter Schwartz, a
contributing writer for the magazine, and Peter Leyden, a senior editor, teamed up to work through the ideas and write the story. Kevin
Kelly, *Wired*'s executive editor, Louis Rossetto, *Wired's* founder and
publisher, and John Battelle, the executive managing editor, challenged our thinking and contributed their ideas throughout the year-
long gestation of the article, which was published in July 1997.

By the winter of 1998, we had started realizing that politics would
be increasingly important in sustaining and extending this Long
Boom. Joel Hyatt, who is an entrepreneur involved in politics, and
who teaches at Stanford University's Graduate School of Business,
joined us in a seminar sponsored by *Wired* in Washington, D.C.,
called "The Politics of the Long Boom." This led to Joel's joining our
efforts to expand the original article into this book. (Just as we were

completing the book, Joel accepted an appointment by the Governor of California to the Public Utilities Commission.)

Meanwhile, the Long Boom idea had been resonating in other countries as well. The article was translated into French, Spanish, Italian, German, and Dutch. The Organization of Economic Cooperation and Development, which represents the United States, Europe, and the developed nations, picked up on the idea, and its Forum for the Future organized a conference called "Twenty-first Century Economic Dynamics: Anatomy of a Long Boom." Wolfgang Michaelski, the driving force behind the conference, brought together government ministers, global business leaders, policymakers and economists to discuss in great detail how to make the Long Boom happen. After two days of formal papers and presentations and group discussions, those attending the conference had advanced the ideas and strengthened their plausibility.

Our early work on the book was spent traveling the world doing research and conducting interviews. Schwartz and Leyden each traveled through Europe, particularly in London, Paris, Berlin, Amsterdam, and Stockholm. We benefited from numerous conversations with many remarkable Europeans, but several stand out: John Browning, former editor of *Wired UK*; Alain Delissen, a history professor at the École des Hautes Études en Sciences Sociales (Paris); Albert Bressand, director of Prométhée, a think tank and consulting firm in France; Torsten Schlabach, a technology journalist in Germany; Duco W. Sickinghe, Managing Director at Kluwer Publishers B.V., the Netherlands; S. J. G. van Wijnbergen, Secretary General, Ministry of Economic Affairs, the Dutch government's top economics official.

Brazil was tottering toward a currency collapse when Leyden visited in the summer of 1998. Roberto Unger, a Harvard professor and adviser to Brazilian presidential candidate Ciro Gomes, was especially thought-provoking, though his radical proposals for a new global economic order challenged many of the fundamental assumptions of our book. Other people in Brazil who gave freely of their insights include Amaury DeSouza, a Global Business Network (GBN) member and consultant; Stephen Kanitz, author of *Brazil: The Emerging Economic Boom: 1995 to 2005* (São Paulo: Makron Books, 1996); Paulo Renato, Brazilian Minister of Education; Peter J. T. G. Anderson,

Director President of Banco Credibanco; José Augusto Guilhon Albur-
querque, Director of the University of São Paulo Research Center for
International Relations; Ben Edwards, consultant and GBN member;
Maximiano Augusto Goncalves Filho, President of Fenasoft, a Brazilian software firm; Fulton Boyd, partner at Boyden, a headhunting
firm; Jairo Cupertino, Executive Vice President at Itaúsa, Investimen-
tos Itaú, a large bank; and Jaqueline Pedreira, former Editor-in-Chief
of *Internet.br* magazine.

Asia's successful recovery and transition to the new global economy is essential to any Long Boom scenario, so Leyden and Hyatt
each separately traveled through the region, ultimately covering five
major countries. In Japan, we are particularly indebted to Kenichi
Ohmae, Japanese intellectual leader, entrepreneur, and writer; Fumio
Kodama, a professor of science, technology, and policy at the University of Tokyo; Tadashi Nakamae, head of Nakamae economic research
group; Hiroaki Kitano, senior researcher at Sony Computer Science
Laboratory; James C. Abegglen, Chairman of Asia Advisory Service
K.K., a consulting firm; Hirotaka Takeuchi, a professor at Hitotsubashi
University in Tokyo; Robin Elsham, an editor in the Tokyo newsroom
of Bloomberg News Service; Reiko Saito, a business and finance reporter at Kyodo News Service; and Karl Schoenberger, former *Los Angeles Times* Tokyo correspondent.

South Korea provided a microcosm of the rise and fall and struggle
to rise again of a proud Asian country. James P. Rooney, President and
CEO of Templeton Investment Trust Management Co., Ltd., in Korea, and a former strategic planner for Templeton Funds, gave a mas-
terful assessment of the state of the global economy and a history of
the revolution in finance that could be its own book. We also greatly
benefited from conversations with Anthony R. Michell, President of
Euro-Asian Business Consultancy Ltd., Korea; Thae S. Khwarg, Chief
Executive Officer of Asset Korea; Wayne T. Cho, Managing Director of
Fritz Companies, Global Logistics Management and Consulting (Korea); Jeff Schroeder, a global shipping and logistics consultant; Han
Sung Joo, former Foreign Minister; and Chang Dal Joong, former
dean of Seoul National University.

A stable, thriving China is indispensable to any twenty-first century
world order, and so we spent much time traveling to Shanghai, Beijing,

and Hong Kong. Mark L. Clifford, Asia bureau chief for *Business Week* and former business editor for the *Far Eastern Economic Review,* gave generously of his many insights into China and the region. Special thanks also go to Melissa Brown, Director, Regional Power and Utilities Equity Research at Solomon Smith Barney in Hong Kong; Ronnie C. Chan, Chairman of Hang Lung Group, a real estate conglomerate based in Hong Kong; Victor Fung, Chairman of Li & Fung, a conglomerate based in Hong Kong; Richard Boucher, U.S. Counsel General to Hong Kong; Thomas M. H. Chan, head of the China Business Center at the Hong Kong Polytechnic University; David N. Devine, Vice President of Overlook Investments Limited, a global investment firm based in Hong Kong; Hans W. Vriens, Vice President for APCO Asia Ltd., the Hong Kong branch of the global public affairs and strategic communicating company; and David Dodwell, author of *The Hong Kong Advantage* and executive at the investment firm Jardine Fleming in Hong Kong.

Indonesia was the Asian country most decimated by the crisis, and we went there to witness the destruction firsthand. In Jakarta, Francis A. Lutz, President of the Association of Foreign Bank Representatives and Country Manager of Toronto Dominion Bank, gave the best explanation of what went on inside the mind of global investors who pumped capital into economies like Indonesia despite the big risks. Other key guides included Mark Winkel, who heads his own communications firm, Prisma Public Relations; Salmona L. Jahja, Senior Staff Planning Analyst for the multinational oil firm ARCO, in Indonesia; and Jessie C. Inman, Canadian investment Adviser for the Canada-Indonesia Business Development Office.

India withstood the crisis but also holds some keys to the future. Alok Vajpeyi, a former stock broker and investor, provided us rare access to Indian society. John Moore, Director of TransTech India Limited and longtime British expatriate, gave us the long-view history of British colonialism in Asia. Other memorable interviews came from Ravi Narain, Deputy Managing Director of the National Stock Exchange of India; S. S. Tarapore, retired top official of India's economics ministry; Ajay Shah and Susan Thomas, both assistant professors at the Indira Gandhi Institute of Development Research; Cyrus J. Guzder, Chairman and Managing Director of Airfreight Limited, India; and Leo Puri, Principal at McKinsey & Company, the Indian branch of the global consulting firm.

Back in the United States, we moved around the country to connect with key sources and crystallize our ideas. Of those people we spoke to on the East Coast, we are particularly grateful to several: Thomas L. Friedman, foreign affairs columnist for the *New York Times,* who shared his insights on globalization on several occasions and read the manuscript, and Michael Porter, a professor at the Harvard Business School, whose generosity extended to reviewing and improving the manuscript. We are also indebted to Robert D. Hormats, Vice Chairman of Goldman Sachs (International); Walter B. Wriston, former CEO of Citicorp; Edward Yardeni, Chief Economist and Managing Director of Deutsche Bank Securities; David Landes, Harvard professor emeritus in economic history; Robert Litan, Director of Economic Studies at the Brookings Institution; Mickey Kantor, former U.S. Trade Representative; Steven Kelman, a professor at Harvard's Kennedy School of Government, who also gave valuable feedback on the manuscript; Kevin Corrigan, partner of Security Atlantic Capital Management LLC; and Tom Martinson, urban planner and designer.

As to those on the West Coast, we relied on the significant work of Paul Romer, a professor at Stanford University's Graduate School of Business, who also read the manuscript. We also drew from the ideas of Michael Fairbanks of the Monitor Company, who spent a few weeks, together with Hyatt, as a visiting fellow at Stanford's Hoover Institution on War, Revolution and Peace; Brian M. Sager, biotechnology analyst for Ernst & Young LLP; Shaun B. Jones, a manager of the Defense Advanced Research Projects Agency; G. Pascal Zachory, a senior writer for the *Wall Street Journal;* Don Norman, former head of Apple advanced research; and Roger H. Cass, head of Cass Research Associates and a longtime proponent of the idea of a major economic boom.

Global Business Network, the think tank and worldwide network of strategists, executives, scientists, and artists that Schwartz cofounded, provided an intellectual home for all of us during the book project. Several GBN colleagues were especially important in developing the ideas, some long before the book began. These include Stewart Brand, Napier Collyns, and Jay Ogilvy, three of the original founders, as well as Richard O'Brien, principal in GBN UK. Collyns and O'Brien also gave feedback to the manuscript, along with Katherine Fulton, a GBN principal, and Steven Weber, a professor of political science at the University of California Berkeley and an independent consultant with GBN. The Global Business Network of interesting minds also contributed directly or indirectly. Those who were especially helpful include Eric Drexler, founder of the Foresight Institute; Amory Lovins, of the Rocky Mountain Institute; Bo Ekman, Chairman of Nextwork; Danny Hillis, Disney Fellow; Doug Carlston, founder of Broderbund Software; and Brian Eno, musician and artist. Individuals from several GBN member companies were especially supportive of the ideas: Johan nic Vold of Statoil, Goren Lindahl of ABB, the European-based energy firm, Doug Glen of Mattel, and Goren Collert of Swedbank.

Herman Kahn and Pierre Wack have been especially important inspirations in the scenario work of GBN and in the ideas in the Long Boom scenario. Kahn wrote of the long-term multifold trend in the sixties, and Wack first published his Belle Epoque scenario in the seventies; both of these were precursors of the concept of the Long Boom.

The Long Boom book depended heavily on sustained help from some core people. Joel Ben Izzy, a professional storyteller and story consultant, helped work through the story lines of two strands of the book and came up with the idea of creating a character to track in time. Nick Philipson, our editor at Perseus, gave judicious feedback and stayed open to the unusual features of our book. Gina Casagrande, the project's assistant and researcher, suffered through the transcription of dozens of tapes of interviews, meetings, and long monologues that worked out the raw ideas. She was indispensable from those earliest stages all the way to getting the final polished manuscript out the door. And John Brockman, our book agent, pushed and continues to push to get the book out to the widest possible audience.

David Bank, a reporter in the *Wall Street Journal*'s San Francisco bureau covering technology generally and Microsoft monomaniacally, met almost weekly with Leyden throughout the course of the book to share everything he knew about technology and the world. Many of his ideas helped shape this book. Leyden also wants to thank his core circle of friends, which includes Bank, as well as Michael Hertz, fellow at the Open Society Institute and founder of Probono.net, a non-profit corporation building virtual public interest legal communities; Dorothy Q. Thomas, founder of the Women's Rights Division of Human Rights Watch and current MacArthur Fellow; and Hal Aronson, multifaceted teacher to everyone. Their stimulation and support were deeply appreciated during the trying times of writing this book.

Leyden wants to give special thanks to Sharon Hawkins Leyden, his wife and partner in life. She gave him the time and space to focus on this project while she dealt with many of the by-products of obsession. Thanks to her, he learned as much about life in the year as he learned about the world. He learned how to let go of past patterns, be open to new ones, and constantly keep growing, while staying connected. Her huge heart helped him fully understand the value of empathy and being inclusive of everyone. Much of what he learned from her has surfaced in this book.

Hyatt wants to thank his colleagues at Stanford University's Graduate School of Business, particularly Chuck Holloway and Irv Grousbeck, for giving him the wonderful opportunity to teach entrepreneurship. Stanford attracts first-rate students from around the world who want to learn about and be involved in the culture of knowledge, innovation, and growth that epitomize this school and Silicon Valley, in which it resides.

Hyatt also wants to thank his wife, Susan Hyatt, who has been his partner in everything he has accomplished in his adult life, including this book. Her sense of adventure—along with her sense of humor–is, thankfully, limitless. As their journey together continues, he is confident so will her patience, support, and love, for which he is everlastingly grateful.

Schwartz also wants to acknowledge his great debt of gratitude to his wife, Cathleen Schwartz. She has been a constant inspiration to him. She challenges him and lifts his spirits. She helps him clearly see the way forward and always asks the right questions.

All three authors also want to apologize in advance to all the sources we consulted in creating this book. We decided to write the story as one flowing narrative, so that few people are tied to their direct contributions even though we are well aware that this book could not have happened without them. This also means that we absolve all those mentioned above for the errors and omissions in this book, and we assume full responsibility.

We believe it was important to synthesize all the input and devise a Long Boom idea that could be disseminated in an accessible form—in the spirit of the Internet and the Long Boom itself. In order for the Long Boom to fully take off, good ideas must be spread as widely as possible. The larger the number of people who adopt better ideas, the better off everyone will be. We offer this book in that same spirit. Take what you can from it, and pass it on. Expand the Long Boom idea to the next level. Let the story of the idea continue . . .

NOTES

I N WRITING *The Long Boom,* we tried to assimilate information from many
sources and create a readable narrative that was accessible to a wide audience. The notes that follow are not meant to comprehensively document all
the information in the book. Rather, they are highly selective. Some refer to
particularly helpful interviews we conducted. Others cite exceptional research material that informed passages or whole sections. And a few do give
the readers specific references about where to find key facts.

CHAPTER 1

19   Peter Leyden, "On the Edge of the Digital Age," *Star Tribune,* Spe-
        cial Report (June 4, 1995), Section T. This four-part series was Ley-
        den's first pass at some of these Long Boom ideas.

25   "The Unwired World, an Insider's Guide to the Future Technolo-
        gies of Telecommunications," *Scientific American,* Special Report,
        vol. 278, no. 4 (April 1998), 69–96.

25   *to handle all communication:* Seth Schiesel, "One Nation, Un-
        plugged," *New York Times* (January 11, 1999), C1.

26   *the previous twenty-five years*: This Gates conversation comes from
        David Bank, the *Wall Street Journal*'s main reporter covering Mi-
        crosoft.

27   "Silicon Valley," *Business Week,* Special Double Issue (August 25,
        1997), 24–85.

28   David E. Sanger, "From Trustbusters to Trust Trusters," *New York
        Times* (December 6, 1998), WK1.

30   David Bank, "Rivals of Microsoft Find Collaboration Is Easier Said
        Than Done," *Wall Street Journal* (November 19, 1998), A10.

CHAPTER 2

42   Stephen B. Shepard, "The New Economy: What It Really Means,"
        Business Week (November 17, 1997), 37–40.

42   "The 21st Century Economy," *Business Week*, Special Double Issue (August 31, 1998), 24–88.

44   Thomas W. Malone, "Is Empowerment Just a Fad? Control, Decision Making, and IT," *Sloan Management,* Review (Winter 1997), 23–35.

45   Steven Weber, "The End of the Business Cycle?" *Foreign Affairs*, vol. 76, no.4 (July–August, 1997), 65.

45   Thomas A. Bass, "The Future of Money," *Wired* (October 1996), 142–205.

46   Louis Uchitelle, "Productivity Gains Help Keep Economy on a Roll," *New York Times* (March 22, 1999), A16.

47   "Happy Days: Are They Here Again?" *Wall Street Journal,* Quarterly Survey of Politics, Economics, and Values (December 10, 1998), A9.

47   Robert D. Atkinson and Randolph H. Court, *The New Economy Index* (Washington, D.C.: Progressive Policy Institute, Technology, Innovation, and New Economy Project, November 1998).

47   Edward Wyatt, "Does the Dow Measure Up?" *New York Times* (March 30, 1999), C1.

47   *Beginning of the Long Boom:* Gretchen Morgenson, "Dow Finishes Day over 10,000 Mark for the First Time," *New York Times* (March 30, 1999), A1. Includes great charts on the Dow's historic rise.

50   "World Economic Outlook," *International Monetary Fund*, World Economic and Financial Surveys (May 1997).

50   G. Pascal Zachary, "The World Gets in Touch with Its Inner American," *Mother Jones* (January–February 1999).

51   "The Global Competitiveness Report," *World Economic Forum*, 1997.

51   Nicholas Kristof with Edward Wyatt, Sheryl WuDunn, and David E. Sanger, "Global Contagion, A Narrative," *New York Times*, Four-Part Series (February 15–18, 1999), A1.

51   Richard Lacayo. "The End of the World!?! Counting Down to Armegeddon," *Time,* vol. 153, no. 2 (January 18, 1999), 60–79.

53   Nicholas D. Kristof, "Experts Question Roving Flow of Global Capital," *New York Times* (September 20, 1999), A6.

53   David Wessel and Bob Davis, "Would-Be Keyneses Vie over How to Fight Globe's Financial Woes," Special Series: Markets under Siege, *Wall Street Journal* (September 25, 1998), A1.

53   Jeffrey E. Garten, "Needed: A Fed for the World," *New York Times* (September 23, 1998), A29.

55   Angus Maddison, "Poor until 1820," *Wall Street Journal* (January 11, 1999), R54.

56   Donella H. Meadows, "The Long Wave," *Whole Earth* (Summer 1998), 100–108.

56   *for twenty years:* "China's Economy: Red Alert," *The Economist* (October 24, 1998), 23.

60   Laura M. Holson, "The Deal Still Rules, Mania for Mergers Defines the Market," *New York Times* (February 14, 1999), A10.

Chapter 3

68   Michael Moynihan, *The Coming American Renaissance, How to Benefit from America's Economic Resurgence* (New York: Simon & Schuster, 1996).

69   Thomas L. Friedman, "A Manifesto for the Fast World," *New York Times Magazine* (March 28, 1999), 40–61.

72   "The Next Politics," *Blueprint, Ideas for a New Century*, vol. 1 (Fall 1998) 1-70. This is a new quarterly published by the Democratic Leadership Council.

73   "The New American Consensus," *New York Times Magazine*, Special Series (November 1, 1998),

73   David S. Broder and Richard Morin, "A Struggle over Values," *Washington Post*, vol. 16, no. 11 (January 11, 1999), 6–8.

74   David Kline and Daniel Burstein, "Is Government Obsolete?" *Wired* (January 1996), 86–105.

75   Peter Applebome, "Dueling with the Heirs of Jeff Davis," *New York Times* (December 27, 1998), A4.

75   Richard L. Berke, "Voters All Over Take the Wheel from Conservatives," *New York Times* (January 31, 1999), WK1.

77   DeAnne Julius, "21st Century Economic Dynamics: Anatomy of a Long Boom," *OECD Forum for the Future*, Expo 2000 conference on the policy drivers for the Long Boom. (OECD; Frankfurt, 1998)

81   Kevin Kelly, the executive editor of *Wired,* expands at length on the networking metaphor in his book *The New Rules of the New Economy* (New York: Viking, 1998).

82   "Education and the Wealth of Nations," *The Economist* (March 29, 1997), 15, 21–23.

82   *The Third Wave:* Alvin Toffler, *The Third Wave, The Classic Study of Tomorrow* (New York: Bantam Books, 1980).

83   *like the best schools:* This concept is based on a conversation Leyden
      had with Roberto Unger, a Harvard professor, in São Paulo, Brazil,
      in the summer of 1998. Unger lays it out in his book *The Future of
      American Progressivism: An Initiative for Political and Economic Re-
      form*, by Roberto Unger and Cornell West (Boston: Beacon press,
      1998).

83   Bob Davis and David Wessel, *Prosperity, the Coming 20-Year Boom
      and What It Means to You* (New York: Times Business, A Division of
      Random House, 1998).

84   *how we learn:* This comes from an interview Leyden had with Bill
      Gross in Los Angeles in the summer of 1997.

87   "Steve Jobs: The Next Insanely Great Thing," Interview by Gary
      Wolf, *Wired* (February 1996), 102-107; 158-163.

Chapter 4

92   *11 percent:* These figures are from Richard L. Hudson, "Investing in
      Euroland, a Safe Haven?" *Wall Street Journal* (September 28, 1998),
      R4, and Thomas Kamm, "Au Revoir, Malaise: Europe's Economies
      Are Back in Business," *Wall Street Journal* (April 9, 1998), A1.

92   Andrew Sullivan, "There Will Always Be an England," *New York
      Times Magazine* (February 21, 1999), 38–45.

93   *for the United States:* The eleven countries are Germany, France,
      Italy, Spain, the Netherlands, Austria, Belgium, Finland, Ireland,
      Portugal, Luxembourg.

94   *the U.S. rich:* See the above Kamm and Hudson *Wall Street Journal* ar-
      ticles.

94   Warren Hoge, "Tony Blair Rides Triumphant as a Visionary and a
      Promoter," *New York Times* (February 2, 1999), A1.

95   Roger Cohen, "Germany's Pragmatic Ex-Radical Thinks Globally,"
      New York Times (January 28, 1999), A3.

95   *by that time:* Barry James, "EU Specter: New Version of Old East-
      West Line," *Herald Tribune* (October 28, 1998), 1.

96   Alessandra Stanley, "For Ambitious Entrepreneurs, All Europe Is
      Just One Nation," *New York Times* (December 24, 1998), A10.

100   *The Spirit of Capitalism*: Max Weber, *The Protestant Ethic and the
      Spirit of Capitalism,* (New York: Scribner, 1958).

100   *developmental success:* Leyden interviewed David Landes at his
      home in Cambridge, Massachusetts, in the summer of 1998. His

book is *The Wealth and Poverty of Nations: Why Some Are So Rich and Some Are So Poor*, (New York: W.W. Norton, 1998).

100   *and 15 in Mexico:* Ben C. Fuller and George Riegel, "Brazilian Trends: 2002–2010," a GBN (Global Business Network) report created for Daimler-Benz in 1997. Society and Technology Research Group, Report #1, Brazil/Palo Alto, 1997.

100   *in the United States:* Diana Jean Schemo, "The ABC's of Business in Brazil," New York Times (July 16, 1998), C1.

100   Stephen Kanitz, *Brazil: The Emerging Economic Boom* (São Paulo, Brazil: Makron Books, 1996).

CHAPTER 5

112   *percent shares:* This McNealy insight comes, once again, from *The Wall Street Journal's* David Bank.

115   *a ponzi game:* Leyden interviewed Lutz in his office in Jakarta after the bottom had fallen out of the market in August 1998.

116   Michael Lewis, "Going-Out-of-Business Sale," *New York Times Magazine* (May 31, 1998), 35–69.

116   Paul Krugman, "Saving Asia: It's Time to Get Radical," *Fortune* (September 7, 1998), 33–38.

117   *crisis they face:* Leyden interviewed Mitchell in the Chosun Hotel in Seoul in August 1998.

117   Steven Radelet and Jeffrey Sachs, "Asia's Reemergence," *Foreign Affairs*, vol. 76, no.6 (November–December 1997), 44–59.

117   *of their earnings:* "China's Economy: Red Alert," *The Economist* (October 24, 1998), 23–26.

118   *incremental innovation:* Leyden interviewed Kodama, who is a professor of science, technology, and industry at the Research Center for Advanced Science and Technology at the University of Tokyo. Fumio Kodama, *Emerging Patterns of Innovation: Sources of Japan's Technological Edge* (Boston: Harvard Business School Press, 1991).

120   Michael E. Porter and Hirotaka Takeuchi, "Fixing What Really Ails Japan," *Foreign Affairs* v78, n3 (May, 1999): 66.

121   Stephanie Strom, "In Japan, from a Lifetime Job to No Job at All," *New York Times* (February 3, 1999), A1.

123   "Scenarios for the Future of Japan," *Deeper News*, Global Business Network, vol. 10, no. 2 (February 1999), 1-107.

125   *will get 1,000 opinions:* Ohmae told that adage to Hyatt in dis-
        cussing the Japanese crisis over dinner in Tokyo in August 1998.

128   *in Southeast Asia:* See Sterling Seagrave, *Lords of the Rim: The Invisi-
        ble Empire of the Overseas Chinese* (New York: Putnam, 1995). He ex-
        plores this phenomenon in depth.

129   *the world average:* All these figures come from Angus Maddison,
        "Chinese Economic Performance in the Long Run," (OECD: Paris,
        1998), 194 pages.

129   Peter Schwartz and Jay Ogilvy, *The Next Leap* (San Francisco: Jossey-
        Bass Inc., 1999).

132   *helps the world boom:* Richard Rapaport, "Bangalore," *Wired* (Febru-
        ary 1996), 112–170.

Chapter 6

135   Russell Working, "Russia's Patchwork Economy," *New York Times*
        (March 18, 1999), C1.

135   Bruce Sterling, "Art and Corruption," *Wired* (January 1998),
        119–140.

136   "Future Scenarios on Russian-American Relations," *The Russian-
        American Center* (California: Esalen Institute, September 1996), 1-18.

136   *capacity for suffering:* This is based on observations of Russia by Jay
        Ogilvy, a GBN founder and longtime student of Russian develop-
        ments.

142   "Seeking Answers to Pressing Issues in Economic Development,"
        The World Bank, Policy Research Department FY96 Annual Report.

Chapter 7

151   *every 1,000 years or so:* Many of the weather anecdotes in this pas-
        sage were complied from Mark Hertsgaard, "Severe Weather Warn-
        ing," *New York Times Magazine* (August 2, 1998), 48-50.

152   *since the mid-nineteenth century:* William K. Stevens, "Earth's Tem-
        perature in 1998 Is Reported at Record High," *New York Times* (De-
        cember 18, 1998), A32, offers these numbers and others in this
        passage.

153   *tipping the balance:* William K. Stevens, "In Ancient Ice Ages, Clues
        to Climate," *New York Times* (February 16, 1999), D1.

153   *another Ice Age:* William H. Calvin, "The Great Climate Flip-Flop,"
        Atlantic Monthly (January 1998), 41–63. This article offers a detailed
        explanation of how another Ice Age could happen.

154   *The Population Bomb:* Paul Ehrlich, *The Population Bomb* (San Fran-
         cisco: Sierra Club, 1969).

154   Hardin Tibbs, "Sustainability," *Deeper News,* Global Business Net-
         work, vol.3, no. 1 (January 1999), 5-73.

154   *can replicate itself:* Barbara Crossette, "How to Fix a Crowded World:
         Add People," *New York Times* (November 2, 1997), WK1. Most of
         the population statistics come from this article and United Nations
         sources cited in it.

156   William K. Stevens, "Expectation Aside, Water Use in U.S. Is Show-
         ing Decline," *New York Times* (November 10, 1998), A1. This pro-
         vides some fascinating figures on multiple efficiencies.

157   William K. Stevens, "In Kyoto, the Subject Is for Climate; the Fore-
         cast Is for Storms," *New York Times* (December 1, 1997), D1.

158   David Harris, "São Paulo Megacity," *Rolling Stone* (December 26,
         1997), 126–134.

159   *to release the image:* Stewart Brand is a cofounder of GBN and a
         longtime friend of Schwartz's. Brand went on to do many remark-
         able things, including founding the Hacker's Conference and the
         WELL, the pioneer on-line community, and writing many books,
         including *The Media Lab.* (New York: Penguin Books, 1987).

160   *gone completely global:* Peter Schwartz and Stewart Brand, *Decades of
         Restructuring.* (Emeryville, Global Business Network, 1989) p. 57.

161   "Drowning in Oil," *The Economist,* vol. 350, no. 8109 (March 6,
         1999), 19, 23–25.

162   *Limits to Growth:* A report for the Club of Rome's project on the
         predicament of mankind, by Donella H. Meadows and others.
         (New York: Universe Books, 1972).

162   *miles per gallon:* This number, like several here, comes from Ernst
         Von Weizsacker, Amory B. Lovins, and L. Hunter Lovins, *Factor
         Four: Doubling Wealth, Halving Resource Use: The New Report to the
         Club of Rome,* (London: Earthscan,1997).

Chapter 8

173   *in the human body:* Much of this explanation of fuel cells comes
         from Jacques Leslie, "Dawn of the Hydrogen Age," in *Wired* (Octo-
         ber 1997), 138–191. Leyden worked closely with Leslie on this arti-
         cle, which was one of the first to lay out the implications of a
         full-fledged hydrogen economy. Many other publications soon fol-
         lowed with similar articles, some of which are cited in the notes
         here.

174   Anthony DePalma, "The Great Green Hope: Are Fuel Cells the Key to Cleaner Energy?" *New York Times* (October 8, 1997), D1. This article gives a very good overview of fuel cell development and prospects but, like many *New York Times* articles, remains fairly skeptical.

174   Rebecca Blumenstein, "Shifting Gears: Auto Industry Reaches Surprising Consensus: It Needs New Engines. Demands for Fuel Economy, Lower Emissions Spur Firms' Research Efforts. But Just What Will Be Next?" *Wall Street Journal* (January 5, 1998), A1. This is a good, optimistic overview.

174   Jeffrey Ball, "Auto Makers are Racing to Market 'Green' Cars Powered by Fuel Cells," *Wall Street Journal* (March 15, 1999), A1.

175   *by 90 percent:* Andrew Pollack, "Toyota to Sell Hybrid-Power Car in Japan," *New York Times* (April 26, 1997) C1.

177   *5,000 miles or more. . . :* This, again, comes from that *Wired* magazine article by Jacques Leslie. Several other important facts in this hydrogen section come from that article, including the discussion on safety.

178   *megawatts by 2001:* "At Last, the Fuel Cell," *The Economist* (October 25, 1997) 89-92. This article was part of a cover package on hydrogen fuel. Several pieces of information given here also come from that package.

178   *Department of Energy:* Matthew L. Wald, "Fuel Cell Will Supply All Power to a Test House," *New York Times* (June 17, 1998), A27.

CHAPTER 9

189   *unusual idea:* Kary Mullis has publicly described the context of his breakthrough, which we retell here.

190   Jeremy Rifkin, *The Biotech Century, Harnessing the Gene and Remaking the World* (New York: Tarcher/Putnam, 1998).

191   *inoperable brain cancer:* Lawrence M. Fisher, "Hope Near the End of the Pipeline, a New Generation of Treatments for Cancer Will Soon Reach the Market," *New York Times* (May 1, 1997), C1.

195   *a single mouse:* Sheryl WuDunn, "South Korean Scientists Say They Cloned a Human Cell," *New York Times* (December 17, 1998), A12. An accompanying chart tracks the progress in cloning.

196   *a single cow:* Gina Kolata, "Japanese Scientists Clone a Cow, Making 8 Copies," *New York Times* (December 9, 1998) A8.

197   *the surrounding tissue:* Nicholas Wade, "Scientists Cultivate Cells at Root of Human Life, Hope for Transplants and Gene Therapy— Ethics at Issue," *New York Times* (November 6, 1998), A1. Also Nicholas Wade, "Blueprints for People, but How to Read Them?" *New York Times* (December 8, 1998), D1.

197   *programming of a worm:* Nicholas Wade, "Animal's Genetic Program Decoded, in a Science First," *New York Times* (December 11, 1998), A1.

197   Nicholas Wade, "Who'll Sequence Human Genome First? It's Up to Phred," *New York Times* (March 23, 1999), D2.

197   Karin Jegalian, "The Gene Factory," *Technology Review*, vol. 102, no. 2 (March–April 1999), 64–71.

198   *control that gene, too?:* See the novel *Mendel's Dwarf*, by Simon Mawer (New York: Harmony Books, 1998), which explores this very question.

198   Sarah Lyall, "A Country Unveils Its Gene Pool and Debate Flares," *New York Times* (February 16, 1999), D1.

199   *fears be resolved?. . . :* The original *Whole Earth Catalog* was reproduced in full in the Winter 1998 *Whole Earth,* which marked the thirtieth anniversary of that inaugural issue. Brand wrote a preface to the new version.

201   *most people think:* Gina Kolata, "Pushing Limits of the Human Life Span," *New York Times* (March 9, 1999), D1.

201   *life span to age 120:* Steve Farrar, "Today's Babies Can Expect to Live to 130," *London Times* (February 14, 1999), 1.

201   *as 50 years ago:* Mary Catherine Bateson, who is a member of the GBN network, gave a talk related to this topic at the company's Emeryville office on January 6, 1999.

203   *December 29, 1959:* This comes from a copy of the original lecture by Richard P. Feynman, "There's Plenty of Room at the Bottom." This material, along with other material on nanotechnology, comes from the Foresight Institute.

204   *like an original thinker:* Leyden interviewed Drexler in the Foresight Institute offices in Silicon Valley in Jue 1998. Drexler is the chairman of the nonprofit institute, which promotes an understanding of the possibilities of nanotechnology.

204   *Engines of Creation:* Eric Drexler, *Engines of Creation* (New York: Doubleday, 1986).

205   *on simple experiments:* Charles Siebert, "The Next Frontier: Invisible: Welcome to the Age of the Microscopic," *New York Times Magazine* (September 29, 1996) 137-146.

205   *devices showcased:* This comes from notes from the conference put out by the Foresight Institute. See [www.foresight.org].

205   "Nanotech: The Hope and the Hype," *Technology Review*, Special Report, vol. 102, no. 2 (March–April 1999), 46–63.

205   *very small particles:* Niall McKay, "A Big Future for Very Small Machines," *Reuters* (November 10, 1998).

208   *our road system:* Several of these examples are from K. Eric Drexler and Chris Peterson with Gayle Pergamit, *Unbounding the Future: The Nanotechnolgy Revolution—The Path to Molecular Manufacturing and How It Will Change Our World* (New York: William Morrow and Co., 1991).

208   One of the best of the recent nanotechnology science fiction books is Neal Stephenson, *The Diamond Age* (New York: Bantam Books, 1996).

CHAPTER 10

213   John Noble Wilford, "Superclusters of Galaxies Shed New Light on Cosmic Architecture, *New York Times* (January 26, 1999), D1.

213   John Noble Wilford, "New Findings Help Balance the Cosmological Books," *New York Times* (February 9, 1999), D1.

214   *and more funding:* Brian Sager made this argument in an interview with the three authors in the fall of 1998. Sager has a Ph.D in biochemistry from Stanford and a postdoc in neurobiology research from Harvard. He is now a biotechnology analyst trying to set up a life sciences practice for Ernst & Young, the consulting group.

217   *take 2,000 years:* This and much of the information on warp drive come from the article by Jeff Greenwald, "To Infinity and Beyond: Warp drive, Wormholes, and the Power of Nothing," *Wired* (July 1998), 90-97. Leyden worked with Greenwald on this project.

218   *negated gravity:* Much of this material comes from Charles Platt, "Breaking the Law of Gravity," *Wired* (March 1998) 170-177; 190-202.

219   *stories of the decade:* Charles Platt, "What If Cold Fusion Is Real?" *Wired* (November 1998), 170-179; 222-230.

220   William J. Broad, "A Tempest in a Test Tube, 10 Years Later," *New York Times* (March 23, 1999), D3.

220   *kind of life form:* John Noble Wilford, "Jupiter's Moon Might Be Cradle for New Life," *New York Times* (April 10, 1997), A1.

221 *200 light-years:* William J. Broad, "Scientists Revive Scan of the Heavens for Signs of Life," *New York Times* (September 29, 1998), D1.

223 Warren E. Leary, "Space Station's First Piece Is Set to Soar at Last," *New York Times* (November 16, 1998), A8.

224 Paul Raeburn, "Manned Mission to Mars," *Popular Science* (February, 1999), 40–47.

Chapter 11

230 Numbers here and within this passage are rooted in "The Emerging Middle Class," a *Business Week* special project (November 18, 1994).

233 *in the mid-1990s:* Chip Walker, "Can TV Save the Planet?" *American Demographics* v18, n5 (May 1996), 42-48. Most figures on television in this passage are from this article.

235 Michael Lind, "The Beige and the Black," *New York Times Magazine* (August 16, 1998), 38–39.

236 *of 7.8 billion:* Barbara Crossette, "Surprises in the Global Tourism Boom," *New York Times* (April 12, 1998), WK1. Some of the travel figures are based on a United Nations report.

236 Ronnie Chan, "Cultural Capability—The Making of an International Person," Keynote, Career Development Seminar, Center for Chinese and American Studies, China: Johns Hopkins University—Nanjing University, April 18, 1994.

Chapter 12

244 *6.9 million men:* Tamar Lewin, "American Colleges Begin to Ask, Where Have All the Men Gone?" *New York Times* (December 6, 1998), WK1.

244 *boys in school:* Tamar Lewin, "How Boys Lost Out to Girl Power," *New York Times* (December 13, 1998), WK1.

246 Nicholas D. Kristof, "As Asian Economies Shrink, Women Are Squeezed Out," *New York Times* (June 11, 1998), A12.

247 Francis Fukuyama, "What If Women Ran the World?" *Foreign Affairs*, vol. 77, no.5 (September-October 1998), 24-40.

248 *8,000,000 firms:* "Small Business Administration Accomplishments for Women-Owned Businesses," a fact sheet from the U.S. Small Business Administration, Office of Women's Business Ownership, September 15, 1998.

249   *and she accepts:* Much of the material in this paragraph comes from
        Dorothy Q. Thomas, the founder of the Women's Rights Division
        of Human Rights Watch. She is a longtime friend of Leyden and
        speaks around the world on women's issues.

249   Elisabeth Rosenthal, "Women's Suicides Reveal Rural China's Bitter
        Roots," *New York Times* (January 24, 1999), A8.

CHAPTER 13

262   *"Everybody":* Leyden interviewed Wriston in his office in New York
        in June 1998. The quote, though, is from an earlier *Wired* magazine
        interview with him. Thomas A. Bass, "The Future of Money," *Wired*
        (October, 1996) 140-143, 200-205.

263   *Emulating the Biological:* Many of the reflections in this section
        come from Kevin Kelly and his book *Out of Control* (Reading, MA:
        Addison-Wesley, 1994).

265   *health services of any kind:* These facts are from Barbara Crossette
        "Kofi Annan's Astonishing Facts!" an infographic from the *New
        York Times*, September 23, 1998, WK 16.

266   *4 percent annual pace:* Sylvia Nasar, "U.S. Economy Grew at Fast 5.6
        Percent Rate at the End of '98: Quickest Pace in 2 Years, Inflation,
        Already Low, Slipped to 0.8 Percent in the 4th Quarter, the Lowest
        in 40 Years," *New York Times* (January 30, 1998), A1.

Selected Bibliography

L ISTED HERE ARE SOME of the books that have influenced our thinking over the years. They are also books that readers might turn to for further information on some of the themes we explore in this book. By no means is this list of fifty books comprehensive. It's a rather eclectic compilation of those books that helped stretch our minds in many directions. May they do the same to yours.

The Age of Spiritual Machines, by Ray Kurzweil (New York: Viking, 1999). Gives a sense of just how profound the information technology revolution could be.

The Americans: *The Democratic Experience,* by Daniel Boorstin (New York: Vintage Books, 1973). Lays out how democracy has helped shape the United States and its vision over the last several centuries.

The Clash of Civilizations and the Remaking of World Order, by Samuel Huntington (New York: Simon & Schuster, 1996). A provocative book that envisions a post–Cold War order defined not by conventional politics, but by the major civilizations of the world coming into collision.

The Commanding Heights, the Battle between Government and the Marketplace That Is Remaking the Modern World, by Daniel Yergin and Joseph Stanislaw (New York: Simon & Schuster, 1998). Explains the shift in power and influence over the economy from the government to the private sector over the course of the twentieth century. It provides a good background for the future orientation of our book.

The Competitive Advantage of Nations, by Michael E. Porter (New York: Free Press, 1990). Explores what makes a nation's industries competitive in the global marketplace, and presents Porter's findings about the importance of "clusters" in creating competitive advantage.

Contact, by Carl Sagan (New York: Simon & Schuster, 1985). A science fiction book that examines what would happen if our contemporary world finally did pick up radio signals from other intelligent life in the galaxy.

The Diamond Age, by Neal Stephenson (New York: Bantam Books, 1996). A science fiction book that broke new ground by envisioning a world where nanotechnology is widespread and the world is organized by cultural tribes that are defined not by geography, but by mentality.

The Discoverers, a History of Man's Search to Know His World and Himself, by Daniel J. Boorstin (New York: Random House, 1983). Describes the amazing story of the great explorers of western Europe who ventured out to circumnavigate the planet for the first time and encountered the New World.

Dynamic Forces in Capitalist Development: A Long-Run Comparative View, by Angus Madison (New York: Oxford University Press, 1991). Provides an in-depth analysis of long-term economic change.

Earth, by David Brin (New York: Bantam Books, 1990). A brilliant science fiction vision of a realistic world in the middle of the twenty-first century that is tightly bound together by a fully developed Internet and largely acting as one global community.

Edge City, Life on the New Frontier, by Joel Garreau (New York: Doubleday, 1988). On the surface, identifies the emergence of a new form of suburban city–and analyzes it positively, as the future being born. On a deeper level, it also makes the case for the ingenuity and adaptability of average Americans.

The Electric Kool-Aid Acid Test, by Tom Wolfe (New York: Bantam Books, 1968). Captures the essence of the northern California ideology of extreme openness and creative exploration by telling the story of the countercultural heyday leading up to 1968. That somewhat moderated mentality partly accounts for the region's high-tech success today.

The End of Work, the Decline of the Global Labor Force and the Dawn of the Post-Market Era, by Jeremy Rifkin (New York: Putnam, 1995). A wrongheaded book that is interesting because of how it completely misinterprets global economic trends and epitomizes the common fears about the future. It warns of computer technology creating massive unemployment in the United States–right about the time the Long Boom began tightening the labor market to historical lows.

Engines of Creation: The Coming Era of Nanotechnology, by K. Eric Drexler (New York: Doubleday, 1986). A groundbreaking book that was the first to make the case that nanotechnology can work practically if we only imitate nature. It opens up an optimistic vision of the future by showing that we could learn to control matter not in 1,000 years, but more like in another 50.

Factor Four, by Ernst von Weizsacker, Amory Lovins, and Hunter Lovins (London: Earthscan, 1997). Gives a highly detailed technical analysis of how we can improve the environmental quality of industrial economies by radical technological change.

The Fourth Turning, by William Strauss and Neil Howe (New York: Broadway Books, 1997). Provides a neat, if mechanical, vision of a crisis that the United States will face when four types of generations will align in a way only rarely seen in American history.

The Future of American Progressivism, an Initiative for Political and Economic Reform, by Roberto Mangabeira Unger and Cornell West (Boston: Beacon Press, 1998). A short, provocative book that raises some healthy challenges to many premises of the Long Boom but also challenges the political Left to let go of its historical baggage, embrace the New Economy, and build on what's truly positive about the United States.

Generations: The History of America's Future, 1584 to 2069, by William Strauss and Neil Howe (New York: William Morrow, 1991). A highly original analysis of generational change as a primary driving force in history that points out patterns in U.S. history in order to try to project future changes.

Global Shift, by Peter Dicken (New York: Guilford Press, 1998). An excellent source of data on what is going on in the world economy today—with charts galore.

Globaphobia, by Greg Burtless, Robert Z. Lawrence, Robert E. Litan, and Robert J. Shapiro (Washington, D.C.: Brookings Institution, 1998). Examines the myths about, and fears of, open trade that have led many Americans to oppose globalization. The authors set forth unambiguous data proving that trade in the global marketplace continues to benefit, rather than harm, the U.S. economy.

Holy Fire, by Bruce Sterling (New York: Bantam Books, 1996). Describes a world where an economically successful society is effected by life extension technology.

How the World Was One, Beyond the Global Village, by Arthur C. Clarke (New York: Bantam Books, 1992). Tells the fascinating history of connecting the planet, starting with the efforts to lay the first undersea telegraph cables in the nineteenth century and moving all the way through the early years of communications satellites.

The Idea of Decline in Western History, by Arthur Herman (New York: Free Press, 1997). Argues that from the fifteenth century on, there have always been misguided elites who see the world as being in inevitable decline. He identifies today's environmental movement as the clearest current example.

Imagined Worlds, by Freeman Dyson (Cambridge, MA: Harvard University Press, 1997). Read anything written by Freeman Dyson, one of the wise people of science and technology. This book, based on a series of lectures that roam through a wide range of fields, is a good start.

The Information Age: Economy, Society and Culture: Volume 1. *The Rise of the Network Society,* by Manuel Castells (Cambridge, MA: Blackwell, 1996). An academic book that gives a deep structural analysis of the implications of network architecture for organizations, society, and politics. It attempts to explain almost everything about this new iteration of capitalism—à la Marx.

In Search of History, a Personal Adventure, by Theodore H. White (New York: Warner Books, 1978). An energized narrative that captures the spirit of the GI generation on their mission of remaking the post–World War II world. An inspiration for us today.

Islands in the Net, by Bruce Sterling (New York: Ace Books, 1988). A science fiction look at how the Net could work for good and for ill. Sterling's preoccupation with hackers and the underworld leads him to explore the dark side of an out-of-control but highly interconnected world.

Japan: A Reinterpretation, by Patrick Smith (New York: Pantheon Books, 1997). A useful antidote to most of the modern literature offering conventional wisdom on Japan. Smith saw years ago many of the problems Japan is facing today.

The Lexus and the Olive Tree, by Thomas Friedman (New York: Farrar, Straus & Giroux, 1999). Explains how the democratization of information, telecommunications, and finance have led to globalization. His thesis that the global economy's strength and impact will only grow in the decades ahead lays the groundwork for a discussion of a Long Boom future.

Life After Television, The Coming Transformation of Media and American Life, by George Gilder (New York: W. W. Norton, 1994). A good encapsulation of Gilder's core ideas. He has been way ahead of the curve in thinking through the inevitable consequences of the coming bandwidth bonanza.

Lords of the Rim, by Sterling Seagrave (New York: Putnam, 1995). Talks at length about the role of the overseas Chinese in integrating the rest of Asia, particularly Southeast Asia, with mainland China.

Moral Politics, by George Lakoff (Chicago: University of Chicago Press, 1996). Provides an understanding of the role of markets in liberal philosophy, and explains how the key difference between conservatives and liberals is their conception of family.

New Rules for the New Economy, by Kevin Kelly (New York: Viking, 1998). Provides a very coherent analysis of how and why networked economics is different from traditional economics.

The Nine Nations of North America, by Joel Garreau (New York: Houghton Mifflin, 1991). An original book that disregards national borders and comes up with a better way to understand how North America is organized: through regional economies and cultural identities. It points the way to a more decentralized future in North America, and by example, shows how the world might reorganize itself throughout the twenty-first century.

On Competition, by Michael E. Porter (Cambridge, MA: Harvard Business School Press, 1998). A collection of articles that extends Porter's thinking on clustering and on enhancing competitive advantage through global strategy.

Out of Control, the Rise of Neo-Biological Civilization, by Kevin Kelly (Reading, MA: Addison-Wesley, 1994). Shows how the shift to a twenty-first-century world is best explained by biological rather than mechanical metaphors. Explains how coherence can develop in very complex systems even if there is nobody in charge.

Parable of the Sower, by Octavia E. Butler (New York, London: Four Walls Eight Windows, 1993). A horrifying science fiction novel set in California around 2025 that gives a chilling look at what will happen if the opposite of the Long Boom comes about and the world is torn apart by a struggle over diminishing resources.

The Prize, by Daniel Yergin (New York: Simon & Schuster, 1991). On the surface, about the oil industry's evolution through modern times, but on a deeper level, about the twentieth-century interplay between politics and energy.

The Reckoning, by David Halberstam (New York: Avon Books, 1986). Courtesy of Halberstam's superb storytelling, the rise of the Japanese auto industry and of Asia in general from post–World War II to the 1980s heyday before the crash.

The Rise and Decline of Nations, by Mancur Olson (New Haven: Yale University Press, 1982). Explains long-run economic dynamics and particularly the interplay between social and economic phenomena.

The Rise and Fall of the Great Powers, by Paul Kennedy (New York: Random House, 1987). A controversial book that predicted the decline of the United States as a world power and typified the pervasive pessimism of Americans in the 1980s. The book proved to be totally wrong.

The Search for Order: 1877–1920, by Robert H. Wiebe (New York: Hill & Wang, 1967). A straightforward history of the rapid transformation from agricultural to industrial society in the United States. Though written in the 1960s, it unwittingly lays out remarkable parallels to our Long Boom–right down to the beginning and ending dates.

Things That Make Us Smart, Defending Human Attributes in the Age of the Machine, by Donald A. Norman (Reading, MA: Addison-Wesley, 1993). Norman has crusaded for designing our technologies to more seamlessly integrate into our world and, in doing so, has helped envision a future of ubiquitous computing.

The Third Wave, the Classic Study of Tomorrow, by Alvin Toffler (New York: Bantam Books, 1980). So far ahead of its time in describing elements of the shift to the global networked society that it's still relevant.

The Unbound Prometheus, by David S. Landes (New York: Cambridge University Press, 1969). Shows the power of technology as a key driving force in long-term economic change, with a particular focus on the industrial revolution.

War and Peace, by Michael W. Doyle (New York: W. W. Norton, 1997). Discusses three different visions of the future: realism, liberalism, and Marxism. He argues for a version of the future of liberalism that is similar to the Long Boom vision.

The Wealth and Poverty of Nations, Why Some Are So Rich and Some So Poor, by David S. Landes (New York: W. W. Norton, 1998). A sweeping history of all of modern capitalism up to the New Economy, giving a frank appraisal of every major culture and laying out why some succeed and others fail.

The Wheels of Commerce, by Fernand Braudel (Berkeley: University of California Press, 1992). Studies the evolution of economics, politics, social change, and many facets of everyday life in Europe over the centuries. He provides a very coherent model for understanding the kind of complex scenario represented by the Long Boom.

When Things Start to Think, by Neil Gershenfeld (New York: Holt, 1999). Gives a sense of just how radical the embedding of information technology in virtually all devices could be.

The Work of Nations, Preparing Ourselves for Twenty-First Century Capitalism, by Robert B. Reich (New York: Knopf, 1991). One of the first books to define the knowledge worker and the implications of globalization, though it frames the developments negatively and warns about creating a two-tier society.

About the Authors

Peter Schwartz is an internationally renowned futurist and business strategist. He is co-founder and chairman of Global Business Network, a unique membership organization and worldwide network of strategists, business executives, scientists, and artists based in Emeryville, California. He is also a partner at Alta Partners, one of the leading biotechnology and information technology venture capital funds. From 1982 to 1986, Peter headed scenario planning for the Royal Dutch/Shell Group of Companies in London. Before that, he directed the Strategic Environment Center at SRI International, one of the best-known futurist groups in the 1970s. Peter received a B.S. in aeronautical engineering and astronautics from Rensselaer Polytechnic Institute. He is the author of *The Art of the Long View* (Doubleday Currency, 1991). He lives in Berkeley, California, with his wife, Cathleen, and son, Ben.

Peter Leyden has written and spoken widely on technology, economic change, contemporary history and the future. He is the former managing editor of *Wired* magazine, which helped define the digital revolution. As a senior editor there, he oversaw key projects and articles that explored the political, social, and cultural impact of new technologies. Leyden now is involved in several web-based projects, including a virtual think tank at Meta-Markets.com. Leyden spent fifteen years as a journalist and has written for many publications, including the *New York Times, Chicago Tribune,* and *Minneapolis Star Tribune*. He watched the rise of Asia as a special correspondent for *Newsweek* magazine while based in Seoul in the late 1980s. Leyden holds two master's degrees from Columbia University, one in journalism and one in comparative politics. He received a B.A. in intellectual history from Georgetown University. Now he lives in Berkeley, California, with his wife, Sharon, and daughter, Emma. You can find out more about Leyden and contact him through the www.longboom.net website.

Joel Hyatt teaches entrepreneurship at Stanford University's Graduate School of Business, where he holds the Class of 1973 Lectureship. He is also executive managing director of idealab!, a leading incubator of internet companies. He was co-founder and senior partner of Hyatt Legal Services, which helped revolutionize the legal services delivery system by making legal care affordable and accessible to middle- and lower-income families. Hyatt was also founder and chief executive officer of Hyatt Legal Plans, Inc., the nation's largest provider of group legal plans, which make legal services available as a fringe benefit to employees. Hyatt Legal Plans was acquired by Metropolitan Life Insurance Company. Hyatt was the Democratic nominee for the U.S. Senate in Ohio in 1994. He received his B.A. degree from Dartmouth College in 1972 and his J.D. degree from Yale University in 1976. Hyatt lives with his wife, Susan, and two sons, Jared and Zachary, in Atherton, California.

STAY CONNECTED

The Long Boom is a positive meme about a better future, but like all memes, it is evolving. We hope we've provided a starting point for an ongoing global conversation about how everyone can take advantage of all the great potential of our era and create a better world. We've also made much of the values of staying connected and expanding the network. With that in mind, we've set up a Web site at www.longboom.net to keep the conversation going after you put this book down.

Index